LATINX POETICS

LATINX POETICS

ESSAYS ON THE ART OF POETRY

EDITED BY **RUBEN QUESADA**

FOREWORD BY JUAN FELIPE HERRERA

University of New Mexico Press | Albuquerque

© 2022 by University of New Mexico Press
All rights reserved. Published 2022
Printed in the United States of America

Names: Quesada, Ruben, 1976– editor. | Herrera, Juan Felipe, writer of foreword.
Title: Latinx poetics: essays on the art of poetry / edited by Ruben Quesada; foreword by Juan Felipe Herrera.
Description: Albuquerque: University of New Mexico Press, 2022. | Includes bibliographical references and index.
Identifiers: LCCN 2022021131 (print) | LCCN 2022021132 (e-book) | ISBN 9780826364388 (paper) | ISBN 9780826364395 (pdf)
Subjects: LCSH: Poets, Latin American. | Poets, Spanish American. | Latin American poetry—History and criticism. | Spanish American poetry—History and criticism. | BISAC: LITERARY CRITICISM / American / Hispanic & Latino | LITERARY CRITICISM / Modern / 21st Century
Classification: LCC PQ7082.P7 L38 2022 (print) | LCC PQ7082.P7 (e-book) | DDC 861-dc23
LC record available at https://lccn.loc.gov/2022021131
LC e-book record available at https://lccn.loc.gov/2022021132

Founded in 1889, the University of New Mexico sits on the traditional homelands of the Pueblo of Sandia. The original peoples of New Mexico—Pueblo, Navajo, and Apache—since time immemorial have deep connections to the land and have made significant contributions to the broader community statewide. We honor the land itself and those who remain stewards of this land throughout the generations and also acknowledge our committed relationship to Indigenous peoples. We gratefully recognize our history.

Cover image courtesy of Vecteezy.com
Cover design by Felicia Cedillos
Interior design by Isaac Morris
Composed in New Caledonia LT 10 / 14.25

Contents

ix   Foreword: The Mindful Space of Joyous Creation
         JUAN FELIPE HERRERA

xiii   Introduction
         RUBEN QUESADA

         ◆

1   The Horse and Rider
         TOMÁS Q. MORÍN

9   Poetry in Concert with the Visual Arts:
         Latinx Ekphrasis and Other Inter-arts Fusions
         BRENDA CÁRDENAS

30   What the Neoliberal Policy Labs Eat and Shit:
         Horrific Fables for a Specific Universe
         DANIEL BORZUTZKY

40   Glorious View: Landscapes of Memoria
         FRANCISCO ARAGÓN

48   Peopleness: Ethnicity and the Latinx Poem
         VALERIE MARTÍNEZ

58   My Latino Aesthetics. Or Not.
         STEVEN CORDOVA

63 An Afro-Latino's Poetic and Creative Hungers
    SEAN FREDERICK FORBES

72 Trauma and the Lyric
    SHERYL LUNA

77 La Desembocada: Healing the Wound That Never Heals
    IRE'NE LARA SILVA

82 Longing for a Language That Joins:
    Class Consciousness in Portuguese American Poetry
    CARLO MATOS

90 Let's Call the Whole Thing Off:
    Or, the Possibilities of a Contemporary US Latin@ Poetry
    RAFAEL CAMPO

100 How I Came to Identify as a Latina Writer
    ADELA NAJARRO

111 A Graffiti Artist in Academia
    MICHAEL TORRES

119 Puerto Rican Poetry and a State of Independence:
    A Family Affair
    BLAS FALCONER

127 Notes on Teaching and Learning the Mother Tongue
    JUAN J. MORALES

138 *Duende* the Poem, or Poetics at
    the Intersection of Realities and Identities
    RAINA J. LEÓN

148 *Testarudo*: An Essay on My Poetic Vocation
    ORLANDO RICARDO MENES

163   To Have and Have Not:
Uncovering the Cultural Identity in Twenty-First-Century
Portuguese American Literature
MILLICENT BORGES ACCARDI

177   Invention as Discovery:
An Essay on Latino/a Poetics
ANDRES ROJAS

186   Notes on Writing Poetry and the Function of Language
EVA MARIA SAAVEDRA

191   Stealing the Crown
LAURIE ANN GUERRERO

201   Knocking on Heaven's Couplets:
The Nature and Function of Poesía
NATALIA TREVIÑO

◆

215   Contributors

223   Index

Foreword

The Mindful Space of Joyous Creation

JUAN FELIPE HERRERA

I salute these writers—

the warrior-seekers, philosophers—survivors, archeologists of the elusive and ungraspable self, that thing related to the other thing called identity, titled "Latino Poetics" or "Latinx Aesthetics" or the "Other Tribe," as Valerie Martínez says in her essay and ire'ne lara silva refigures, questions "American?" Or is there "such a thing?" Raina J. León ponders. I salute them. They all have dedicated their art-lives deciphering the elusive phenomena of *Word, Self, Writing, Identity, Aesthetics, Culture, Power,* and ultimately, *Being.*

The practice, creation, and analysis of a "Latinx" (?) poetry are no longer the devotees of solely cultural content or class protest, or simply, the scoured "text" as tackled by the early "Chicano" (?) lit critics of the early '70s and '80s. Here we have deep examinations, personal stories, senses of a damaged cultural self and the "war" to reclaim and honor our injured self, as Blas Falconer writes. Here we enter the quarks and fissions of multiple identities, the out/in transcendent channels of word, body, and memory, as Francisco Aragón keenly interlaces in his piece.

I am astounded by this anthology, its writers, their mind work and investigations. Tomás Q. Morín calls this search for the poem, at times, a place where you "dig into the dark." Latinx poetics is a complex, tremulous rite of passage—identity is key, yet it is not overarching.

The question of brown identity—can we call it "brown"? We can also call it "Afro-Latino," Forbes says. This ID friction has been around for a while. Who are we? Are we truly "cursed by racial ambiguity" as Saavedra states? What is our proper name? This Other we carry on our bodies, or is it the paint of power that has slapped us? Who is this San Francisco "Ayankado/Yankee-ized one," notes Mexican journalist Miguel Prieto in his travel journal as he tours the USA. In 1877, Prieto publishes *Viajes a los Estados Unidos*.

We are plagued by identity borders, or possibly "wounds," as Gloria Anzaldúa would say, who is mentioned in this anthology, and by Lorca's duende, also noted here—the night-fiery bolt, jolting the poet's sudden act and fall into creative bursts and exposures. Part naked search, part unleashed desire.

In 2010, I was pulled by a long-time yearning for my uncle Roberto Quintana's story as a member of *El Barco de La Ilusión*, an XEJ radio comedy segment in the early '30s of Juárez, Chihuahua. I headed to meet one of the last post-revolution poets of the art renaissance on the Mexican *frontera*—to the wary and resilient borderline crackling on the edge of El Paso. Ninety-two-year-old Cuca García (Aguirre) recounted at her home her early XEJ days with her performance partner, Germán Valdez (famous as Tin-Tan in Mexico's golden age of cinema). They were both members of a band of new poets, singers, dancers, radio actors, and artists affiliated with the new radio station border boom. In the makeshift radio studio, Tin Tan rushes in from the streets of Mexican youth dressed in zoot suits, hollers at sixteen-year-old Cuca Aguirre—singer, dancer, poet—"From this day on, Cuca, I am a Pachuco!" A Pachuco? A new kind of Mexican appears, a rebel, a culture-border warrior, slick, cool and upright, a fiery artist. Just like that, like rebel youth, he re-created himself.

Perhaps in similar fashion, at the beginning of the new phenomenon of "Chicano poetry," in 1966, on 14th and B Street, San Diego, Alurista surprised me, six years before he installed a radical Chicano poetics frame with three identity keys of "Flor y Canto / In Xochitl In Cuicatl," the Mexican term for poetry; "Aztlán," the forgotten homeland of the Southwest (with Luis Valdez); and the hemispheric Latin American macro-self, "Amerindia," all central to the meanings and sources of what we now call Latinx poetry. Alurista turned and faced me in his spare apartment, one block from mine, as we listened to *Brazil 66* on his phonograph. "Juan Felipe, from this day on, I am a Chicano." A rare term in those days. Just like that, it seems, identity and poetics can be structured, claimed, absorbed, fused, and enacted.

What are the ingredients of a Latinx poetics? Is there such a thing? How do we go about it? These concerns are tackled in every essay in this most wisdom-deep and visionary collection.

Indeed, each poet digs deep. Perhaps it is not the terms and answers these thinkers are after. Perhaps it is their humanity, our humanity—a poetics of humanity? Is it possible—to attain a miraculous, porous, ever expanding and ringing radius of life-creative, redefining itself in its ever vibrating spirals?

Solid identity, the Static Self, the One Defined Thing, a demarcated cultural habitat, a pure poetics, is not possible in today's churning dynamics of cultural change. These author-warriors seem to be battling for the possibility of space.

The space is personal. There is trauma, there are ancestors to be called upon, there is the shedding of ethnic requirements, there is a "war" that had to be waged with many ascribed, familial, and violent cultural forces, as Blas Falconer admits in his essay. There is an unleashed raw graffiti slamming against the walls to release the relentless spark, Michael Torres paints. And there are "brutal specificities" that had to be carved into a poem, on a book, into our being, at all costs—the names and more names, on the street-sized lists of killed girls on the bleeding border, Daniel Borzutzky outlines. Where do we go now?

Move into this anthology and you will get closer to the findings. Discoveries are abundant in these texts; they overflow with this collective of restless poets. Each one is concerned and pioneers with a consciousness-lab tearing out of their body, experiments of and for a "new territory of Latino aesthetics," as described by Rafael Campo. How can we dislodge the fixed and false summations and ethno-screens projected over our skin, thought and word of being?

These questions are open. Yet being breathes through the micro-memoirs of these writers as they speak of aesthetics, poetics (poetry as "story," writes Adela Najarro), and the slippage of language and the fluid fibers of poetry. Francisco Aragón keenly treats these queries with his notions of language fragments "entered and passed through my body." I find these discussions and idea-liberations in this anthology exhilarating—new ways to speak, examine, and feel the making and motion of an ever-changing Latinx poetry.

These writers are defining Latinx poetics as they write. They are sketching out the new contours of being Latinx and/or Chicana—the poems find a new self, just as the writers do, hopefully "without having to prove myself," as Eva Maria Saavedra says out loud.

What is sculpted on these pages may be a kind of Latinx poetics prosopopoeia. Brenda Cárdenas mentions this particular process and practice in her examination of ekphrastic poetry. Perhaps we can take her findings another step: "How do we *speak to, for and about our self-imaging and naming* whether as social out-scapes or as reflective inscapes?" The question: *How have we created ourselves, the text, and the world around us?*

Brilliant, revolutionary, mega-inspiring. Let us salute these poets.

Each writer, each poet, embarks on a quest. Each poet grapples with their beginnings. Each one tackles the once-upon-a-time border walls of language, speaking, writing, and like Frederick Douglass, the liberation of being and Others in front of multitudes. If this is possible, then such being, such humanity, such a cause for an inclusive life poetics makes the collective being of a people a reality where we all engage in the "mindful space of joyous Creation."

—Juan Felipe Herrera
Poet Laureate of the United Sates, Emeritus
March 6, 2021

Introduction

RUBEN QUESADA

In her essay "Peopleness: Ethnicity and the Latinx Poem," Valerie Martínez remarks on the proliferation of Latinx poets; it is a "phenomenon that reveals the complexity of our voices, styles, perspectives, and literary identities." Martínez reminds us that we live in a world that would be poorer without these complex identities. The proliferation of Latinx poetry adds to our ongoing understanding of the human experience.

The cultural experiences found in Latinx poetry are new to many readers. Latinx culture encompasses people with connections to and from the Caribbean islands, Mexico, and Central and South America who are living in the United States. Poetry by Latinxs reflects complex and varied identities of class, education, and social mobility. The intersection of voice and style makes Latinx poetry a phenomenon. There is no singular voice or common theme among the culture or poetry beyond a connection to the Spanish language. Latinx culture is as varied as the cultures of the Irish and the Kiwi, who happen to share the English language.

This is the first time these contemporary voices have been collected in an anthology of essays on poetry with such breadth and scope. Contemporary Latinx poets at all stages of their career provide scholarly and personal insight on what it means to be a poet, but more importantly on what it means to be a Latinx poet. These essays are for educators, writers, and lovers of poetry.

Poetry reminds us that our human experience has always been complicated. We live in a time when people are reading and writing more than ever in the history of humanity. For writers and for poets who are the makers of worlds—the curators of history—words carry the weight of calling the world to action, to awaken its readers to both the beauty and the ugliness that surrounds us today.

Poetry enlarges our view of the world and expands our understanding of the human experience. For poet Orlando Menes, the very tools poets use—words—kept him from fully realizing his potential. He remembers, "One of my linguistic handicaps was having an inadequate vocabulary, so I took it upon myself to memorize new words from the dictionary or any other text, keeping a vocabulary journal." It is words endowed with power through faith and science in composition—the compression of sentences into lines waiting to be unpacked by readers—that gives us permission to realize more than we imagined we were capable of understanding.

Poems are a record of time, and the numerous collections of poetry written by the largest ethnic and racial minority in the United States demonstrate that Latinx poets are vastly documenting the American experience. The essays in this anthology are an examination, not a polemic. These essays further record what Latinx poets observe as the nature and function of poetry in their lives and in the fabric of American literature.

Of those who rise to tell their stories, a poet (a rhetorician) is distinct from a journalist, a politician, or a celebrity, though we know, in retrospect, that "literature is news that STAYS news" (Pound 1960, 29). The word *news* as defined by the Oxford English Dictionary is a "new thing"—the definition dates back to late Middle English as the plural of *new* or medieval Latin *nova*. Human emotions in literature are not new, but the depicted experiences are, and it drives readers to return to literature to discover how a writer has made those emotions new for them. When turning to contemporary American poetry, we find the new in poetry of the Latinx community.

The news of poetry is not gossip, not rumor, but a form of communication that informs and persuades through narrative or lyric imagination, preserving through language the life and times of the poet. As Ezra Pound reminds us, "These things are matters of degree. Your communication can be more or less exact" (29). That is, the experience is not a report. The focus of the poet may reveal experience and emotion, and it is up to the common sense of the poet where the focus will be. A poem is a witnessing. There is a fine line between providing a reader evidence and proof of a situation and having the poet be the focal point of the poem. Is this poem about the poet or is it about the situation, or both? In our post-internet age, the act of telling is often best left to reporters and the act of showing to video or photograph. The poet is best left to provide a response to the events of the world, to be allowed to make the world new.

As reflected since the mid-nineteenth century, American poetry has focused its singular attention on the cultural landscape, the birth of the American idiom. In the spirit of individual liberty through language, the rise of idiomatic expression, in particular free verse and the democratization of poetic subject, readers were given a view of culture and place not widely seen since perhaps Phillis Wheatley's *Poems on Various Subjects* (1773). Walt Whitman's *Leaves of Grass* (1855) and Paul Laurence Dunbar's *Oak and Ivy* (1893) are notable for their responding to their nineteenth-century world.

The ambivalence of identity and displacement of home is a defining characteristic of the Latinx collective. In recent years, that sense of unity, a growing sense of belonging to a collective ethnic group of Latinx, has begun to foster a growing awareness of Latinx in American literature. In thinking about the social fabric of the Latinx experience in American literature, I wonder, then, what is the social function of our cultural contribution to American poetry? For millennia poetry has been seen as the sister art to painting, but poetry is not composed of "static objects extended in space but the life that is lived in the scene that it composes" (Stevens 1942, 25). Poetry is dynamic, and to understand the varied human experiences, one must examine the stories it tells from those telling the stories.

The tradition of American poetry as a social function is rooted in nineteenth-century American poetry. Consider the importance of Phillis Wheatley, Walt Whitman, or Paul Laurence Dunbar, whose poetry encompassed the unacknowledged man or woman, sex worker or drug addict, slave or servant. Too often, contemporary poets charge ahead without acknowledgment of their predecessors or those poets who have enabled their own stories to be told. It is the non-white poets who wrote among and in response to literary giants who have given us a foothold for our own historical impression—then, now, and for the future. Acknowledging the past is not the sole focus of this argument. More important is the potential of the poet to challenge, or find alignment with, the establishment.

A century after Wheatley, Whitman, and Laurence, poets like Tomás Montoya, Jayne Cortez, Gloria E. Anzaldúa, Sonia Sanchez, Leslie Marmon Silko, Cherríe Moraga, Sandra Cisneros, Tomás Rivera, Jimmy Santiago Baca, Gary Soto, and Juan Felipe Herrera, to name but a few, began to tell our varied stories, to open a path for us today who find the watermarks of these predecessors on each page of our poetry.

As a poet, this self-awareness makes me acutely aware of my own resistance to or alignment with tradition and contemporaneous trends in American poetry. Emerson has said that while mankind is capable of sensing or being aware of the world, not everyone is moved to tell their story. Though everyone's experiences should be depicted in poetry, and while everyone may manifest memory with sufficient force to arrive at the senses, they may not be capable of compelling the reproduction of themselves in speech (Emerson, 1844). We must think back on the origin of poetry. Turning toward our contemporary and future state of the poetry, I look to a past even further than this nation's.

I turn to the oral tradition and the importance of storytelling through poetry. Writing on the oral poetic tradition and history, linguist and scholar Ruth Finnegan explained that there is a common assumption that the "oral tradition" is a monolith, a self-evident entity, but that actually, there are "three main classes of oral tradition: recognized literary forms, generalized historical knowledge, and personal recollections" (Finnegan 1970, 195). These varied essays perfectly describe the variety of experiences of Latinx poets. The Latinx community is not a monolith. These contributions account for an increasingly pluralistic representation in contemporary writing, where the life of the individual constantly evolves into an uncertain and complex ethos.

I turn to essays on the art of poetry to find the resiliency of poetic composition that will outlast us all. I turn to ideas on poetics that have served to forge the social function of poetry for millennia, the classical ideas of Aristotle and Horace. Verisimilitude and the emotional charge of language enable the poet to compose poetry that both delights and instructs readers about the human experience. It is through the commonality of language and associative meaning where readers find a connection to a depicted experience.

In the spring of 2007, Francisco Aragón published *The Wind Shifts: New*

Latinx Poetry. The anthology, which collects poetry by twenty-five Latinx poets, was featured on the Poetry Foundation Podcast in July of the same year. In an interview, Aragón acknowledges the importance of contemporary Latinx poets assimilating into American culture. Aragón notes that contemporary poets have acculturated into the American tradition without losing sight of their own Latinx identity by drawing on the social and political movements of the 1970s via "code switching," through an artful use of language to create a mosaic of emotion and story. A recent anthology called *Angels of the Americlypse: An Anthology of New Latin@ Writing* (2013), edited by Carmen Giménez Smith and John Chavez, was the first major mixed-genre anthology of Latinx writing that acknowledged and focused on Latinx literature's innovative and experimental strand. Over the last decade, Latinx poets have created a written world of experiences. In a series of lectures, W. H. Auden claimed that the job of the poet is to create secondary worlds and that a love of the primary world leads the poet to create those secondary worlds. Latinx poets create not only out of love of their primary world but also, perhaps more importantly, out of the challenges they face because of their Latinx cultural and racial identities.

The most recent edition of the *Princeton Encyclopedia of Poetry and Poetics* recognizes that studying poetry of the past, in the information age, is sometimes conceived as an antiquarian field, a field of theoretical issues or reflections on the practice of writing poetry. As a Latinx and a poet in the United States, I recognize the importance of my Latinx predecessors, the influence that history and American literature has had on their work, their intersection into my own history, and our impact on the American literary tradition. The essays in this anthology are a spectrum of voices and varied understandings. These essays offer a deeper perspective on the richness and excellence of Latinx poetry.

SOURCES

Emerson, Ralph Waldo. 1844. *Essays: Second Series*. Boston: J. Munroe.
Finnegan, Ruth. 1970. "A Note on Oral Tradition and Historical Evidence." *History and Theory* 9 (2): 195–201. https://doi.org/10.2307/2504126.
Pound, Ezra. 1960. *ABC of Reading*. New York: New Directions Paperbacks.
Stevens, Wallace. 1942. *The Necessary Angel: Essays on Reality and the Imagination*. New York: Vintage.

The Horse and Rider

TOMÁS Q. MORÍN

WHAT COULD I possibly have to share about writing that could be of any interest, much less helpful? The little that I know I either picked up as a student, in my reading, or here and there during conversations with others or myself. Poetic wisdom was never revealed to me by a burning bush speaking in pentameter. Even when I was lucky enough at times to have something revealed to me by a person far smarter than me, I was either not ready for that knowledge or too stubborn to accept it and so went on and made my mistakes and learned it the hard way.

◆ ◆

It seems to me that one of the most basic things necessary in making art is curiosity. Most of the artists I have come to know are endlessly curious people. Their curiosity runs the gamut from the subject of Big Foot's existence to wondering how and when the word *fly* came to mean a soaring baseball, an insect, and the place where zippers and buttons hide on a pair of pants. If you're not curious about the world, then you will never be curious about words. And if you're not going to be curious about words, then spare yourself a miserable life chasing publications, grants, and prizes. Build a bridge, mow lawns, or become a plumber instead; these and any number of other worthwhile pursuits will surely bring you more satisfaction. If you are chasing fame, get out of the race now. Or don't.

◆ ◆

An author's materials often seem magical to beginning writers. Legal pads, typewriters, fountain pens, computers, phones, pencils, all appear to have some sort of talismanic power to the fledgling author. I know because I used to believe this. Before I knew what it took to make a poem, I would hunt interviews with poets for the part where they would answer the question about their writing routines and the tools of their trade. There were two things that I didn't realize until much later.

The first was that no pen or keyboard or special paper was ever responsible for the creation of a single line of verse. Believing so was just as silly as an apprentice carpenter duplicating the master's toolbox right down to the bumblebee-black-and-yellow DeWalt measuring tape. Just as one hammer is as good as most any other hammer in the world of carpentry, so is one journal as good as any another in the world of writing.

The second realization is that all of these tools—even the hammer of the master carpenter—do have power, but only for their owner. This power is not transferrable. One cannot underestimate the effect of a pen that fits comfortably in the hand in a way that no other pen does or the way that a certain computer screen feels welcoming and warm. Even an agitated genius creates under the spell of a certain measure of calm.

These tools do not create art; they facilitate it by giving us a sense of comfort and ease so that when we raise our arm to strike the first nail into the first board of the poem or story we are about to build, our aim will be true.

◆ ◆

Genre, school, movement. These are all the jargon of literary critics, who, like biologists, work diligently to classify what they encounter. If an artist is to have any chance at making something that will last—and let's face it, the odds are long—then they must be like the mole that is ignorant of the phylum, class, genus, and species we have assigned it. Dig into the dark and let others worry about what you are and where you're going. There will be time enough at the end for the critics to dissect you. Don't give them a head start by climbing onto the examination table and tearing yourself open.

The Horse and Rider

◆ ◆

Some years ago while drafting the first stanza of a poem whose last line I intended to be "until laughter did us part," something unexpected happened. I had been playing with the extended sentence for some time before this poem but had never managed to keep a sentence alive for much longer than seven or eight lines. In this poem I decided to push the sentence as long as I could. The result was forty lines, three hundred plus words. While the stamina of my sentence was unexpected, my surprise came as I prepared to move on to the second stanza and that last line I was working toward. I must have watched the cursor blink for hours. I walked away, came back, and nothing. The poem would not budge. Eventually, I realized that the first stanza was in fact its own poem. Frustrated, albeit grateful to have written a poem accidentally, I decided to start over the next day with the same end line in mind.

The second day began with another long, winding sentence. Thirty-two lines and almost three hundred words later, I set down a period at the end of my stanza, and the poem was done. Just like that, the poem was sealed. That period was like a roadblock I couldn't get around. Unwilling to accept this, I stubbornly hit return twice and started typing what I was going to force to be the second stanza. A few hours in, I realized that I had simply begun a new poem. Defeated, I gave in to the reality that I was not in charge as I had foolishly led myself to believe and transferred this poem to a new page with the hope that "until laughter did us part" would finally find its home as a last line. And it did. In order to avoid another roadblock period, I decided to stop playing with the extended sentence and to just use shorter clauses. Two stanzas later, I had my poem with the last line I wanted. Only my lesson was not quite over. The poem had problems that persisted for some time, until it dawned on me that the two stanzas needed to be separated because they were in fact separate poems.

◆ ◆

It was a while before I discovered the proper amount of gratitude for the gift I had been given; from one line, I was given four poems, three of which I had never planned to write. What's more, I found that I liked the first two poems more than the one whose last line I had so desperately chased. Don't get me wrong. I love all the poems I have finished. I just don't like them all the same. Parents who get along better with one child over the others, though all are loved equally, can surely relate.

◆ ◆

Someone once asked me, "Where do your poems come from?" "My crazy brain," is all I could think to say. If it had occurred to me, I would have added that I am no more in charge of what ideas escape from that three-pound lump of tissue between my ears than a beaver is when its lighter, but by no means less impressive, brain devises the blueprint for its next home. But where both the beaver and I do have control is in the execution of those blueprints. All we can do is try, and either fail or succeed.

Robert Frost famously said, "Poetry is play for mortal stakes." Therein lies the crucial difference between the beaver and the poet. If the beaver's dam is poorly constructed, both it and its mate might not survive the winter or marauding wolves, whereas a poorly constructed poem will at worst bore you to pieces. I can think of no better counterargument to the Auden line "poetry makes nothing happen" that the haters of culture like to trot out. If they would only look in the mirror at the froth around their mouths, they might reconsider their opinion about the power of poetry. Poems and beaver lodges are a mystery, and the obvious is often hidden in plain sight.

◆ ◆

Poetry doesn't owe anyone anything. Ever. Sometimes one book is all we get. And not even a good book at that. Even so, how much more fortunate is the writer of a single book than the earnest souls who submitted their work to every venue and publisher for decades until rejection beat the joy out of them?

◆ ◆

Charles Wright once wrote, "Every line is a station of the cross." This suggests that each line of a poem should correspond to different, increasing levels of suffering. What are the stations of the cross, after all, if not a testament to ancient Rome's highly developed attention to the nuances of human suffering and endurance, not to mention drama. The crucifixion of Christ was a spectacle, one that would have been ruined had the flogging, crown of thorns, and long walk been skipped. Every word and gesture—even every pause and silence—should contribute to the spectacle. Any comedian worth their salt knows this.

◆ ◆

Poetry as story is an idea that has been around longer than it has been out of fashion.

◆ ◆

One summer when I was in high school, I worked as a stable hand. My responsibilities entailed the cleaning of the living quarters and corrals of a small group of thoroughbreds and miniature horses. I was also expected to maintain the peace. In addition to being snippy with one another, the thoroughbreds also liked to bully the miniatures. I remember the name of only one of the thoroughbreds: Rosita. She was elegant, mischievous, and that creamy shade of brown after bananas have turned.

One day while in the corral, I found myself suddenly caught between the fence and her massive flank. Realizing the danger I was in, I pushed against her and told her to move. She responded by taking a half-step toward me so that I could feel a fraction of her weight and power. A few panicked seconds later, she released me and walked off. She had made her point.

A strong image should make us uncomfortable because it presses against our assumptions and our relationship to the world. It forces us to redefine ourselves. It is both a threat and a gift. William Carlos Williams knew this; many of his imitators did not. They trotted out the same miniature pony to press against a reader. Had laughter been their goal, they would have succeeded. Choose your horses wisely, and always examine their teeth. It's better to be considered rude than a hack.

◆ ◆

When I first began writing poetry seriously, I was in the grip of a deep depression. Far away from home and lost in darkness, poetry was one of the few lights in my life. During this time, I received a box in the mail from my mother containing a small dreamcatcher. Her letter contained instructions on how to use it, as well as an explanation that it would catch all my bad dreams while I slept. I hung it on the wall above my pillow and thought nothing of it. The next morning, I woke to find that my sleep had been filled with dream after dream. This was unusual because I rarely dream. What was also strange was that my mind was now eerily calm. Where before I had felt like everything sparked with the potential for a poem, now there was nothing. It was something akin to having the stars disappear from the night sky. I felt empty, uncreative, and more alone than ever.

A week of this went by during which I sadly passed from one muted day to another. The hope that I might become a writer was gone. All the while, my dream life had been more vivid than it had ever been. It took five days before it occurred to me there might be a connection between these two extreme states. Without hesitation, I threw the dreamcatcher in the trash and hoped for the best. The next morning, after a night of no dreams, the world spoke to me once more. My imagination was alive again, as it had been before.

What I took from this experience was that while patience, surely, is a virtue for any artist, you have to be grateful for every moment and write everything that occurs to you to write. Whether your work fails or succeeds doesn't matter. The point is to do it and appreciate it, because tomorrow you might step on a four-leaf clover and it will all be gone. Death bringing an end to this life of art is not what worries me; rather, it's the premature loss of this great gift that has been given to me and that has brought me more joy than any one person deserves.

◆ ◆

Ezra Pound proclaimed, "Poetry is a centaur. The thinking word-arranging, clarifying faculty must move and leap with the energizing, sentient, musical faculties." The conscious and unconscious must unite and move as one in the making of art. One can surmise that if an artist is merely a rider, the work might feel overdetermined and uninspired. If the reverse is true and an artist is the horse, what is created might seem sloppy and emotionally indulgent. Of course, the world of art is rife with exceptions. Melville seems more bear than horse, while Goya more horse than man. Geniuses are beasts of another color; they can break the rules because it is their right. But for us mere mortals, a centaur is a sufficient challenge; such a union of emotion and thought is suitable for making interesting art. The best we can do is squeeze tight enough with our legs the barrel of our horse so that when we run and jump, stop, start, and go again, we do so as one heart and one mind.

◆ ◆

It used to be that I would casually sit down and dash off the first draft of a poem easily. I would then, over the next several months, revise until it was done. When I gave up writing year-round to better manage my energies as a teacher, something changed. The first time I sat down to write in late May, as the two past semesters of teaching were becoming a weak memory, I stalled. No poetry came. I looked back over the notes I had taken for poems I wanted to write and tried to find a poem whose subject would be easy to engage. Days went by, and I dipped in and out of books, took long naps, watched Seinfeld marathons, and mostly walked to my desk and then walked away.

When that first line was finally anchored, I moved on to the next. Unlike in the past, I found myself no longer able to move on from one line to the next until I had fully revised the previous lines. I had never revised while composing before. To keep track of my changes and to be able to work backward if I hit a dead end, I began numbering the files—Poem 1, Poem 2, Poem 3—so that by the end of the first full draft of a poem, I might end up with a file titled Poem 72. While all of this was unfamiliar territory, I trusted the impulse and followed obediently.

But this was not the only thing that was new. I was now hungry—famished, in fact. It didn't matter if I had eaten a heavy meal before sitting down to write; my body demanded food. And so began the frenzied process of hunting the kitchen for raisins, apples, granola bars, chips, and peanuts. And I wasn't looking for just one of these items; it was all of them and more that I would consume. When they were gone, I would resort to eating slices of bread. After a month, and realizing that this was not going to stop, I made sure the apartment was stocked with healthy snacks so that I wouldn't balloon up by the time the fall semester began.

The other odd thing that changed was that when I was writing and in this ravenous state, I was also hot. By the time I would knock off working on a poem for the day, my shirt would be soaked with sweat. I don't know what my temperature would rise to, but it was enough to make me feel itchy all over. Before that summer, I would have never imagined that ice water, tank tops, and a towel for wiping the sweat from my face would be necessary for me to write a poem.

Maybe someday, someone who knows more about the body than I do will explain it all to me. Regardless, I don't need to understand it any more than woodpeckers understand their compulsion to pound their beaks ten thousand times a day, every day, until there is a safe place to bring something new into the world.

Years from now, it will probably all be different. For all I know, I'll be draped with blankets because I'm freezing, and I'll be using a recorder to compose my poems. My only hope is that I have the good sense to keep embracing the change. And to be worthy of it all.

Poetry in Concert with the Visual Arts

Latinx Ekphrasis and Other Inter-arts Fusions

BRENDA CÁRDENAS

AS A THIRD-GENERATION Mexican German American growing up in Milwaukee, Wisconsin, in the 1960s, mine was a world of lively fusions, juxtapositions, and cross-pollinations. English mixed not only with Spanish but with the Purépecha words in my paternal grandfather's dialect and the Slovenian of a close uncle-in-law who had emigrated from Yugoslavia and married my Mexican aunt. It was he, rather than she, who nicknamed me Cacahuate Mantequilla—Princess Red Cheeks—and it wasn't unusual in our home to eat sauerkraut on Sunday and mole on Monday.

These mixes were nothing new. My paternal grandparents had immigrated to Milwaukee from Michoacán and Jalisco in the late 1920s and settled on the near south side—then, simply a neighborhood of immigrants from various countries. In fact, my grandmother used to say that neighbors spoke so many different languages, when folks went to the butcher to buy meat, they would gesture to communicate what they wanted. A slap to the right thigh meant, "I'll take some leg of lamb, please."

For my grandparents—brown immigrants with only third-grade educations—making do demanded reenvisioning in order to retool, combine, and craft new items with whatever materials they could salvage from what they had broken or others were throwing away. They passed this creativity onto their children and grandchildren. Anything could be reimagined and remixed, could find itself newly affixed to a strange surface. My family's was a practical *rasquachismo*, but the objects they made always bore an artistic flourish, emerged from a craftsperson's hand, an artist's eye. Perhaps this is one reason that despite their humble backgrounds, two uncles, a brother, and several cousins became either visual artists or artisans, such as furniture makers and fine leather smiths. Whether painting a coffee can to use as a planter or a large canvas that would hang above a mantle, they paid attention to detail.

I didn't inherit their talents for visual art or their craftsmanship. Instead, I trained my ear and eye on language, filling my blank handmade books with stories and, eventually, poems. Yet their influence has cultivated in me an abiding interest in both the visual arts and the unconventional assemblages that often form in and emerge from liminal spaces.

In the years directly after graduate school, such leanings led me to collaborate with choreographer Evelyn Velez Aguayo on a performance-art piece that braided together dance, theater, poetry, and visual art. This and other collaborative inter-arts ventures had such a positive impact on me that a few years later, I moved to Chicago to serve as a teacher and coordinator for the National Museum of Mexican Art's youth initiatives in the heart of the Pilsen barrio. From 1998 to 2001, I worked with visual artists who lived in the community to codesign and teach workshops such as Printmaking and Poetry Writing, Mural Painting and Collaborative Writing, and Mask-Making and Storytelling. This was one of the more formative experiences of my adult life. For one, it immersed me in activist cultural work that had an immediate, profound impact on Latina/o youth and the community in which we lived. Second, it opened a space conducive to forming friendships with visual artists and musicians that resulted in a number of our own inter- arts collaborations.

During those years and since, I've found myself increasingly drawn to conversations between poetry and visual art, both ekphrastic and other inter-arts mergings, with their third- mind sensibility. Formally and often thematically, those created by Latinx poets and artists tend to reflect and respond to the liminal and hybrid spaces of transcultural experience. Along with the examples I discuss later in this essay, consider Maria Melendez Kelson's poem "A Chingona Plays Miss Dinah Brand," written in response to Asco's (a conceptual art collective of the 1970s and 1980s) *A la Mode*, which is one of their "No Movies"—fabricated stills from movies that were never made. Just as the photograph centers Asco member Patsi Valdez playing a Chicana femme fatal (a character who never appeared in movies of the 1940s to the

1970s), Melendez Kelson's persona poem gives voice to the character who "Kitten-posed / on a tabletop in Philippe's / Original Sandwich Shop, / Los Angeles, '76," tells her future viewers:

> I take in the unedited
> numbers that tumble
> in one continuous shot
> from my Now to yours,
> and there's a mestiza
> born every minute, I
> know where I sit:
> right on top of a
> pretty warm piece
> of sweet American pie. (Melendez Kelson 2016, 614–15)

In transgressing neat categorizations and divisions, such projects help to subvert static notions regarding Latinx cultures and arts while also contributing to community building. Rather than trading in the elitist indifference of aesthetes, as might be assumed, many Latinx poets turn their engagement with the visual arts to sociopolitical and ethical concerns.

As literary critic Stephen Cheeke reminds us in *Writing for Art: The Aesthetics of Ekphrasis*, since Horace's *Ars Poetica*, in which he put forth the notion of *ut pictura poesis* ("as in painting, so is poetry"), theorists have been speculating about the relationship between the so-called "sister arts," and at least since Gotthold Lessing's *Laocoön: An Essay on the Limits of Painting and Poetry* in the eighteenth century, many have focused on the distinctions between them, claiming that visual art belongs to the spatial arena and poetry to the temporal—a gap that neither can cross (Cheeke 2008, 21–22). However, they attach to these domains a number of assumptions that ignore the fluidity of social constructions: "image as bodily, present, replete, still, silent, natural, and feminine; and word as abstract, rational, active, eloquent, and male" (Loizeaux 2008, 14).

Ekphrasis (from the Greek *ek*—out—and *phrazein*—tell, declare, pronounce), which scholar James A. W. Heffernan defines as "the verbal representation of visual representation," thus framing the exchange as mimesis or translation, has been fraught with controversial theoretical concerns (1993, 3). A number of scholars, Heffernan and W. J. T. Mitchell among them, argue that this rhetorical mode, which can be traced back to the description of Achilles's shield in *The Illiad*, is inherently paragonal—that is, it presents a confrontation or "struggle for dominance between the image and the word" (1) that emerges from what each art is perceived to lack, as well as from the problem of representation itself. Since, according to Plato, "every thing or object in the world is already a copy of an ideal and unchanging form or essence beyond the world . . . , then every artistic representation of that object will constitute a copy of a copy. It follows that a verbal description of a work of art produces a copy of a copy of a copy" (Cheeke 2008, 25).

Mitchell (1995) posits that the ekphrastic poem's attempt to bridge a perceived gap between media by speaking to, for, or about a work of visual art is based on an illusion. Although the visual and the verbal use different signs, "'speech acts' are not medium-specific" (160). Images, which are never completely reducible to language, can tell stories and make arguments of their own. For Mitchell, ekphrasis portrays "'the visual' as other to language" (163) and reveals, as it participates in, "the social structure of representation as an activity and a relationship of power/knowledge/desire—representation as something done to something, with something, by someone, for someone" (180).

If, then, ekphrastic poems are merely mimetic, their makers envious for the attention viewers bestow upon works of visual art (Cheeke 2008, 15), and worse, if the goal is chiefly to speak *for* visual art, often obscuring or dominating it, why would so many contemporary poets, let alone Latinx poets who are usually at least somewhat sensitive to systems of power and oppression, wish to immerse themselves in it? Why would we have seen in recent years a number of ekphrastic poems and projects by Latinx poets? Of course, the answers are as varied as the poets' approaches to ekphrasis, but I think they lie partly in questioning the limitations of the paradigms framing this "genre" and partly in considering the more nuanced (and often subversive) critical lenses through which some Latino/a poets view and "read" visual art. Finally, poems written by Latinas/os often serve to identify and champion works of Latinx and Latin American art that may be unknown to the wider United States public, including readers of poetry.

Some literary critics, such as Elizabeth Bergmann Loizeaux in *Twentieth-Century Poetry and the Visual Arts*, have recently sought to reconsider the paradigms surrounding ekphrasis. Although she agrees with Mitchell that this mode is dialogic, ethically charged, and "all about otherness," Loizeaux adds that ekphrasis is also "about how one engages" that otherness (2008, 9). She notes that poets often explain their ekphrastic aims in terms of sincere companionship or friendship, and she is skeptical of the *paragone*. She states:

> Under its lens every ekphrastic relationship looks like linguistic appropriation, every gesture of friendship like co-optation, every expression of admiration a declaration of envy by the word for the unobtainable power of the image. . . . While ekphrasis depends on the difference between word and image and can stage their representational contest and opposition, it also stages relations across difference. Otherness is not always "rival." (15–16)

Even Stephen Cheeke considers the potential in the border crossing that ekphrasis requires for true conversation between the arts when he writes, "Sometimes the encounter with alterity takes on a special charge when it is not merely an occasion for the discovery of difference but a place of relation and therefore of the possibility of exchange" (2008, 6).

In *Museum Meditations: Reframing Ekphrasis in Contemporary American Poetry*, Barbara K. Fischer makes a space for ekphrasis as "an interpretive occasion and a critical tool—a mode that involves description, enumeration, analysis, comparison, citation, questioning, critique, assessment, summation and judgment" (2006, 2). She points out that a number of contemporary ekphrastic poems address non-representational visual works, while some "may not represent their subjects at all, riffing off of their visual sources more tangentially or interrogatively" (ibid.).

These important insights are in keeping with Katie Geha and Travis Nichols's notion of ekphrasis as "a process of correspondence between words and images, between signs, between marks on the page and marks on the canvas, between texts" (2007, 16). In their introductory article to the catalogue *Poets on Painters*, they discuss the poems in their exhibition as "non-sites" that re-present the paintings without resembling them (16–17). Geha writes:

> I like to think of this as a constant correspondence, or the constant reflection of any one origin. Instead of having a discrete painting on the wall or finished poem on the page, both points are charged and constantly representing one another . . . allowing the word and the image to constantly shift, illuminating the other's trace, while refusing to act as static objects. (18)

This more dynamic and nuanced spectrum of relations between word and image—especially notions of ekphrasis as conversation, correspondence, riff, or critical tool—applies to much of the contemporary ekphrastic poetry written by Latinas/os in recent years. Yet it is important to note that Latinx ekphrasis may have deeper roots outside of Euro-American literature and theory and inside a long tradition of Latinx interdisciplinary arts that bring together word, image, and music. One of the very first invitations I received to give a public reading of my own poetry outside of my home state was to participate in a 1993 *flor y canto* celebration in Fort Collins, Colorado, with such literary luminaries as Lorna Dee Cervantes and Lalo Delgado. The *flor y canto* (flower and song) festivals, popular in Chicana/o artist-activist communities, especially in the 1960s and '70s, derive from pre-Columbian Aztec feasts called *in xochitl in cuicatl*, which included poetry recitation, writing-painting, and music. Historian Miguel León-Portilla explains that *xochitl* (flower) and *cuicatl* (song) "are a recurring semantic couplet" in Nahuatl poetry that means "poetry," "art," "symbolism" (1992, 54). Certainly, the concept shifted in various ways when adapted to the Chicana/o project of cultural reclamation, but my sense of that era's *flor y cantos* from the stories shared by those who attended them is that they often combined poetry writing and recitation, mural painting, music, dance, and feasting. During the same period, inter-arts cultural festivals and venues flourished in other Latinx communities as well. For example, New York City's El Museo del Barrio, Taller Boricua, and Nuyorican Poetry Café, while focusing in the first two cases on the visual arts and in the third on poetry, all became spaces that host multiple arts, both as separate exhibitions or performances and as inter-arts fusions.

A number of contemporary US Latinx poets, including Xanath Caraza, Eduardo C. Corral, Blas Falconer, Carmen Giménez Smith, Laurie Ann Guerrero, Juan Felipe Herrera, Valerie Martínez, Iyawó (Kristin Naca),

Carmen Tafolla, and Roberto Tejada, have written more than an occasional ekphrastic poem, engaging seriously with the mode. Single ekphrastic poems by several more Latinx poets have also begun appearing in literary magazines, partly as a result of Letras Latinas's *Pintura : Palabra*, "a collaborative, multi-year initiative, which is fomenting the creation of art-inspired writing through workshops held in tandem with the Smithsonian American Art Museum's traveling exhibit, *Our America: The Latino Presence in American Art* ("Announcing," 2015).

Aside from William Carlos Williams's 1962 *Pictures from Brueghel*, a series of ten poems regarding paintings by the Flemish artist Pieter Brueghel the Elder, two of the earliest substantial series of ekphrastic poems by a US Latino author are Juan Felipe Herrera's *The Roots of a Thousand Embraces* (1994), regarding Frida Kahlo's life and work, and his and Artemio Rodríguez's *Lotería Cards and Fortune Poems: A Book of Lives* (1999).

The latter, a handsomely printed hardcover book, contains 104 reproductions of Rodríguez's linocuts on pages facing Herrera's poems. The inclusion of the artwork in the book and the names of both artist and poet on its cover speak to the equality of the participants and their art forms, framing it as collaboration. In an interview with Frederick Luis Aldama, Herrera explains that he loved the process of writing in response to Rodríguez's prints so much that he produced about eighty more poems than the publisher originally requested. He says:

> Nothing was forced. Nothing was artificial for me. . . . Rodríguez gave me a lot of room to respond creatively . . . More than anything, his art just hit on all those areas that I hadn't written about but wanted to. It was like he found that musical key—like a D diminished or an augmented ninth with a lot of luscious chords—that I'd always wanted to sing in but hadn't had a chance to. (quoted in Aldama 2006, 137)

It is as if Herrera had found a kindred spirit with whom to converse, or better yet, with whom to jam. The poems are imbued with a sense of improvisation and performativity, several of them written in slick urban voices to jazzy tempos that at first appear to contrast Rodríguez's ornate and precise black-and-white prints. That is, until one considers the surreal sensibility and often satirical tone of both prints and poems. Rodríguez's linocuts recall medieval European and Mexican Revolution–era Guadalupe Posada woodcuts as well as velvet paintings and pre-Columbian codices, some characters even breathing Aztec speech glyphs.

Rodríguez's prints are based on Mexican *lotería*, a game of chance popular in Mexican and Mexican American communities. In his introduction to the book, art historian Rupert García explains, "There are actually two Mexican games of chance, one indigenous and ancient—*patolli*—and the other European and colonial—*la lotería* . . ." (quoted in Rodríguez and Herrera 1999, xi–xii). To win *patolli*, a player has to cover fifty-two spots painted in a cruciform design, the player's moves determined by a "roll of dice made of beans" (xi). *La lotería* is similar to bingo, but rather than matching numbers and letters, *lotería* uses a deck of cards, each portraying "a colorfully illustrated character whose name is printed at the bottom of the card" and playing boards containing the same (xiii). "When the *lotería* announcer chooses a card from the deck, he doesn't simply call out its name, but rather, he either improvises a short poem or uses a stock phrase that makes a poetic allusion to the character on the card" (xiv). The player has to figure out which character the announcer is invoking in order to cover a matching spot on their playing board. Thus, visual art, poetic composition, improvisation, and interpretation are inherent components of the *lotería* game, and the announcers' cleverness often predicts their popularity. Many iterations of the game have been produced since its inception, but as García notes, the most well known is the 1887 Don Clemente version (xv). While its cast of characters is engaging, the drawings are simple, similar to those one might find in a grade-school primer.

Rodríguez includes some of the Don Clemente characters, but his versions are much more surreal, often macabre and marked by black humor. For example, in the current version of the Don Clemente game, La Botella holds ketchup. By contrast, Rodríguez's La Botella holds Mata Perros (kills dogs), 100-percent agave tequila añejo, along with the drunk who lies contorted at the bottom of the bottle. The artist's insistence on the presence of the ugly is an important statement, for as poet and critic Alfred Arteaga observes, "Art differentiates the beautiful from the ugly, the civilized from the primitive, art from kitsch, the subject from the nonsubject. For not only does artistic discourse fashion the representation of peoples, it also discriminates who is to be represented and who represents" (1997, 79).

Many pairs in the Rodríguez/Herrera deck are striking for their nuanced sociopolitical commentary forged of polysemic signs. In the poem "La Muerte," Death says that it is her nature "to spell Integration with an X" (Rodríguez and Herrera 1999, 8), suggesting at once Malcolm X, the *x* an illiterate person might mark as a signature, the unknown, and the Nahuatl *x* in *Mexica* (pronounced "meshica") and *Mexico*, later replaced in Spanish by the hushed *j* sound. It might even recall the cruciform design on which the Aztecs played *patolli*. On another card, Rodríguez ironically depicts El Caballero (the gentleman) as a conquistador on horseback trampling a native person. Herrera's corresponding gentleman taunts the person he looms over, saying, "You are in my way aren't you, you are / thinking about rising up, about speaking" (164)? It is almost as though Herrera, in a metacognitive moment, is poking fun at his own ekphrastic practice of prosopopoeia.

In addition to reenvisioning standard *lotería* characters, Rodríguez also adds a number of new ones, further modernizing and hybridizing his deck. Many of them address issues relevant on both sides of the border. In the introduction, García points to the print-poem pair titled *La Migra* (the immigration officer); Rodríguez depicts a "Schwarzeneggerian U.S. border patrolman with a buzz haircut and handcuffs at the ready" (xx) whom Herrera calls "the child- eye dipped in soldier oil" (Rodríguez and Herrera 1999, 94). This purposefully ambiguous phrase conflates border-patrol officer with soldier, notes how young some officers and soldiers actually are, and may also allude to the artist's "child eye"—one that can humorously and imaginatively meld the officer with his dragnet vehicle and the back half of a horse but that must also confront the war waged by the United States against undocumented immigrants.

La Migra follows *El Mojado* (the wetback) on the preceding page spread. If placed side by side, these two prints make one continuous image. They and their poems fall almost exactly at the book's center, giving them added weight. *El Mojado* depicts a skinny, barefoot man running alongside a barbed wire fence while being chased by a horse and a human hand holding an open handcuff. Only when readers turn the page do they see the full-on pursuit of *la migra*. Herrera's poem again envoices the silent image, but I find this a counter-hegemonic move since *El Mojado* represents the undocumented, who in the United States are repeatedly subjected to systems of silencing. As Elizabeth Loizeaux points out:

> Prosopopoeia can . . . be understood as the collapse of subject and object, the inhabiting of another body and voice by the poet, equally an objectification and an exercise of empathy. As a closing of the gap between poet and image, prosopopoeia can be seen variously as the most hegemonic of moves (language taking over the image, inhabiting it) or as the most altruistic (language liberating the frozen image to tell its story). (2008, 24)

In this poem, Herrera not only gives voice to those often silenced; he also creates a satirical, knowing voice that toys with the reader:

> . . . the tiny fever bones under
> my naked feet, these I know.
>
> Call them Matamoros–New York
> Call them Agua Prieta–Seattle
> Call them Tecate–West Liberty, Iowa
> Call them Aguililla–San Quintín
>
> I count shadows, I follow them, wherever I go.
> They adjust their little mirrors, they guide me,
> You want to run with me, esta noche? (Rodríguez and Herrera 1999, 92)

The tiny fever bones belong to those migrants who have died crossing the desert. Furthermore, Herrera's use of hyphens between the names of towns/cities in Mexico and those in the United States at once link and separate them, mirroring the seesaw migration between them and suggesting that they are much closer than some might think. The last pair of place names cleverly links Aguililla, a city in Michoacán, to San Quintín, an agricultural town in Baja California, subtly erasing the line between the two Californias and also providing an eye rhyme with San Quentin, the state prison in northern California that houses the state's only death row.

In Herrera's hands, the toll of *La Campana* is both surprising and empowering. Rodríguez portrays a church bell with a human head for its clapper. On its left, an aloof child holds the rope that could ring it; on its right, a horned creature grins; and atop its supporting beam walks another creature with a dog's body and a serpent's tongue. One might expect Herrera's poem to interpret the clapper as a slave, lynched man, or forced convert to Christianity. After all, this head has lost its body, has a rope connected to its neck, and is surrounded by sinister onlookers. Instead, Herrera's hip clapper is quite the optimist, empowered by his recent acquisition of gainful employment dealing in the mysteries of time. The poem begins:

> Say baby, so I got a job. Yeah
> no more cheese lines, no more dead
> quesadillas, mango flakes or blintz-wanna-
> be's. See me? Hey don't pity me, Jack. I am
> on. (12)

He's on because instead of being controlled by time, space, or anything else around him, he brags, "They snap at my command" (12). Plus, as the town crier, he knows everyone's secrets:

> . . . You want to know
> how long you got to live? You want to know
> about the last homicide, the Rice Festival,
> the grimace inside this building. Listen up. (12)

Herrera flips the script—and the power dynamics along with it—on the victim narrative one expects when first casting eyes on the print.

In this collaboration, partners do speak—image and word, visual artist and poet, each individually on its/his own terms, and together as a third mind. García writes, "Seemingly opposing and competitive modes of creating have resulted in a collaboration that transcends the usual prejudices of perception" (xi). The volume—with its visual art, pre-Columbian motifs, poetry, and myriad references to music—is an innovative *lotería*, but it is also a contemporary *flor y canto*.

Chicana poet Carmen Tafolla and Mexican artist Catalina Gárate García's *Rebozos* (2012), which began as an exhibit of paintings and poems at the University of El Paso's Centennial Museum, is the only other collection of US Latinx ekphrastic poetry I have found that contains reproductions of the images, in this case color paintings in an art book format. As is the case for *Lotería Cards*, the names of both poet and visual artist grace the cover of *Rebozos*. A prefatory essay by Tafolla, the poet's and artist's closing statements, and a detailed afterword by anthropologist Hector García Manzanedo provide historical and cultural contexts for the collection's subject, the rebozo or Mexican shawl. They explain that it has been used by Mexican women, especially in rural and indigenous communities, for over four hundred years as a sling to carry children, wood, and foods; a shield to protect against the weather or to provide privacy; and a shroud to cover the dead (Tafolla and Gárate García 2012, ix, 37). In addition, García Manzanedo explains that the garment "became incorporated into the dance of Mexico as well, twirled above the head or wrapped around the shoulders; from the festivity of La Bamba to the solemnity of Zandunga, the rebozo became an integral part of the folkloric culture of Mexico" (40).

Dancer Rosa Guerrero was invited to participate by choreographing a dance titled *Rebozo Rojo* for the multi-arts exhibit, once again reminiscent of a *flor y canto* celebration. Of their truly collaborative effort, Guerrero says, "We are stirring this all together, like cultural revolutionaries, for identity, stirring it como un mole, then weaving it, como un rebozo" (41). Gárate García felt strongly that "people should see this art and these poems together" (xiii). Just as the linocuts in the *Lotería* project are inspired by other works of art, Tafolla stresses:

> This book [*Rebozos*] cannot be traced solely to the artist, the poet, and the dancer that co-created, weaving into and out of each other's expressions. The central work of art celebrated here is the rebozo itself and the many centuries of women on this continent— Indigenous, Mestiza, Criolla, Pre-Columbian, Colonial, Revolutionary, Modern Feminist—who used their rebozos as creative instruments in their lives (ix).

Tafolla and Gárate García celebrate the rebozo as a cultural icon imbued with the power to reach across borders of race, ethnicity, class, epoch, and nation to unite Mexican and Mexican American women. While I question the totalizing potential of such a utopian perspective, I appreciate the many different roles—soldadera, laborer, curandera, mother, artist, lover, bruja, planter of literal and figurative seeds—and the wide range of emotional experience the project assigns to women.

One of the most powerful features of the collection is that Tafolla provides both English and Spanish versions of the poems that are not translations, thereby privileging the bilingual reader. She says, "I wrote each poem authentically in its own language, and insisted . . . that each poem should have its freedom to be unique, even from its counterpart in the other language" (43). If one also conceptualizes visual art as speaking its own tongue, the book becomes a uniquely polyvocal text.

Gárate García's impressionistic paintings with their broad strokes poignantly capture the gestures, movements, and moods of their subjects. Yet very rarely does she show the full faces of the woman depicted. They are often turned away from the viewer's gaze, covered by the rebozo, or rendered abstractly. The tone is respectful, as though the artist had been careful not to intrude, wishing to reduce the sense of spectacle while enhancing the role of the rebozo in the depicted woman's everyday life. Gárate García writes, "The rebozo of a Mexican woman will always be for me a symbol of her strength against the hardships of life, and a protective mantle that covers her throughout her existence" (34).

At first, Tafolla's poems may seem to do the opposite, as she draws on the paintings' titles and moods to suggest many potential details the viewer does *not* see: time animated as a shy, gold-eyed coyote that the pregnant woman in "Waiting" tries to coax with "morsels, sabrositos, / open hands" (8) or the old woman's "crackles like dried leaves in ancient bottles," "half-blind eyes," and "shuffling slippers" in "Curandera, Your Voice" (18). These verbal images do not appear in the paintings, but neither are all of them in the Spanish versions of these poems, while the Spanish versions contain elements that the English do not. This paradoxical inclination on the part of both collaborators to simultaneously celebrate and shield the women wearing the rebozos belies a desire to gain visibility for Latinas without fully exposing them and relinquishing their secrets to the colonizing gaze that would exploit and erase them. Theirs is, perhaps, a kind of strategic essentialism. As with *Lotería Cards*, this text complicates the problems of ekphrasis rather than simply perpetuating them.

A number of my own recent ekphrastic poems have responded to the life, praxis, and earth-body works of Cuban American artist Ana Mendieta, so I was delighted to learn that Mendieta is also a favorite of poet Carmen Giménez Smith, whose 2013 collection *Milk and Filth* includes a long poem regarding Mendieta's work. Mendieta was born in Havana in 1948 and sent at age twelve with her sister to the United States under Operation Peter Pan, which sought to "protect" Cuban children from Fidel Castro's communism but ultimately often orphaned them. The Mendieta sisters "were shuttled between foster homes, orphanages, and juvenile correction facilities" (Blocker 1999, 52). In Iowa, where there were few people of color, their difference was noted, and they were often subjected to racism (53).

Mendieta's work combines ritual performance, body art, earth art, sculptures, and installations, as well as archival photographs and film that become works of art themselves. She often uses her own body as part of the piece, to mark her silhouette in the earth, and/or to shape figures on the earth's surface with various natural objects. In her insightful analysis *Where Is Ana Mendieta?*, art historian Jane Blocker explains that Mendieta's works "invoke disappearance, movement, and indeterminacy," emphasizing "liminality over legibility and change over fixity" (1999, 24). She asserts that due to Mendieta's "short life, aesthetic choices, gender, ethnicity, and politics," she is absent "from a variety of discursive sites" (3). Critics have often marginalized her work by suggesting "that the meaning of her art is contained by the particularities of her own life rather than by larger political and cultural contexts and questions" (12).

Giménez Smith's poem in eight parts "A Devil Inside Me" addresses this absence. It takes its title from Mendieta's performance film *Untitled (Blood Sign #1)*, during which the artist finger paints "There's a devil inside me" on a white wall in blood. The film illustrates the transgressive nature of Mendieta's work, particularly as a method to critique stereotypes that cast Latinas as aggressive and hot tempered, effectively silencing their expressions of anger at injustice. Within this context, Giménez Smith's title links Mendieta to second-wave feminists, like Gloria Anzaldúa and Cherríe Moraga, who were pioneers in analyzing the intersections between multiple systems of oppression. Because Giménez Smith's book as a whole pays tribute to the influential strategies and accomplishments of the second wave, the title "A Devil Inside Me" resonates throughout the book.

Although the title alludes to a single work of art, the poem is in conversation with Mendieta's entire oeuvre. Rather than representing a representation by describing specific pieces, Giménez Smith presents a montage of images that refer more broadly to processes Mendieta performed throughout her career—processes that suggest the world view and politic behind her work. Furthermore, in Giménez Smith's hands, the ekphrastic poem becomes the "interpretive occasion and critical tool" that Barbara Fischer describes (2006, 2). It serves as corrective to critics' depoliticization of Mendieta's work and argues for an analysis that acknowledges Mendieta's resistance. Thus, the last three lines of the poem's very first section present an especially important petition: "Olofi, I trust/in the words 'the personal/is political.' Let it be so" (Giménez Smith 2013, 57).

Jane Blocker (1999) argues that the liminality in Mendieta's work suggests she "occupied her exile as a discursive position from which to create her art . . . [and] interrogate nationality, color, ethnicity, and gender" (27). Linking herself to the earth—and through it, to the universe—rather than any nation, she resists normative "concepts of belonging, borders, margins, and centers" (73). The poem contains several passages in which Giménez Smith situates Mendieta's work in the non-national limen. In section two, for example, she points to Mendieta's purposeful illegibility and constant movement:

> The bodyprint
> is an illegible surge:
> of leaving trace
> of self in route. (58)

And later, she suggests that Mendieta's fusion of her own body with the earth's may be a negation of borders or a reclaiming of land as it was conceptualized before them:

> The body, a territory.
> From inside the territory,
> call for reversal. The call
> for reversal is native, first. (59)

In a section of the poem that alludes to Mendieta's *Tree of Life*, Giménez Smith emphasizes the regenerating power of Mendieta's praxis as well as her agency:

> ... the body
> schemes with verdure
> and mud ambrosia,
> in a tree trunk,
> that baptismal consecration.
> Art history banished
> the body and its sopping glut in
> customary expulsion.
> The body pushes back.
> She is found *embedded*, heart *exuded* ... (60)

The "sopping glut" may refer to women's bodies in general but also to any number of pieces in which Mendieta covered herself in blood, often to call attention to violence against women. For this she is expelled and "found embedded" in the earth or a tomb with an animal "heart exuded" atop the blood drenched sheet that shrouds her body. Rather than focusing on the trauma of Mendieta's exile from Cuba, Giménez Smith points to her exile from the art world and her will to push back (60).

Finally, the poem also proposes links between Mendieta's work created thirty-plus years ago and current horrors. At the beginning of section six, Giménez Smith connects both the artist's and the earth's bodies to this decade's wars and environmental wreckage:

> The body is a battleground. Drone attacks
> on it. If it's broken, they buy it.
> If it's splayed on the table
> for dissection, they bought it. Blood
> is the enterprise (62)

At the same time, these lines refer to Mendieta's *Untitled (Rape Scene)*, a performance created to protest the rape of a woman on the college campus she attended. Rather than obscuring the subversive nature of Mendieta's art, Giménez Smith foregrounds it. Her nuanced approach meets the work on its own terms, opening a discursive site for more complex readings of it.

There are other excellent examples of Latinx ekphrasis to which I could point. In fact, the myriad approaches that Latinas/os take to this mode convince me that it is time to expand its definition and complicate its paradigm. With this, I turn to a different kind of inter-arts correspondence. Consider Kenneth Patchen's painted poems where visual art and poetry interact on the same canvas. In Latinx literature, I can think of few whose practices exemplify this better than poets/artists Carlos Cortez and Cecilia Vicuña. Cortez's poetry collections, such as *De Kansas a Califas & Back Again*, also showcase reproductions of his linocut prints that, in turn, often contain words, both the visual and verbal reflecting his lifelong political activism. In many of Vicuña's books, *Precarious/QUIPOem*, *Cloud-Net*, and *Instan* among them, any borders between the arts disappear. Vicuña has created installations both inside of buildings (from farmhouses to galleries) and outdoors. Usually, they contain no written text, although while inhabiting them, she might recite poems. Sometimes different manifestations of these pieces—part archival and part new work—find their way to print. For example, Vicuña might photograph one of her installations and then lay short poems over or next to the photos when placing them in a book. This occurs frequently in *About to Happen*, *Cloud-Net*, and *QIUPOem*, the latter's title a play on the word *quipu*, the Andean system of intricately knotted cords that was used to store information significant to Andean culture and civilization.

Vicuña's piece "Sendero Chibcha" is spread across two pages of *QUIPOoem*. In the bottom left corner of the left-hand page rests a photograph of two yellow strings anchored to the earth. One stretches across the ground to the right, and the other reaches into the sky. In the upper right corner of the right-hand page, a different photograph, this one a close-up, shows two crossed sticks, bound together with red string, standing among foliage. From one of them, a yellow string pulls toward the left. Neither photo covers its entire page. The poem's typed words stretch across the pages as if an extension of the yellow string attempting to literally tie the two pages and places together. They read, "The sun spins the thread of life around the world the earth is a loom and the sun weaves the night and the day. / The Chibchas weave lines, birds lose feathers and being makes its offering to immensity. Two or three lines, a mark, and silence begins to speak" (1997, 66–67). Interestingly, Johanna Drucker, one of the foremost scholars on verbo-visual texts, has written, "It may well be that there is no human urge more fundamental than that of mark making—just as there is no activity which characterizes human culture more distinctly than that of language" (1998, 57). In Vicuña's poem, the marks are their own language; they speak.

Vicuña's work not only fuses poetry and visual art; many poems are inter-textual as well, incorporating quotations from myriad sources. They layer and juxtapose images of knots, the warp and the weft, entanglement, and weaving to treat the larger theme of interconnection. Although some of them are written completely in Spanish, others combine it with Quechua, Nahuatl, Latin, and/or English. For example, Vicuña once chalked the invented word *partisipasión* in three separate chunks—"parti," "si," and "pasión"—across a highway, photographed it, and then placed another poem beneath the photo. The poem reads:

> Sex is dust,
> el polvo,
> the sí
> in passion
> And to parti si pate
> is
> to partake of suffering
> (passion from the Latin *patire*, to suffer) (1997, 56–57)

This piece illustrates how Vicuña breaks open words and turns them inside out, uncovering their derivations to expose their internal metaphors in what become poems as textured as the weavings that also play a role in much of her work. The poem's visual performance on the page is integral to its meaning.

In fact, some are concrete poems—one in the shape of a radiating sun and another in that of a warp and weft. The book's context is key, for throughout it, Vicuña has strung photographs of yarn, thread, or string creating webs or tying one element to another, such as a thread and its shadows crisscrossing a bedroom (24–25) or two strings stretched from rock to rock across a river as if to tie its banks together. In *QUIPOem*, as in Vicuña's other books, the pages flow seamlessly into one another. The *quipu* is the poem is the art. Hers is both a literal and figurative weaving of visual and verbal.

I have not yet fused the arts on the page, only in performance, but I have written poems in response to prints, paintings, drawings, earthworks, installations, glass art, sculptures, performance art, photographs, and assemblage by artists living and dead, artists whom I have known personally and locally as well as those I have never met. They have included Jeff Abbey Maldonado, Roberto Valadez, Rene Arceo, Guillermo Gomez Peña, Maria Magdalena Campos Pons, Charles "Chaz" Bojorquez, Ana Mendieta, Graciela Iturbide, Remedios Varo, Erik de Luna Genel, El Anatsui, Roy Staab, Harvey Littleton, Amy Cropper, and Linda Howard, among others. Some of these engagements have been more successful than others, but they have always led me to a more multifaceted understanding of the artist's work and a deeper appreciation for the concerns it expresses.

Some poems have been inspired by multiple kinds of art. I still relish the experience I shared with Chicago artist Roberto Valadez when he asked me to write a poem in response to his painting *Arbol de Blues*, which he conceived as an *ofrenda* (an offering and elegy) to the Delta blues musician Jimmy Davis. I wrote "At the Base of the Blues Tree" only after listening to Valadez's stories about how he first came to know the blues and the Chicago musicians who played at the Maxwell Street market where the borders between Mexican American and African American communities became a bit less pronounced. We shared those stories while listening to recordings of Davis and live jams by other Delta blues men. The poem incorporates images from the painting to be sure, but it also riffs on the music and the stories that Valadez wanted to share.

More recently, I participated in *Mind the Gap*, a project curated by artists Tim Abel and Sara R. Parr. They invited nine writers to contribute ekphrastic pieces on any artwork in the world. They then turned the poems and micro-fictions over to nine printmakers who created new works based on the literary pieces. The result was an ekphrastic chain-link or relay of visual and verbal encounters that landed in a portfolio of prints with an accompanying letterpress booklet of poems and stories. What if a project like this were to travel forward to another writer and then again to a new visual artist? What if it traversed many borders to reach its participants? Which traces of each interaction would remain?

I am inspired by a profound love of collaboration forged in respect for difference. A true merging of minds—a third mind—does not erase the thoughts of either or the contexts in which they arise. It embraces the overlaps and the intersections, but it also checks and challenges. It knows when to pause. Moreover, it seeks (and often finds) that which could only emerge in the exchange. The various projects I have described here involve different degrees of collaboration. And because traditionally, an ekphrastic poem comes *after* the visual art and the artist may not be available for consultation, one could argue that it is not a true collaboration at all. My goal, however, is to treat it as such to the fullest extent possible—to put "the ekphrastic power of the word," as Loizeaux has phrased it, "to the service of connection that here and there, now and then, self and other not be isolated" (2008, 177).

SOURCES

Aldama, Frederick Luis. 2006. *Spilling the Beans in Chicanolandia: Conversations with Writers and Artists*. Austin: University of Texas Press.

"Announcing the Pintura: Palabra DC Residencies." 2015. *Letras Latinas* (blog). Institute for Latino Studies, University of Notre Dame, April 22. http://letras latinasblog.blogspot.com/2015/04/announcing-pinturapalabra-dc- residencies.html.

Arteaga, Alfred. 1997. *Chicano Poetics: Heterotexts and Hybridities*. New York: Cambridge University Press.

Blocker, Jane. 1999. *Where Is Ana Mendieta? Identity, Performativity, and Exile*. Durham, NC: Duke University Press.

Cheeke, Stephen. 2008. *Writing for Art: The Aesthetics of Ekphrasis*. Manchester: Manchester University Press.

Cortez, Carlos. 1992. *De Kansas a Califas & Back Again*. Chicago: MARCH/Abrazo Press.

Drucker, Johanna. 1998. *Figuring the Word: Essays on Books, Writing, and Visual Poetries*. New York: Granary Books.

Fischer, Barbara K. 2006. *Museum Meditations: Reframing Ekphrasis in Contemporary American Poetry*. New York: Routledge.

Geha, Katie, and Travis Nichols, eds. 2007. *Poets on Painters*. Wichita, KS: Wichita State University.

Giménez Smith, Carmen. *Milk and Filth*. 2013. Tucson: University of Arizona Press.

Heffernan, James A. W. 1993. *Museum of Words: The Poetics of Ekphrasis from Homer to Ashbery*. Chicago: University of Chicago Press.

Herrera, Juan Felipe. 1994. *The Roots of a Thousand Embraces: Dialogues*. San Francisco: Manic D Press.

León-Portilla, Miguel. 1992. *Fifteen Poets of the Aztec World*. Norman: University of Oklahoma Press.

Lessing, Gotthold Ephraim. 1887. *Laocoön: An Essay upon the Limits of Painting and Poetry with Remarks Illustrative of Various Points in the History of Ancient Art*. Boston: Roberts Brothers.

Loizeaux, Elizabeth Bergmann. 2008. *Twentieth-Century Poetry and the Visual Arts*. Cambridge, UK: Cambridge University Press.

Melendez Kelson, Maria. 2016. "A Chingona Plays Miss Dinah Brand." *Poetry* 207, no. 6 (March): 614–15.

Mitchell, W. J. T. 1995. *Picture Theory*. Chicago: University of Chicago Press.

Rodríguez, Artemio, and Juan Felipe Herrera. 1999. *Loteria Cards and Fortune Poems: A Book of Lives*. San Francisco: City Lights Books.

Tafolla, Carmen, and Catalina Gárate García. 2012. *Rebozos*. Chicago: Wings Press.

Vicuña, Cecilia. 1997. *The Precarious/QUIPOem: The Art and Poetry of Cecilia Vicuna*. Hanover, MA: Wesleyan University Press.

———. 1999. *Cloud-Net*. New York: Art in General.

———. 2002. *Instan*. Berkeley, CA: Kelsey Street Press.

———. 2017. *About to Happen*. Los Angeles: Contemporary Arts Center and Siglio Press.

Williams, William Carlos. 1962. *Pictures from Brueghel*. In *Pictures from Brueghel and Other Poems*, 1–14. Cambridge, MA: New Directions.

What the Neoliberal Policy Labs Eat and Shit

Horrific Fables for a Specific Universe

DANIEL BORZUTZKY

> *My translational intent has nothing to do with personal growth, intellectual exercise, or cultural exchange, which implies an equal standing of some sort. South Korea and the U.S. are not equal. I am not transnationally equal. My intent is to expose what a neocolony is, what it does to its own, what it eats and shits. Kim Hyesoon's poetry reveals all this, and this is why I translate her work.*
>
> —DON MEE CHOI, *Freely Frayed, ㄱ=q, & Race=Nation* (WAVE BOOKS, 2014)

I

THINKING ABOUT THE US reception of translated Chilean poems of historical horror, a useful starting place is Jack Schmitt's translation of Raúl Zurita's *Anteparaiso*. The review is written by the US poet David Kirby, and it was first published in *Library Journal*. Kirby writes:

> Perhaps first-hand experience of Chile is necessary before the reader of these poems feels anything close to the translator's reaction to them. When he was first introduced to Zurita's poetry, Schmitt writes, it "haunted me, even gave me nightmares," but the emotions that affected him so strongly may not be felt by others. . . . [He recommends it] for libraries with large Latin American collections only. (Kirby, 1986).

Reception: Kirby's reading is one where there is a distinct "here" (the United States) and a distinct "there" (Chile). The two do not intersect, and as Kirby would have it, the book cannot be understood without "first-hand experience" of the nation. He cannot access the poetry, he claims, because he cannot access or imagine the national context in which it is written. For Kirby, the poetry is too specific, too specifically tied to nation.

On the other hand, some critics argue that poetry in translation should not be used to draw conclusions about a nation and its cultural and political histories. I am thinking of a recent review in *Book Forum* of the great Korean poet Kim Hyesoon's new book *Sorrowtoothpaste Mirrorcream*. The reviewer, Mia You, laments the way in which reviewers have depended on Korean history and politics to situate Kim's poetics. Mia You concludes:

> In reading the criticism on Kim's poetics, I've been struck by how often the same bullet-point history of South Korea is recounted: the Korean War, the military dictatorships, the Gwangju Massacre, the nuclear race. The implication is that Kim comes from a bloody culture, so how can she help but write bloody poetry? . . . —I would say that Kim is no more predisposed by her context to such violence than Billy Collins or Charles Bernstein. After all, we could say that their context comprises of over 30,000 gun violence-related deaths each year and a president who announces on television, "We tortured some folks." Kim is a singular poet in Korea, just as she is in America, but we can only fully appreciate this when we see that, for her, such violence is not the end but a means (You, 2014).

Here we have two problems regarding reception of dissidence and translated poetry. Kirby, on one end, can't understand Zurita's poetry without knowledge of the historical and political context through which he writes, while Mia You tells us that it is *wrong* to read Hyesoon through the historical and political context through which she writes. We make a mistake, Mia You argues, when we read her poetry as something that helps us understand the culture. Or perhaps more accurately, we make a mistake when we conclude that Korea's culture and its history tell us something about Hyesoon.

Thus, if Kirby's argument is that Zurita's poetry requires specific historical or cultural knowledge to be understood, then Mia You's argument is that it is dismissive to frame Hyesoon's writing with the specifics of history and culture. At first, these positions seemed like binaries to me, but now I think they more or less lead to the same place: we should not turn to poetry, and specifically translated poetry, to understand, analyze, or critique historical, political and national events. Such specificity either alienates readers (Kirby) or it misguidedly turns the poet into a mouthpiece for her culture (You).

Mia You's essay on Hyesoon is provocative, and I don't think she's wrong to say that a poet translated into a foreign language can easily become a sociological specimen whose poetry becomes subsequent to her nation-based identity. But on the whole, I find neither position particularly compelling, nor would I argue that Zurita's writing offers a counterargument to the aforementioned positions in regard to specificity versus universality. It asks to us to occupy both positions; it asks us to position him as a Chilean within a given context while also asking us, especially in his recent poetry, where "the plains of Hiroshima and Nagasaki pass before the Chilean sky," to consider the Chilean dictatorship as just another moment in a violent universe whose history does not allow us to distinguish one atrocity from another. For Zurita, then, the Chilean dictatorship sits within a global continuum of international and transhistorical violence. Its specificity, he might say, is both fundamentally important and fundamentally irrelevant. As he has told me in conversation, it could have happened now, or it could have happened a thousand years ago.

II

In the United States, poetry and translation generally operate in a border-contained isolation. We like to use the rhetoric of how translation is something that makes the world a bit smaller, but we don't really want to see translation through the lens of transnationalism, where the work in translation can dialogue with, can critique, can shed light on several national identities at once. One notable exception comes from critic Michael Dowdy in his 2013 book *Broken Souths: Latino/a Poetic Responses to Neoliberalism and Globalization*. And one big mission of Dowdy's book is to connect English-language Latino writers in the United States with Spanish-speaking writers in Latin America. To this end, Dowdy writes specifically about Martín Espada's poem "Not Here," which is dedicated to, and in dialogue with, Raul Zurita:

> The other poets tell me: electricity was involved / 7 years later, Zurita blinked to save his eyes, and wrote: / in the name of our love let even the steel-toed boots / that kicked us be loved. (Dowdy 2013, 113)

According to Dowdy, what Espada is up to here is the creation of "radical intersubjectivities between North and South among Latino and North and Latin American poets to contest official narratives of the coup. . . . And if Zurita reconstructs the imaginary community of the Chilean nation, Espada makes Chile the site for launching an imaginary transnational 'republic'" (Dowdy 2013, 111). Furthermore, Dowdy calls attention to the image of electricity flowing through Zurita's body to illustrate how Zurita's "poetic project is grounded in sensory experience and the strength to withstand the 'shock treatment' also figuratively given to the Chilean state and body politic by the Chicago Boys" (Dowdy 2013, 113).

In other words, the broken body of the poet is the container for the physical violence caused by the Chilean government and the economic violence born in my hometown of Chicago.

III

I come from a Chile and a Chicago that have both been labeled as "neoliberal policy labs"; a Chicago that copies Chile's "hypermarketized governance that denigrates collective institutions," which, according to University of Illinois at Chicago Education Policy scholar Pauline Lipman, involves:

> gutting social welfare and privatizing public assets as the new urban dogma. [privatizing] bridges, parking meters, public parking garages, schools, hospitals, and public housing," while driving down the cost of labor through deregulation, outsourcing unionized jobs, [and]

casualized and contingent labor. To deal with the contradictions produced by neoliberal policies in Chicago and nationally, the privatizing state is also a punitive state that polices and contains immigrants, homeless people, the dispossessed, and low-income communities of color, particularly youth, and their political resistance. Chicago is notorious for its police torture scandals and brutal policing of African American and Latino communities. In short, neoliberal urbanism has set in motion new forms of state-assisted economic, social and spatial inequality, marginality, exclusion and punishment. (Lipman, 2011)

These are policies designed forty years ago at the University of Chicago, tested out in the neoliberal policy lab created under the smoke screen of murder and torture by the Pinochet dictatorship, policies that included mass privatizations of education, health care, and public services, which destroyed the labor unions and created a brutal financial dictatorship where the consolidation of wealth and power destroyed the working class, destroyed the environment, caused massive poverty and homelessness. These were policies that began in Chile forty years ago, and these police thrive in Chicago today. We could, in fact, take Pauline Lipman's paragraph above and, with the exception of the discussion of race, replace Chicago with Chile. And while some might say that my comparison of violence in Chile and Chicago is hyperbolic or inaccurate, to understand the discussion more broadly, one need only look at the numbers of people tortured and abused by the Chicago police, the number of people killed on the streets each year, the literally hundreds of thousands of poor children left to struggle in impoverished public schools that lack the most basic of resources. And the recent reporting about police torture centers in Chicago, where unregistered prisons are "disappeared," only further justifies this point. I know, of course, that there are differences between the two places. But I am sick of comparisons, of playing the which-apocalypse-is-worse game. All the brutal neoliberal policy labs are murder zones. And someone tortured or killed by the Chicago police is someone just as dead or tortured as someone tortured or killed by the Pinochet regime.

Or as Dowdy writes, the economic policies of the Chicago boys "were designed to erase specificities of places and to displace socialist as well as Keynesian versions of economy and society." An erasure that, in my view, traveled from Chicago to Chile and now back to Chicago again.

IV

I want to conclude by mentioning three works of poetry that are unabashedly specific in their discussions of local violence while at the same time asking us to situate this violence within a broader global continuum: Valerie Martínez's 2010 book-length poem *Each and Her*; Juan Felipe Herrera's poem "Señorita X: Song for the Yellow-Robed Girl from Juárez"; and Mexican poet María Rivera's "Los Muertos," translated by the inexhaustible poet and activist Jen Hofer.

In *Each and Her*, Martínez documents with facts, names, and narratives the deaths of hundreds of young Mexican girls and women along the US-Mexico border. Many of these women worked in the maquiladoras; they were murdered, tortured, raped, and mutilated.

Here is one section of *Each and Her*:

> the number of girls and women
> working in the post-NAFTA
> maquiladora industry
>
> 472,423
> while they can't be hired legally
> at the age of 16, it is common for these girl-women
> to get false documents
> start work at 12, 13, 14 (Martínez 2010, 21)

And here is another section from *Each and Her* :

> Jessica Lizalde Leon (3.14.93)
> Lorenza Isela Gonzalez (4.25.94)
> Erica Garcia Morena (7.16.95)
> Sonia Ivette Ramirez (8.10.96)
> Juana Iñiguez Mares (10.23.97)

> Perla Patricia Sáenz Diaz (2.19.98)
> Bertha Luz Briones Palacios (8.2.99)
> Amparo Guzman (4.2.00)
> Gloría Rivas Martinez (10.28.01)
> Lourdes Ivette Lucero Campos (1.19.02)
> Miriam Soledad Sáenz Acosta (3.28.03) (Martínez 2010, 32)

In *Each and Her*, there is love for the dead communicated through an inferno-rendering poetry that always brings us back to the ways in which the abstractions of bureaucracy and government and capital destroy real, actual, human bodies. We have the names of those who died, but we do not have the names of their killers. The absence of the names of the killers perhaps amplifies the presence of the names of murdered women. In doing this, Martínez forces us to confront the names, the individuals, the lives obliterated at the conjunction of the military-police state, narco-trafficking juntas, border and immigration politics, and the exploitative practices of international capitalism.

To name the names of the dead and to write them as poetry is not to aestheticize them. Rather, it is to force the reader to witness the dead. It is to prevent the dead from disappearing permanently. It is to ask us to consider what it means for our bodies to live knowing that these other bodies have been slaughtered, knowing that are own bodies are complicit in their slaughter, knowing that are own lives are, if we care enough to think about it, intricately connected with their deaths.

And this approach to naming the names is also used by Juan Felipe Herrera in his poem "Señorita X: Song for the Yellow-Robed Girl from Juárez":

> This report, writes Herrera, has been filed in accordance with
> the proper policy for
> identifying the dead
> Who's the killer Brenda Berenice Delgado?
> Who's the killer Alma Chavira?
> Who's the killer Verónica Martínez Hernández?
> Who's the killer Esmeralda Herrera Monreal?
> Who's the killer Mayra Reyes Solís?
> Who's the killer Guadalupe Luna De La Rosa?
> Who's the killer Griselda Mares? (Herrera 2010, 79–80)

Herrera's poem names the names of the dead, perhaps, so that we might look for their lives, so that we might understand them as individuals, as girls and women whose lives and deaths ought to mean something to us. The first name on Herrera's list is Brenda Berenice Delgado, who according to the website of *El Universal Nación* was only five years old when she was found murdered and sexually abused in 2003. Words fail me here. It is a darkness I can barely consider.

Admittedly, I am engaging with the poem in a way that most readers would not. But in reality, I am doing no more than accepting an invitation the poem offers.

One way, then, of understanding the naming of the names is as a means of maintaining a public record, of giving the dead more respect than they were given by the state, by their employers, and by their unnamed and anonymous murderers. It honors the people who were disposed of. It is a memorialization and a condemnation. A record of an atrocity, a communal and horrific failure that is at once local and global.

And to conclude, I want to look at a few lines from Mexican poet María Rivera's great poem "Los Muertos," translated by Jen Hofer and published in *Jacket2*:

> There they go
> María,
> Juana,
> Petra,
> Carolina,
> 13,
> 18,
> 25,
> 16,
> their breasts bitten,
> their hands tied,
> their bodies burnt,
> their bones polished by desert sand.
> They are called
> dead women nobody knows nobody saw being killed,

they are called
women who go to bars at night alone,
they are called
working women who leave their homes at dawn,
they are called
sisters,
daughters,
mothers,
aunts,
disappeared,
raped
burnt to ashes,
thrown away,
they are called carne, flesh,
they are called carne, meat.
There
with no flowers
with no gravestones,
with no age,
with no name,
with no tears,
they sleep in their cemetery:
It is called Temixco,
it is called Santa Ana,
it is called Mazatepec,
it is called Juárez
it is called Puente de Ixtla,
it is called San Fernando,
it is called Tlaltizapán,
it is called Samalayuca
it is called El Capulín,
it is called Reynosa,
it is called Nuevo Laredo,
it is called Guadalupe,
it is called Lomas de Poleo,
it is called México

What can be said?
　What can be said?

In one way, nothing at all.

And in another way, for these poets, it is the poem's job to attempt to say as much as possible, and to do it with a horrific and brutal specificity

SOURCES

Dowdy, Michael. 2013. *Broken Souths: Latina/o Poetic Responses to Neoliberalism and Globalization*. Tucson: University of Arizona Press.

Herrera, Juan Felipe. 2010. *187 Mexicanos Can't Cross the Border: Undocuments 1971–2007*. San Francisco: City Lights.

Kirby, David. 1986. "Book Review." *Library Journal* (July): 89.

Lipman, Pauline (2011). "Contesting the City: Neoliberal Urbanism and the Cultural Politics of Education Reform in Chicago." *Discourse: Studies in the Cultural Politics of Education* 32 (2): 217–34.

Martínez, Valerie. 2010. *Each and Her*. Tucson: University of Arizona Press.

Rivera, María. 2010. "Los Muertos." Translated by Jen Hofer and Román Luján. *Jacket2* (July 8, 2011). https://jacket2.org/commentary/speak-or-speak-what-cannot-be-spoken.

You, Mia. 2014. Review of *Sorrowtoothpaste Microscream*, by Kim Hyesoon. Translated by Don Mee Choi. *Bookforum* (September 29). www.bookforum.com/culture/sorrowtoothpaste-mirrorcream-by-kim-hyesoon-13761.

Glorious View

Landscapes of Memoria

FRANCISCO ARAGÓN

RECENTLY, I HAD the pleasure of breaking bread with a talented young poet from Massachusetts who had settled in Inverness. She is one of the coeditors of an eclectic, soulful journal, *Inverness Almanac*, a magazine vested in the stories from and about this coastal region north of San Francisco. But she had taken a job in Berkeley and so found herself commuting to, spending significant time in, the East Bay. As dinner progressed, she expressed the belief that her writing would likely change as a result, even though she preferred the rural landscapes of Northern California she had grown to love. I understood; our meal took place in Point Reyes Station, where I was spending time at a residency for writers, Mesa Refuge. My second floor room's wall-sized window looked out onto tidal flats fed by Tomales Bay. Depending on the tides, my balcony had an expansive view of either mudflats or a shimmering estuary. I would sit and read in the one wooden chair, gazing up from time to time, a fragrant wind moving through the trees, often tinged with the intermittent chattering of birds—not one of which I could identify to save my life. But it sounded and smelled like paradise. Was this because I was a native of San Francisco, whose regions still feel like home?

And yet, as a poet, I often write about a place without being *in* that place. I will call this *accessing deep memory*. In other words, I have found that it can take years after I have left a place before aspects of that place appear in a poem. I just completed an ekphrastic prose poem that morphed into a vehicle for revisiting my time in Barcelona in 1987–1988, my year abroad in college. So: more than immediate landscapes, this strand of my poetics is rooted in the landscapes of memory. There is a poem of mine that I consider emblematic in this regard. Here's how it begins:

> The path off the West Crescent that turns
> briefly into the small
> wooden bridge, and above it a canopy of leaves
> —crossed and recrossed
> through the years,

From that one time I played hooky in high school (1982)—taking BART across the bay to see and hear the poet-priest Ernesto Cardenal—to my fifth and final year in college (1989) when I commuted to class from San Francisco, I absorbed and internalized this bit of geography–the pavement from the Berkeley BART station, up Center Street to the edge of campus bordering Oxford Street, the foot path that forks from the curved west entrance ("The path off the West Crescent") before shortly arriving at a footbridge that crosses a creek. "Bridge over Strawberry Creek" is a poem from my first book, *Puerta del Sol* (2005). Notice those years: 1982, 1989, 2005. In other words, it took a while. And so this poetics of memory is also a poetics of prolonged gestation. The poem continues:

> , never pausing once for a peek
> over the edge,

For years I never glanced down into that stagnant patch of creek on the fringe of campus, crossing that footbridge time and time again. Or maybe I *did* peer over the railing, but what I saw ("concentric rings it's / beginning to rain // or water-striders skating") never registered as compelling enough to include in a poem. Or rather, as compelling enough to be the basis for an entire poem.

More fruitful, I find, is when something *involuntary* occurs; one or more of the five senses is engaged in a memorable way. It is *that* kind of experience that dislodges a fragment of *memoria*, causing it to float to the surface of consciousness in a manner that jars, spurring one to take note. This strand of my poetics, then, is a waiting for, being available for, those moments—and attentive enough to know when it's happening, disciplined enough to record it: a phrase, a word, a syllable. One such moment took place in a classroom in Dwinelle Hall on the Berkeley campus:

> And when I chose my place that morning
> at the open window—redwoods
>
> framed against June's day blue—it wasn't
> the wind in the trees which
> if I closed my eyes, had me on a balcony
> in Sitges those summer nights
>
> listening to the Mediterranean breathe

The summer after I graduated from Berkeley, before I returned to Spain to pursue a master's in Spanish, I took an intensive course of college French—a year's worth in ten weeks. Our instructor was Madam Boucher. For reasons I don't precisely recall, I was determined to read Paul Éluard *en français*. Once I got to Madrid, I would add Apollinaire and Pierre Reverdy and proceed to immerse myself in literary cubism and other manifestations of the European avant garde. I digress.

That summer, in French, I would sit in the back, at an open window in order to gaze at campus Sequoias, to listen to the sound that leaves make in a breeze. One day, eyes closed, that breeze blew me back to Sitges, a white-washed coastal village south of Barcelona. A friend, in the summer of 1988, had loaned me his beachfront apartment for two weeks while he was away. At night, before and after hitting the bars, I would sit on the balcony and just listen. But again, it wasn't enough to be a catalyst for a complete poem. Which is not to say that it wasn't deposited into my memory bank. It most certainly was.

French class that summer was held daily. And then, one morning, Madam Boucher uttered the words that triggered it—cascade of memoria that prompted the poem I have been walking us through, here:

> but rather the fact
> of her voice, Madam Boucher's—meaning & sound
> meshing in a phrase

And so it was not a sensory perception per se, but a fragment of language, or rather: *how a fragment of language entered and passed through my body*. It's interesting to note that the phrase in question (" . . . *a la belle étoile* . . .") came to serve as this poem's epigraph. It blindsided me. And the way I attempt to convey that force is by how I punctuate this particular line, or rather, the *lack* of punctuation in that transition from the present ("meshing in a phrase") to the past ("I'm 12") to mimic the velocity with which the speaker is hurled back to his adolescence:

> meshing in a phrase I'm 12
>
> and lying on a bed of chipped wood, warm
> snug in the bag
> facing the stars,

Summers growing up, my mother had to figure out what to do with me when school wasn't in session. From the age of seven to fifteen, a church day camp was a congenial solution, first as a camper (age seven to twelve), then as a junior camp counselor (age thirteen to fifteen). One of the principal annual outings was a trip, for a few nights, up to the Russian River, our yellow bus crossing the Golden Gate Bridge, venturing into Sonoma County, north of San Francisco. In fact, earlier in my childhood, let's say from age three to six, I have memories of my family going on vacation *to* the Russian River. There's a color snapshot of my older brother and me crouched at the river's pebbly edge. Our family would live in a wooden cabin for a week. Even so, it was my church-sponsored summer-camp trips to the Russian River that held a particular place in my pantheon of memory. We would sleep outside, arrayed across a large tarp. Our contingent numbered in the dozens, and we would be divided into various groups according to age, with two counselors in charge of whatever group they were assigned to. I remember often gazing up at the night sky while in my sleeping bag, mesmerized.

And yet: there was something about Madam Boucher's utterance *that* summer day during college French. Her voice—the timbre and pitch of her "*a la belle étoile*"—sparked the memory of something *else* swirling inside a boy nearing puberty, fixated on the stars:

>, my head sifting
the day: a morning hike, a dip

in the Russian River before lunch,

We had two swimming options: the river or a pool—which, no surprise, inevitably entailed occupying physical spaces where one would have to change into and out of bathing suits, swimming trunks; where inevitably we took showers with varying degrees of exposure:

>, before
the doorless stalls, the dank
cement on the soles of my feet, the towels
the soap,

Lidia Torres, in her book *A Weakness for Boleros*, has a piece titled "Adrift" that comes to mind right about now. In it, a female speaker engages in friendly banter one evening with the male lifeguard of the local community college pool. Here is a passage in the middle of the poem:

> Our voices carried over the nearby pool.
> Going to the showers, we glimpsed
> each other's bodies. His modest
> shrunken penis, my forgotten breasts. (2005, 42)

Some of my students, in a literature class I teach on Latino poetry at Notre Dame every fall, have persuasively written about "Adrift" as a poem of sexual awakening. What I admire about this poem is how it poignantly evokes this theme in a subtle, yet unflinching way—unflinching in how it handles issues to do with the body, gazing at the human body.

"Bridge over Strawberry Creek" includes a shower stall setting, as well, but in a way that only begins to hint at, scratch the surface of, sexual awakening, sexual attraction. The poem concludes:

>, the rich lather
lacing his chest

But unlike in Torres's poem, the two characters in "Bridge over Strawberry Creek" are of the same gender—male. Also, whereas Torres's speaker is a young adult ("I was 22."), my speaker is twelve. And although we don't know a precise age of the male this twelve year old is gazing at, the speaker notes a "rich lather / lacing his chest," suggesting, I would argue, chest hair abundant enough to seem interspersed with soapy suds. What we have here is an adolescent boy staring at an adult hirsute man taking a shower.

In the spring of 2007, after a reading I gave at the College of Santa Fe, I was approached by a faculty member, a man, who expressed something approaching frustration at how "Bridge over Strawberry Creek" ends. He felt as if he was taken to the cusp of a description of a man whose hairy chest was laced with lathered-up body gel and then *denied* that description. In other words, he wanted more. He wanted to be *satisfied*.

I have come to be of two minds about this. On the one hand, I acknowledge a certain reticence, on my part, when I have explored the homoerotic in my poems. I see myself as part of a particular lineage. In that spectrum of forefathers, I am more Cavafy than Ginsberg. On the other hand, I also recognize (I address this in my essay "Flyer, Closet, Poem" in my second book, *Glow of Our Sweat*) that it is entirely possible that when I wrote this poem, and others, there may have been some unconscious "covering," a not wanting to disclose too much, because I was not wholly comfortable in my skin—a sentiment, I would argue, that is *also* part of this lineage I belong to.

It is a lineage that includes voices lesser known than Cavafy or Ginsberg. Recently, I discovered one: Dunstan Thompson, whose life and work has been rescued and brought back to us by D. A. Powell and Kevin Prufer. But it was not until I read Dana Gioia's substantive essay on Thompson in the *Hudson Review* that I began to think of him as a kindred spirit. Specifically, it prompted me to reexamine and deeply consider another strand of my poetics—a strand beyond the poetics of memory that we have been focusing on thus far.

Gioia titles his piece "Two Poets Named Dunstan Thompson," making light of the fact that his admirers typically fall into two camps: those who swear by his first two books and consider him a "pioneering poet of gay experience and sensibility" (books whose homoerotic passages are "elaborately coded"), and those who strongly prefer Thompson's later work and view him as "one of the important English-language Catholic poets of the twentieth century."

And yet what I found refreshing about Gioia's thesis is that both these characteristics—Thompson's identity as a gay man, Thompson's identity as Catholic—are not, in Gioia's view, at odds with each other but rather intricately linked. He writes: "What unites Thompson's early and later work is his personal identity as both gay and Catholic. The expression of that complicated double identity differs significantly, but it persists as an animating presence."

In February of 2015, at the conference "The Future of the Catholic Literary Imagination," I convened and moderated the panel "Latino Catholic Writers." Reading Dunstan Thompson, reading Dana Gioia *on* Dunstan Thompson, and the experience of walking us through "Bridge over Strawberry Creek" has complicated how I view my poetics. I am finally easing into it—jacket of one aspect of my particular lineage: gay Catholic Latino poet.

When I read and reread the poem today, I hear a string of memories, paradoxically casual *and* purposeful. Let me call it a rosary of *memoria* leading to something like a moment of unarticulated truth. I can't help but feel empathy and tenderness for that boy, away at camp: in his shower stall, gazing into the doorless column of space across the way, secretly exhilarated by the sight, the glorious view.

Bridge over Strawberry Creek

"*. . . A La Belle Étoile . . .*"

> The path off the West Crescent that turns
> briefly into the small
> wooden bridge, and above it a canopy of leaves
> —crossed and recrossed
>
> through the years, never pausing once for a peek
> over the edge, the surface
> blooming with concentric rings it's
> beginning to rain
>
> or water-striders skating around a stagnant
> section of the creek.

And when I chose my place that morning
at the open window—redwoods

framed against June's day blue—it wasn't
the wind in the trees which
if I closed my eyes, had me on a balcony
in Sitges those summer nights

listening to the Mediterranean breathe
but rather the fact
of her voice, Madam Boucher's—meaning & sound
meshing in a phrase I'm 12

and lying on a bed of chipped wood, warm
snug in the bag
facing the stars, my head sifting
the day: a morning hike, a dip

in the Russian River before lunch, before
the doorless stalls, the dank
cement on the soles of my feet, the towels
the soap, the rich lather

lacing his chest (2005, 86)

SOURCES

Aragón, Francisco. 2005. *Puerta del Sol*. Tempe, AZ: Bilingual Press.
———. 2010. *Glow of Our Sweat*. Kansas City, MO: Scapegoat Press.
Gioia, Dana. 2015. "Two Poets Named Dunstan Thompson." *Hudson Review* 69, no. 1 (May). https://hudsonreview.com/2015/05/two-poets-named-dunstan-thompson.
Torres, Lidia. 2005. *A Weakness for Boleros*. Woodstock, NY: Mayapple Press.

Peopleness

Ethnicity and the Latinx Poem

VALERIE MARTÍNEZ

I

IN THE AUTUMN of 1993, I flew from Tucson to New York to Johannesburg to the small nation of Swaziland for a job teaching elementary school. The small plane wobbled unsettlingly as we approached the single runway at the Matsapha airport. Below, I saw dozens of Swazi children run from their homesteads to climb the fence that lined the tarmac. They cheered and waved as we descended the airstairs in the hot afternoon sun.

I had never visited southern Africa, nor did I speak more than a few words of si-Swati, nor had I ever taught elementary school. On the drive to the capital city of Mbabane, my host father thought it a good idea to drop me off, alone, at the nearest open-air market, with instructions to buy one fresh pineapple. Immersion as an introductory gesture. I fumbled my hello to several Swazi women, their pineapples piled high, pyramid-like. It got a gentle laugh from everyone.

During the three years I lived and worked in Swaziland and traveled in South Africa, Zimbabwe, and Botswana, I was not able to convince many that I am "brown." No matter how I tried to explain my ethnicity, most southern Africans saw me as a white woman, and everything—good and bad—associated with white people was projected onto me. I was—alternately—colonizer, wealthy expat, Trustafarian, liberal do-gooder, Peace Corps volunteer. It was one of the most profound experiences of otherness I have ever lived.

Here are additional facts-of-my-life that have deepened my sense of otherness:

- I was molested when I was seven years old.
- In the 1960s, elementary school teachers urged my parents not to speak Spanish at home
- so that we "would be able to succeed." My parents did their best to comply.
- In 1979, I left our close-knit Latino/a community in Santa Fe to attend college in New York State. I did not return to settle in New Mexico until 2003, after visiting and/or living in eight US states and ten foreign countries.
- In 1980, I resolutely left the Catholic Church.
- The poems in my first book of poetry (1999) did not resemble much of the Latino/a poetry that I was taught or that I read in high school, college, or graduate school.
- I married an atheist descended from Russian Jews.
- I do not have children.
- A DNA test in 2018 revealed that I am as much Native American as Hispanic/Iberian, that rumors on both sides of my family of our Native antecedents are undoubtedly true.

The above explains, in part, the restlessness that has characterized much of my life. On the other hand, it confirms a kind of *rootedness in otherness* that resonates with many people of color.

Other is my tribe, my language, my religion.

II

I became particularly interested in how ethnicity is expressed in Latinx literature after the publication of my first book of poetry. In 1999, after reading from my first collection, someone in the audience asked how my work could be considered Latino—presumably because he didn't find in it the recognizable "markers" of ethnicity:

> Orange, orange. And the hand arching up
> to hold it. The woman's hand. The arching.
> Up. And the star exploding, seeing it
> where it wasn't, a telescope on the night sky.
> The thermonuclear flash.
> The explosion.
>
> She had her hand out; it fell
> like an explosion into her fingers.
> It wasn't the scope and the eye,
> was hand, fruit. It was what I saw.
> It was what I imagine I somehow saw.
>
> Out on the horizon of stars beyond the gigantic sun.
> Beyond the measure of the sun the star bursting.
>   (Martínez, from "And Seeing It," 1999)

Unprepared for the question, I answered with the best I could do at the time: "Well, I am Latina, and these are the poems that come out of my body."

III

During the second half of the twentieth century, anthologies issued by major publishers popularized the "Latino Poem" that tended to signal ethnicity with recognizable "markers"—subject matter, narrative style, and the use of Spanish:

> I scramble over the wire fence
> that would have kept me out.
> Once, I wanted out, wanted the rigid lanes
> to take me to a place without the sun,
> without the smell of tomatoes burning
> on swing shift in the greasy summer air.

> Maybe it's here
> en los campos extraños de esta
> ciudad where I'll find it, that part of
> me mown under
> like under a corpse
> or a loose seed.
> (Cervantes, from "Freeway 280," 1981)

> Since I was on his time, I ran
> And became the wag to a short tail of Mexicans—
> Ran past the amazed crowds that lines
> The street and blurred like photographs, in rain.
> I ran from that industrial road to the soft
> Houses where people paled at the turn of an autumn sky.
> What could I do but yell vivas
> To baseball, milkshakes, and those sociologists
> Who would clock me
> As I jog into the next century
> On the power of a great, silly grin.
> (Soto, from "Mexicans Begin Jogging," 1981)

These poems, many of which have been vitally important to me as a writer and reader, contributed to a postmodern wave of women writers and writers of color whose narrative and/or confessional work evoked powerful personal stories. These stories introduced a larger readership to lives and landscapes theretofore ignored, silenced, suppressed—a significant literary accomplishment. And it makes perfect sense that editors and publishers wanted to feature Latino/a poems that signaled Latinidad in recognizable ways. I have no doubt that the publication of these poems both opened doors for other Latino/a writers and encouraged a wider readership for poetry in general.

But what, then, of poems by Latino/a writers that did/do not "mark" ethnicity in these ways?

> The sensibilities in speech of winter
> where process is undressed
> of all history. The matter with fact
> bankrupt theories to her blue dress
> lifting in the crisp marina.
> Here then are the engine plumes
> living among us in a relative manner,
>
> resemble beak proportion to appropriate capacity.
> The ancient computer mothering in the hamlet sighs:
> How old are you, then, when is it a good time
>
> to call and dictate a list of imperatives for the lyric hero?
> (Gomez, from "This Particular Season," 2007)

I imagine an editor discovering Gomez's "This Particular Season" in a stack of blind submissions. Let's say this editor understands the disproportionate publication of work by white writers compared to writers of color. S/he wants to publish exemplary work and to be inclusive. Does s/he not look for the more obvious markers of ethnicity in the poem? Does the absence of these markers relegate a poem to some sort of "non-ethnic" status? How and where does ethnicity "reside" in poetry, and how do we recognize it?

IV

For a moment, I'd like to turn to the fields of ethno- and sociolinguistics to begin addressing how ethnicity is "marked" in general. Joshua A. Fishman, in *Language and Ethnicity in Minority Sociolinguistic Perspective*, acknowledges what we all know to be true, that the use of an "ethnic language" is a powerful marker of identity:

> Language is more likely than most symbols of ethnicity to become *the* symbol of ethnicity. Language is the recorder of paternity, the expresser of patrimony, and the carrier of phenomenology. (1989, 32)

Even so, Fishman and others agree that an ethnic language can remain significant within a group even if all its members do not use it for communication. John Edwards, in his essay "Symbolic Ethnicity and Language," writes that among minority groups, or within groups, in which language shift has occurred in the reasonably recent past, the value of language as a symbol can remain in the absence of communicative example. (1996, 227)

He cites the example of Gaelic as what he calls an "associated language" that is connected with a group identity but is not used regularly or, for some, known at all (227). Fishman also writes:

> Indisputably, many ethnic groups do not have a distinct language or lose it along the way. Although the strength of their bonds may suffer as a result, their certainty that their language is essential to them may also remain undiminished. (32–33)

In other words, the loss of a "distinct language" may indeed affect the bonds within a group (the fact that, for example, I was not able to communicate fluently with my paternal grandparents, who were bilingual but favored the use of Spanish) but does not necessarily mean that this distinct language is not important to a sense of group identity. Of course, the loss of an ancestral language is tragic; language is the bearer of much more than a "communicative example." But it is comforting to know that language can remain significant whether widely spoken or not and that one's sense of ethnicity endures beyond the loss of language.

Hutchinson and Smith, in their introduction to *Ethnicity*, affirm that "we should expect public and non-symbolic characteristics to be relatively early casualties in assimilative or modified pluralistic contexts" (2). Examples of "public" characteristics include speaking of one's ethnic language in public, speaking English with an "accent," and/or wearing "traditional dress." While one may do all these, particularly in the context of family and community gatherings and celebrations, younger generations of US Latino/as may not enact these characteristics inside or outside the home or ethnic community.

Edwards affirms, on the other hand, that "private and symbolic markers continue to exist because they promote the continuation of group boundaries without hindering social mobility and access" (228). Unfortunately, we continue to live in a country in which public markers of ethnicity do hinder social mobility and access. The reality of racism and the fight for equality and justice in so many ways argue *for* public markers of ethnicity. At the same time, "private and symbolic markers" also carry the literary DNA of ethnicity, what Rosalyn Negrón (2014) calls "different strategies of affiliation."

V

The word *ethnic* descends from the French *ethnie*, which is derived from the Greek *ethnos*:

> A named human population with myths of common ancestry, shared historical memories, one or more elements of common culture, a link with a historical homeland and a sense of solidarity among at least some of its members. (Hutchinson and Smith 1966, 6)

Many textbook and theoretical definitions of *ethnic* refer to issues of "paternity," "patrimony," and "phenomenology"—biological kinship, communal behaviors/rituals, and a sense of ethnic meaning and belonging. Juan Flores, in "The Latino Imaginary," describes group identity as "a collective self-consciousness drawing on shared memories and desires" that encompasses "both the junctions and disjunctions of Latino histories, migratory experiences, economic positions, and processes of racialization" (2000, 194).

My favorite definition of ethnicity comes from Fishman:

> Ethnicity is "peopleness," i.e. belonging or pertaining to a phenomenological complete, separate, historically deep cultural collectivity, a collectivity polarized on perceived authenticity. This "belonging" is experienced and interpreted physically (biologically), behaviorally (culturally) and phenomenologically (intuitively) . . . it is a very mystic, moving and powerful link with the past and an energizer with respect to the present and future. (216)

Fishman's "historically deep cultural collectivity" especially resonates with me, affirming that ethnicity is grounded, above all, in one's sense of biology, history and community—a powerful, personal sense of belonging. I imagine how this is multiplied both in number and complexity within the diversity of a pan-ethnic US Latino/a diaspora.

VI

At the same time, Fishman notes that ethnicity is "fraught with moral imperatives, with obligations to one's 'own kind,' and with wisdoms, rewards, and proprieties that are both tangible and intangible" (216). Negrón refers to these as the "broader debates about what it means to be Latino, who can and cannot make claims to a Latino identity, and the ways Latino identity can be performed" (2014, 89). Writers might ask themselves, How does my work "perform" my Latinidad? Does this happen consciously or unconsciously? Do I have an obligation to signal ethnicity, and if so, how? As for editors and publishers—how do they navigate the complex terrain of public and private markers of ethnicity, external and internal signifiers, and more?

VII

I do not have definitive answers. What I do know is that the Latinx diaspora in the United States includes writers self- and other-identified as Mexicana, Mestizo, Hispanic, Cubano/a, Boriqueno, Bicho/a, Blaxican, Chicanx, Hondureño, and more than a half-dozen other terms. We are gay, straight, bisexual, poor, affluent, assimilated, and semi-assimilated. We are immigrants. We are descendants of Spanish colonizers who arrived in the fifteenth and sixteenth centuries and of our Mayan, Aztec, Diné, Tewa, and other Amerindian ancestors. We are Mestizas, Pardos, Zambas. We are bilingual and monolingual, dispossessed and privileged, political exiles and the politically powerful. The contemporary landscape of published Latinx poetry includes writers with a wide range of styles and aesthetics. I laud this expansion, a post-postmodern phenomenon that reveals the complexity of our voices, styles, perspectives, and literary identities.

If markers of ethnicity are going to appear in the body of Latinx poetry, they are going to be as complex and diverse as we are. They have to be.

> It happened gradually. My hands, always behind me, sore
> from picking at ropes, went first.
> They began to feel light and hollow, though something
> prickled
> beneath the skin. My fingers closed and fused,
> my arms grew narrow and long
> until they were twice the length of my body.
> Then, my heart. It raced ahead of me
> and tried to thrash its way out—
> philomel, philomel—
> I listened, afraid to speak.
> I thought the hush could do me no harm.
> But in silence my tongue was severed.
> I'd watched it writhe on the ground in front of me,
> murmuring,
> dividing, becoming forked it slithered off.
> When feathers finally appeared in patches, I saw
> that you can live, mute and still, with a sharp desire
> for your father's country, which is power.
> Or you can deny your name until it feels like strength,
> and give away all but your scarlet hair,
> for it might bring recognition
> when you feel murderous, waiting, impatient to do nothing.
>   (Franco 2007)

I want to push away from the idea that literary Latinidad can be codified by a few recognizable markers and that poems by Latinx authors will reveal ethnicity in repeated and similar ways.

It is true that this may mean that editors, publishers and readers accept a body of literature that both embraces and defies familiar signs of ethnicity. This might be confusing, frustrating, and even mystifying. But with acceptance of this complexity, we will encourage a much more nuanced and accurate understanding of the contemporary Latinx community.

VIII

Early in this essay, I listed nine "displacements" from myself. Of course, the list instead embraces my complex identity and communicates the depth of my *mestizaje*. Whether my experience is common or foreign to most Latino/a is secondary to its primacy as my own "ethnic story"—mystic, moving, and powerfully linked to the past. This is the well that feeds the images, rhythms, music, and content of my poetry. This is my peopleness. And the vibrancy of Latino/a literature depends on the complex expression of our multitudinous ways.

SOURCES

Cervantes, Lorne Dee. 1981. "Freeway 280." In *Emplumada*, 39. Pittsburgh, PA: University of Pittsburgh Press.

Edwards, John. 1996. "Symbolic Ethnicity and Language." In *Ethnicity*, edited by John Hutchinson and Anthony D. Smith, 227–35. Oxford: Oxford University Press.

Fishman, Joshua A. 1989. *Language and Ethnicity in Minority Sociolinguistic Perspective*. Bristol: Multilingual Matters.

Flores, Juan. 2000. *From Bomba to Hip-Hop: Puerto Rican Culture and Latino Identity*. New York: Columbia University Press.

Franco, Gina. "Darkling." 2007. In *The Wind Shifts: New Latino Poetry*, edited by Francisco Aragón, 112. Tucson: University of Arizona Press.

Gomez, Gabe. 2007. "This Particular Season." In *The Outer Bands*, 8. Notre Dame, IN: University of Notre Dame Press.

Hutchinson, John, and Anthony D. Smith, eds. 1996. *Ethnicity*. Oxford: Oxford University Press.

Martínez, Valerie. 1999. "And Seeing It." In *Absence, Luminescent*, 8. Marshfield, MA: Four Way Books.

Negrón, Rosalyn. 2014. "New York City's Latino Ethnolinguistic Repertoire and the Negotiation of Latinidad in Conversation." *Journal of Sociolinguistics* 18 (1): 87–118.

Soto, Gary. 2001. "Mexicans Begin Jogging." In *Contemporary American Poetry*, edited by A. Poulin Jr. and Michael Waters, 489. New York: Houghton Mifflin.

My Latino Aesthetics. Or Not.

STEVEN CORDOVA

I NEVER THOUGHT I'd hear myself say this, but I try to avoid the political when I read, and when I write.

I mean a lot of things when I say that.

I mean that once upon a time, I was politically active, very politically active, then I burned out on being politically active.

I mean that though I've burned out, I try to stay abreast, but that really, I'm happy to lead a life of reading and writing.

I mean I have a TV, but I don't watch TV, don't watch the news.°

I read—I read on the bus that takes me to work Monday through Friday.

Later in the day, I read crossing the Manhattan Bridge on a Manhattan-bound D. I am headed to the gym.
    In winter the crossing is dark, in summer it is light, variably clear or cloudy. I look up from my reading.
    In the distance I see other bridges.

Most evenings I waste time working out—time I could be reading or writing.

My Latino Aesthetics. Or Not.   59

Working out, I pace myself. I think about form, I think about repetition.

Working out, I look at the forms of other men and women changing their forms.

I mean that it's a kind of ecstasy: to control the form at the same time that it–the form–the repetition and the rhyme–controls you.

Saturdays I write. Sundays I write.

Mondays,
   Tuesdays . . . ,
   I write
   but only when
   the moment strikes.

The more I read and write, the more the moment strikes.

I mean that I rely on friends who keep up with the news. They keep me up.

I mean that everything I do, everything I do and don't do, adds up to an aesthetic. I mean, I hate to admit it, but I rely on my Facebook feed.

Lucky thing that many of my Facebook friends are ACT UP veterans who keep up.

Sometimes when I see one of those ACT UP veterans walking down the street toward me, I know him or her to be crazy.

Was s/he always crazy or did I not notice it until now?

No matter. I greet him/her warmly anyway.

Sometimes I greet him/her less than warmly. It depends on how his/her craziness manifests itself. Sometimes it depends on my ever-changing mood.

Cloudy or clear.

Other veterans are thunderstorms of ego. Seeking cover I cross the street.

I mean that despite my attempts to avoid the political, the political finds its way into my life, into my poems, sometimes in the form of thunderstorms;

and that, therefore, trying to resist something is a way of letting something (or someone?)
   in.

I mean, too, that I worked in social-service and advocacy organizations longer than I was on the street raising placards above my head, shouting chants, getting arrested.

I mean in the arena of activism, as in the arena of nonprofit advocacy and social services, I've seen a lot of "leaders" and a lot of "heroes" behave badly.

I mean I don't write to create heroes;

don't write to "speak out" or to "heal myself."

I mean that if my identity is so fragile that I can't read anything that doesn't affirm it, then it's not much of an identity, now is it?

I mean I do, on the other hand, write to exorcise myself.

I mean I try not to give in to sentimentality, to nostalgia, and to the media.

I mean that while tricks and tropes will sometimes break my poems, words will always hurt me.

Sincerity—especially sincere sincerity—can be the most annoying thing in the world.
   I mean there is no such thing as a hero, only a heroic act.
   I mean everything nostalgia gives, nostalgia takes back;
   that she who is a hero one moment is a hypocrite the next.
   I mean when I wear my heart on my sleeve, I never wear it with anything that doesn't match.
I mean I, I have behaved badly.

I mean to be a moral writer I must be, when I write, without morals, completely without
    morals.

I mean politics and activism once changed my life. I mean art changed it in a different way.
    I mean art seldom lets me down.

Reading and writing are solitary enterprises; activism is a group enterprise. The latter can seem to disappoint more than the former.
    I mean activism and art speak to each other even though I cross the street to avoid a character from my past.

I mean that when making art, I try to put art above activism;

but that when I'm engaging in activism, I put activism above art strictly on a case-by-case basis.

I mean that I didn't appreciate it when I bumped into a "beloved" San Antonio author who urged me to write about "our" San Antonio.

I mean that activism and art are both about "freedom"; freedom to read what I want; freedom to write what I want;

I mean that while art may lead to change, art itself is not at the service of change, social or otherwise;

I mean that I appreciate a good satire, even when it is directed at "my own."

I mean that I already have a younger brother and that I don't like anyone else calling me "brother," especially if I've only just met him/her.

Sister?—ah, yes, well, sister is an entirely different story.
I mean that I wanted to get through this essay without using the word Latino or gay.

Survivor or addict or HIV-positive;

I mean the last thing I need is one more identity.

I mean that I "pass" and I will use that passing to spy what I can spy. I mean that time is "passing" and "passing" is a euphemism for death.
    I mean that when I read and write I change my aesthetic at the rate at which I can read and write and that, therefore, I have no one particular aesthetic.

I mean that a room of one's own exists only in the heaven—the foolhardy heaven—of our minds. I mean my mind. Or yours.

I mean that if I stop at the political, I may never reach the poetry.

I mean I sometimes dream a dream of a poem, which, waking, I can never write. I mean it's all in the unveiling. . . .

An Afro-Latino's Poetic and Creative Hungers

SEAN FREDERICK FORBES

A POET AT THE CROSSROADS

AS AN AFRO-LATINO poet, I often feel some apprehension when I mention to my colleagues my minor familiarity with Latino/a poets whose works appear in most anthologies we use in our English composition and literature courses. Canonical authors such as Julia Alvarez, Sandra Cisneros, Martín Espada, and Rigoberto González stand out in my memory. At the same time, my knowledge and teaching of additional writers include Julia de Burgos, Pablo Neruda, and Octavio Paz, who define identity—as well as the United States and Latin America—in a more expansive, hemispheric imaginary. As a voracious reader across continents, I turn for guidance to poets who are African American or Afro-Caribbean in origin with themes about our human diaspora. Is this a result of my growing up in a largely African American community in Southside Jamaica, Queens, New York City, or that Spanish was rarely spoken in my household? Perhaps it is the combination of these two, or maybe it is rooted in the murky description of my racial and ethnic ancestry as being "mixed" with colonial and international influences.

When I first read Gwendolyn Brooks's poem "To the Diaspora," I was in college and struggling to understand my racial and ethnic identity. I was beginning to learn about the black diaspora in the Caribbean. In the opening line of the poem, Brooks writes, "You did not know you were Afrika" (1994, 499). She employs a different spelling of the vast continent, one that does not contain a European ethos and sensibility. The use of the directive in the poem engages the reader, and it is highly suggestive that Brooks only addresses a black reader, but in many ways, she is highlighting the fact that the African continent has played a major role in cultural, global, historical, political, and social contexts around the world. In rereading this poem, I began to think about the ways in which blackness/Africanness is highly significant and relevant in terms of defining Latino people and culture. Furthermore, Brooks writes, "You did not know the Black continent / that had to be reached / was you" (499). The directive becomes a rhetorical device, one that inspires the reader to engage in a deeper discourse that aids in a broader understanding of the self. In my case, my reading of literature from African American and Afro-Caribbean writers has led me to question and accept my own Afro-Latino identity and the ways in which it informs and complicates my thinking and writing.

My maternal and paternal grandparents and mother were born in Isla de Providencia, Colombia, a mountainous island that is located off the eastern coast of Nicaragua in the Caribbean Sea. It is a part of the Colombian department of the Archipelago of San Andrés, Providencia, and Santa Catalina. Providencia's two-hundred-year history is complex and includes the following empires and realities: it was under British and Spanish colonial powers; there were major political battles between Nicaragua and Colombia over which nation has rightful ownership, and a native English-based patois is spoken even though Spanish is the official language. The island is ethnically diverse, with inhabitants claiming West African, European, and, of course, mainland Colombian ancestry.

Much like the geographic, racial, ethnic, and cultural ambiguity of the island of Providencia, I too am a poet at the crossroads, with many lenses from which to gain vision and depth. To stand at the crossroads is to experience two worlds at once and to be informed by them as both observer and actor. Sometimes one can slide back and forth easily between these two worlds, other times not so easily, but the intended action is justified and always carried out. The trickster, too, is a "boundary crosser" or, as mythologist Lewis Hyde puts it, an "on-the-road" figure, a traveler with a fierce appetite that drives his wandering spirit and inquisitiveness (1998, 8). The very fact that the trickster has this intense appetite and is a wanderer is suspect; hence s/he operates under a highly dangerous and disruptive guise. Yet in the introduction to his book *Trickster Makes the World*, Hyde writes that "in spite of all their disruptive behavior, tricksters are regularly honored as the creators of culture" (8). As a gay Afro-Latino poet, I am drawn to the trickster figure, a boundary crosser who engages in positive disruption and creative boundary crossing.

Ultimately, as a poet committed to documenting the diaspora of diverse peoples, Michelle Cliff's and Audre Lorde's poetry appealed to me as a young gay Afro-Latino male while I was an undergraduate student. Long before I contemplated a career in academia and also as a poet, their writing spoke to me in ways that were uniquely personal and relevant about race, sexuality, and discovery of the true self, which are all interconnected to the African diaspora. I discovered many poets, like Gwendolyn Brooks and Robert Hayden, who are goddess and god to me, respectively, but it wasn't until I read Cliff and Lorde that I was struck by their hunger to create female-voiced speakers. Through their poetic genius, they introduced women's voices that challenged notions of patriarchal, historical, societal, and cultural constructs that too often exclude women. The speakers in their poems refused to be silenced and thus became a chorus of mischievous, yet serious, voices to be heard with resonating thoughts and situations. Reading their works became influential to my formation as a close reader and later in my apprenticeship as a poet. Their writing fueled my own hunger for presenting multifaceted speakers—both male and female and sometimes inanimate—in my own poetry.

As a poet, perhaps the most useful way to read this "hunger" is through a psychoanalytic or Jungian lens, as an image for creative desire. Paul Radin's text *The Trickster* includes commentaries from Karl Kerenyi, a scholar on Greek mythology, and psychoanalyst Carl Jung. For Radin, Kerenyi, and Jung, the trickster's developmental growth within cultures operates alongside an individual's psychological growth: "The trickster is an inchoate being of undetermined proportions, a figure foreshadowing the shape of man" (1972, xxiv). This assessment suggests that a creative hunger exists in the human psyche, borne of his desire to see his own image reflected in the world. Like the trickster, my poetic hunger was rooted in a desire to create my own world, one that was not predicated on a preconceived definition or understanding of Latino/a poetics.

LORDE INVOKES THE TRICKSTER

Published in 1978, *The Black Unicorn* established Lorde's creative and spiritual hunger and her search for a new name. It also showed the beginning of the trickster sensibility in her poems. The title of the collection most likely is inspired by a French series of six tapestries, woven of silk and wool, titled *La Dame à la licorne*, translated as *The Lady and the Unicorn*, from the late fifteenth century. Each of the six tapestries depicts a noble lady with the unicorn on her left and a lion on her right; some also include a monkey in the scene. Lorde's title poem opens with an image that is central to the book: "The black unicorn is greedy. / The black unicorn is impatient" (3). Initially, the words "greedy" and "impatient" suggest that the black unicorn is a figure driven by self-indulgent desires. Indeed, Lorde seems to be playing explicitly with this idea of trickster's divine hunger, for images of hunger appear repeatedly in the book.

The tone of the first two lines establishes an insistent urgency that demonstrates, as Hyde points out, that "trickster starts out hungry," thus illustrating the strong urges within the trickster's inquisitive nature (1998, 17). These feelings of "greed" and "impatience" represent hunger pangs that help show the female speaker where the black unicorn's powers rest. This knowledge allows the speaker not only to connect with this uniquely beautiful mythic creature but to become aware of her own creative hunger.

Lorde's focus on the black unicorn's greed artfully illustrates that animal hunger, its need to be fed, will help the speaker become mentally swift. This in turn allows her to become trickster-like and, as Hyde would put it, "adept at creating and unmasking deceit" (17). In the poem, Lorde employs images of a "cold country" and of the black unicorn's horn to represent a deeper awareness and understanding of history that the speaker acquires through this hunger.

This "cold country" perhaps refers to human slavery and the icy stings of racism under this oppressive system that "painted mockeries" of the speaker's fury. In this instance, these "mockeries" refer to a system of white male oppression that ignores the black female presence. Lorde then invokes the figure of the maiden when she writes, "It is not on her lap where the horn rests / but deep in her moonpit / growing." Here Lorde's image suggests that the black unicorn's horn is not where the source of power resides; rather, that power grows deep within the maiden, representing not only fecundity but also strength and creativity. The final stanza symbolically brings the images of hunger and the "cold country" together:

> The black unicorn is restless
> the black unicorn is unrelenting
> the black unicorn is not
> free. (3)

Lorde ends the poem with an image of a fiery creature that refuses to be tamed despite its imprisonment. She employs the word *is* three times in this stanza to emphasize that the black unicorn's struggle for freedom is constant. While the black unicorn is indeed *not* free, the words *restless* and *unrelenting* suggest that there still remains a creative, if not physical, hunger to be free, which is a recurring theme for not only my poetry but for Latino poetry as well.

CLIFF EMBRACES THE TRICKSTER AT THE CROSSROADS

Michelle Cliff's largely autobiographical collection of prose and poetry, *The Land of Look Behind*, was published in 1985 and was dedicated to Lorde. It can thus be surmised that Cliff's work was influenced by Lorde's trickster sensibility even though Cliff's trickster tropes are less explicit. Her narrator is logistically, historically, and mythically situated in a place where she is actively engaging with "the land of look behind." Similar to Lorde's, Cliff's interests in a crossroads or trickster figure becomes evident through her hunger for a female-voiced speaker. This hunger allows her to employ a poetic-prose form that questions conceptions of history, life writing, and storytelling. Cliff traces her discovery and acceptance of herself as a lesbian of color.

Cliff's trickster-like hunger causes her "to liberate her 'tongue' from the woodenness of an enforced colonial language" (Russell 2009, 82). It is this strong desire to be liberated, to speak with an honest "tongue," that Cliff thinks about writing in a nonlinear and poetic-prose manner. She notes that as a Jamaican, she was writing out of colonialism's historical legacy, which informed her thinking and understanding of her national, racial, and sexual identities. She writes, "One of the effects of assimilation, indoctrination, passing into the Anglocentrism of British West Indian culture is that you believe absolutely in the hegemony of the King's English and in the form in which it is meant to be expressed. Or else your writing is not literature; it is folklore, and folklore can never be art" (1985, 13). Ultimately, Cliff found her artistic female voice by mixing aspects of linear and nonlinear constructions of storytelling and essay writing to express her split consciousness as a writer. She freely admits that when she began to understand her subjectivity outside of academia, her "writing was jagged, nonlinear, almost shorthand" (12). This jaggedness is appropriate for her content, however. She presents a narrative form that is disruptive and unsettling. These characteristics remind readers that her female speaker's journey and understanding of her position in the world cannot be defined as neat and simple.

In "Claiming an Identity They Taught Me to Despise," Cliff writes halfway between poetry and prose, between traditional linear life writing and experimental self-exploration, between Africa and England, and between white and black. By operating rhetorically as a "halfway" figure, Cliff is able to isolate, observe, and question the ways in which such binary structures operate within and between cultures. Timothy S. Chin argues that writers such as Cliff offer a stark contrast to either/or choices by "frequently deploy[ing] narrative strategies that privilege ambiguity and the ability to negotiate contradictions" (2008, 89). Cliff's narrative strategy disrupts conventional linear models of life writing, especially in a sequence titled "Passing," in which her writing style shifts back and forth between poetry and prose to negotiate contradictions, most notably about the notion of passing. Cliff writes:

> In Jamaica we are as common as ticks.
> We graft the Bombay onto the common mango. The Valencia onto the Seville. We mix tangerines and oranges. We create mules.
>
> Under British rule—Zora Neale Hurston writes about this—we could have ourselves declared legally white. The rationale was that it made us better servants.

> This symbolic skin was carried to the United States where
> passing was easy. (22)

In this particular passage, the stanza breaks exemplify the narrator as a crossroads figure. The stanza breaks physically and rhetorically position her simultaneous embrace of insider and outsider status. After each statement or comment is posed for the reader, the narrator rhetorically pauses to suggest that the information presented must be carefully considered and thought about. The white space invites the reader to question what is being said; for instance, is the narrator ashamed of being able to pass? Or is the narrator glorifying the fact that she can pass easily for white, especially in the United States? In a passage that follows, Cliff writes:

> Isolate yourself. If they find out about you it's all over. Forget
> About your great-grandfather with the darkest skin—until
> You're back 'home' . . . Go to college. Go to England
> To study. Learn about the Italian Renaissance and forget that
> They kept slaves. (22–23)

William Doty and William Hynes note that "the role of the trickster is primarily that of a delicate balance between creativity and destructiveness" (1993, 19). Indeed, Cliff's balancing of form and of the topic of passing in both general and personal terms allows her to become both creative and destructive. The idea of passing suggests that one has to be highly creative about one's past, one must "forget" the past and must not divulge too much information, but this ultimately leads to the destruction of the self. While passing is an act of survival, a camouflage that protects the individual, the narrator questions the idea of passing. I, too, question the idea of passing, if not choosing, to identify myself as black or Latino because the intersection between these two identities runs too deep to ignore.

In his keynote speech "To the Writer, to the Activist, to the Citizen," delivered on May 10, 2010, at the National Latino Writers Conference in Albuquerque, New Mexico, gay Chicano writer Rigoberto González provided advice to the young Latino members of the audience by stating:

> Learn who your literary antepasados are—know their names and read their works. This will keep you humility in check and your esteem on fire. Recognize that your influences are from a variety of bookshelves, not just writings from Chicano/a and Latino/a writers, but also the writings from our Latin American cousins, plus the works of translation from African, Europe, and Asia. Embrace your town or village or city but locate it within a larger map—world literature. (2013, 114)

I take González's advice and guidance to heart because it is the writer who is willing to read, to learn from writers from other cultures and backgrounds as a means of engaging in conversations that are meaningful and purposeful. While it is cliché to say that inspiration can come from virtually anywhere, it is definitely true from my perspective. As I began to write the poems for my book *Providencia*, I was voraciously reading Lorde's and Cliff's poetry, along with others, to understand how writers capture the often forgotten, messy, and murky facets of the African diaspora. When I traveled to Providencia, Colombia, in 2009, I conducted archival and genealogical research, interviewed distant relatives, and toured the island on foot, as a passenger on a motorbike, and on a boat, chronicling my initial impressions of the landscape. Since my grandparents spoke so fondly and longingly of their birthplace, the island holds mythic power to me. As I wrote, I immersed myself in an intricate poetic process of selecting the precise words, sounds, images, narrative voices, and poetic forms and styles to write in, and the writings of Cliff and Lorde offered me both humility and confidence to express my poetic and creative hungers in written form.

SOURCES

Brooks, Gwendolyn. 1994. *Blacks*. Chicago: Third World Press.
Chin, Timothy S. 2008. "'Bullers' and 'Battymen': Contesting Homophobia in Black Popular Culture and Contemporary Caribbean Literature." In *Our Caribbean: A Gathering of Lesbian and Gay Writing from the Antilles*, edited by Thomas Glave, 78–96. Durham, NC: Duke University Press.
Cliff, Michelle. 1985. *The Land of Look Behind*. New York: Firebrand.
Doty, William, and William Hynes, eds. 1993. *Mythical Trickster Figures: Contours, Contexts, and Criticisms*. Tuscaloosa: University of Alabama Press.

Forbes, Sean Frederick. 2013. *Providencia*. New York: 2Leaf Press.
González, Rigoberto. 2013. *Red-Inked Retablos*. Tucson: University of Arizona Press.
Hyde, Lewis. 1998. *Trickster Makes the World: Mischief, Myth, and Art*. New York: Farrar Strauss and Giroux.
Lorde, Audre. 1978. *The Black Unicorn*. New York: Norton.
Radin, Paul. 1972. *The Trickster: A Study in America Indian Mythology*. New York: Schocken.
Russell, Heather. 2009. *Legba's Crossing: Narratology in the African Atlantic*. Athens: University of Georgia Press.

Trauma and the Lyric

SHERYL LUNA

I AM A survivor of childhood sexual abuse and a Latina. Poetry helps me live and thrive in this world by healing the wounds of the past so that I can move on to a new place. Lyric poetry helps me heal with strong emotions to live contemplatively and fully. Poetry can help an individual who has suffered from trauma or abuse. It can also help a collective group such as Latinos heal and reclaim a sense of power rather than one of victimhood, oppression, or shame.

Some people argue that poetry is not therapy and telling the story of abuse (whether rape or communal oppression) is not popular in some schools of thought in contemporary American poetry. However, such tellings are necessary political and personal acts of courage; the lyric can bring awareness of suffering and alleviate suffering, and the alleviation of suffering is a beautiful thing. The transformative emotional power of poetry can help people move beyond victimization to a place of pride, power, and agency.

Trauma creates a sense of shame that is internalized, and sometimes this shame affects one's confidence. Individual trauma survivors often struggle with survivor's guilt and blame themselves for the abuse. Rather than developing a strong sense of identity, a person feels fragmented or dissociated and can even forget the events that created the trauma. Jeffrey C. Alexander defines trauma in the following manner: "Trauma occurs when individuals and groups feel they have been subjected to a horrendous event that leaves indelible marks upon their consciousness, will mark their memories forever, and will change their future in fundamental and irrevocable ways" (2004, 1).

Trauma does not occur in a vacuum. An individual's trauma often occurs within the context of a community. Such shaming lives in the overall consciousness of the Mexican American culture (Burnett 2006). Internalized racism, or hatred of one's own culture, can occur when one begins to feel ashamed of his or her ethnicity or race. Oppression by the dominant Caucasian culture can lead an oppressed people to feel shame. For instance, darker skinned people may be ostracized, and lighter skinned individuals may be praised by one's own family, as well as by the dominant culture. People of color can *collectively* react to a trauma, whether the trauma is to an individual or to a cultural group. Entire communities can be shaped by violent or oppressive histories. Many Latino/as have forgotten past traumas, such as the dousing of Mexicans with toxic chemicals before they crossed the border into the United States. Members of an oppressed or marginalized group may feel it is a dangerous world and find it difficult to trust white people or people outside of their culture. This hyper-vigilance is a symptom of trauma. Individuals and communities can also be re-traumatized and triggered by situations similar to earlier trauma, whether it is recognized or goes unrecognized (SAMHSA 2014).

Some people argue that the past should simply be left behind, but the integration of the fragmented parts of one's psyche or one's cultural identity help a person, or a society, to change, and the restoration of identity can raise self-esteem. The relationship between the individual and the larger oppressed group is that the larger group is made up of individuals who must take back their power collectively and seek healing and empowerment.

I forgot many of the details and, in some cases, relevant parts of the abuse I experienced.

Dissociation is a separateness or disconnection from oneself. It often involves detachment. The Mental Health America website describes dissociation as "a mental process that causes a lack of connection in a person's thoughts, memory and sense of identity. Other forms of dissociation include 'psychogenic fugue' (memory loss characteristic of amnesia, loss of one's identity and fleeing from one's environment" (Mental Health America, n.d.). This inability to remember left me in a constant state of anxiety. We are all driven by instinct. We freeze, fight, or flee. It wasn't until my perpetrator died that the memories flooded back. I would dissociate when faced with something that triggered me back to that time and place. I would drift off to a place where I felt safe, numb. This was not productive.

Resiliency comes from the process of recovery, and often this involves telling the story of the trauma. The relationship between individual trauma and culture is one of shame. Recovery consists of taking back one's sense of power and agency. Both individual trauma and cultural trauma effect one's sense of pride. Restoring a lost sense of self-respect and confidence is an essential part of the healing process for both the individual and the community. This can occur through reading and celebrating a community's history and literature or through the process of writing.

These traumatic experiences can be manifested in a poem through imagery and tension. But how does a person manage to write from such a place? Writing from the first person can be both empowering and healing. The first person "I" and the lyric are vehicles that can help poets explore both personal and cultural trauma and move beyond victimization to a place of strength and confidence. In *A Borderlands View on Latinos: Latin Americans and Decolonization*, Pilar Hernández-Wolfe asks, "How does epistemic privilege play out in our thinking and approaching trauma, resilience and resistance?" (2013,122). Privilege is often blind to the reality of those who are less privileged. To better communicate our experiences to those who have not experienced trauma, it is vital for us to sing our own songs.

Using the first person "I" and taking a subjective stance is necessary when one is sharing his or her trauma. A collective trauma can also be shown via subjective experience and the first person "I." Appropriation of another's experience does not hold the weight that someone relating tangible details of their own trauma-related injury does. Experiencing becomes a necessary component, because the whole point is to share the traumatic experience to make it more real for readers. Creating a disturbance in the mind of a reader is not a bad thing. The whole point of telling is to help oneself and society heal. Helping readers get outside of their comfort zone can help bring awareness to the political and personal ramifications of war, rape, violence, and a long history of oppression. It can cause a reader to question authoritarian stances about aesthetics and societal privileging. A person who has not experienced trauma may not understand wholly the fragmentation and dissociation involved, much less the long path to recovery.

The traumas of ethnic and cultural groups can be witnessed around the world. Poems about the Holocaust, war, and colonization are well documented. Carolyn Forché in her anthology titled *Against Forgetting: Twentieth-Century Poetry of Witness* presents a number of poems that show both the mourning and resiliency of trauma survivors. The anthology explores suffering and how we can sing about dark and difficult times as artists and writers. Bearing witness to trauma and past events of historical oppression is a means for us to survive and thrive. Rather than being victims, these poets are survivors.

Telling our own stories, and using our own language and customs rather than the stories, languages, and customs of others, is one way we can process what has happened to us and move forward (SAMHSA 2014). Writing as medicine is what the lyric can be about for Latinos/as. A poem written from the first-person perspective need not be labeled confessional or self-absorbed.

Confessional implies that there is some guilt involved on the part of a speaker. The first-person perspective is a means to personal and social change. Personal emotions such as grief and anger must be expressed. To argue against the subjective experience is a way of silencing and dismissing trauma. Is it any wonder that anti-lyric sentiment has come about when minorities and marginalized groups are now finding their voices and publishing their stories?

It is imperative that Latino/as create for themselves a place of safety and community in the literary world. Marginalization in contemporary literature is still prevalent even though minority groups have created their own presses and contests. Writers and poets filing grievances against what has occurred in the past, in the minds of some, is unnecessary and an example of behaving as a victim. The lyric voice can constitute survival, resistance, and resilience for those who have endured or witnessed violence. This is true along the Mexican border, where many have been violently killed, as well as in many Latin American countries, where dictators have terrorized their people. Many of these people who have a violent and tumultuous history have fled to the United States. The echoes of violence are often absorbed by later generations, and it is vital that their experiences be told. Abuse at the hands of those in more powerful positions, historically and in the present, must be voiced if are Latinos/as to heal.

It is vital that poets and writers speak to those silences and give those traumatized a voice. My own use of the lyric and the first person "I" was a necessary component in facing and processing the violence in my childhood. It is my hope that my poems help survivors process trauma and let go of shame. Bringing attention to the devastating effects of trauma offers hope for recovery and helps us process our histories, both personal and cultural, so we can, as human beings, begin to change lives on this planet.

SOURCES

Alexander, Jeffrey C. 2004. "Toward a Theory of Cultural Trauma." Berkeley: University of California Press, California Scholarship Online. doi:10.1525/california/9780520235946.003.0001.

Burnett, John. 2006. "The Bath Riots: Indignity along the Mexican Border." National Public Radio, January 28. www.npr.org/templates/story/story.php?storyId=5176177.

Mental Health America. n.d. "Dissociation and Dissociative Disorders." www.mhanational.org/conditions/dissociation-and-dissociative-disorders.

Forché, Carolyn, ed. 1993. *Against Forgetting: Twentieth-Century Poetry of Witness*. New York: W. W. Norton.

Hernández-Wolfe, Pilar. 2013. *A Borderlands View on Latinos, Latin Americans and Decolonization: Rethinking Mental Health*. Lanham, MD: Jason Aronson.

SAMHSA (Substance Abuse and Mental Health Services Administration). 2014. *Behavioral Health Trends in the United States: Results from the 2014 Survey on Drug Use and Health*. October 22. www.samhsa.gov/data/sites/default/files/NSDUH-FRR1-2014/NSDUH-FRR1-2014.pdf.

La Desembocada

Healing the Wound That Never Heals

IRE'NE LARA SILVA

TO BELONG

"WHERE ARE YOU from?" both English- and Spanish-speaking people ask me. My best answer is in Spanish—"*Soy de aquí. De la frontera. Mexicana de este lado. Indigena.*" In English, it always seems my answer is longer—because each label means something different to different people—"Tejana. Chicana. Latina. Mexican American. De-tribalized Native."

People from both sides look at me and think "immigrant," but I have no memories of other places, no concept of a foreign homeland. My parents were born here, as were most of my grandparents and great-grandparents and so on and so on. I might as well be made of this Texas earth, this earth that birthed me, this earth I will return to.

My parents spoke Spanish. Neither received more than a couple of years of elementary education. They were migrant workers their entire lives, in the fields and as truck drivers. I attended three or four schools every school year as we traveled on the harvest circuit, from onions and cantaloupe and cabbage and watermelon to sorghum to rice to silage to sugar beets to cottonseed and back again. We never traveled "North" as many others did—we stayed in Texas, Oklahoma, New Mexico. We worked the land. We traveled and re-traveled the roads. We were always "home."

I fell in love with words the first time a book was read aloud to me, in kindergarten. But it was also books that told me I did not belong. That named me outsider, other, foreign; that told me all these words I loved were not mine.

LA DESEMBOCADA

Our annual circuit always led back to South Texas, and in the Rio Grande valley, everything was defined by the river—which side you lived on, which side you had been born on, which side your parents were from. At different points, the river was a muddy trickle or a concrete wall or green and flowing as it was in the crossing I was most familiar with—the bridge into Nuevo Progreso, Tamaulipas.

I have crossed that bridge at least a thousand times, and each time, we always paused for a second as we passed the marker that divided Mexico from the United States. Perhaps we felt the most whole standing there, breathless on a bridge, the river below, at the line of demarcation.

But if you go farther south inside Texas, you find yourself in front of the ocean, at the Gulf of Mexico. As a child and as an adult, I spent many hours on South Padre Island and at Port Isabel. One a busy tourist spot. The other almost completely deserted. The road went straight to the sand, to the ocean. Where almost no one ever went, though, was to the mouth of the river.

The place where the Rio Grande/Rio Bravo met the ocean. *La desembocada*.

Anzaldúa speaks of the *herida abierta* that the Rio Grande is, and it is an open wound, always bleeding, always throbbing. Poverty. Violence. Drugs. But the mouth of the river is another place. No one who lives in the valley goes there or speaks of it, but it is like nothing else. The wind is different there. The birds are different there. Salt water and fresh water come together, an opposition that creates verdant life. Birthing and tumbling and turning. The mouth of the Rio Grande is like the end of the world, where transformation and choice and imagination are physical and visceral things.

How to draw a line there, where one thing is always becoming another? Roar of saltwater. Sigh of freshwater.

What is a poet if not the mouth of the river, channeling language, pouring it into the ocean of the world?

THE DREAM

I am on the beach. Cloudy sky. My mother. My father. My youngest brother.

My mother sitting fully clothed on the beach, warily eyeing the waves as if she fears a sudden tidal wave. My father striding toward the waves. My brother I can barely see. He met the ocean and lost his human body. Now he is a manta ray skimming the surface of the ocean, heading toward the open and the deep. Me, immersed but treading water, closing my eyes and holding my breath when the waves intensify.

I wake. Wonder at the symbolism. What does this dream say about my writing?

My mother is the fear that lives behind, beneath, before, after writing—the unwillingness to immerse myself—to channel emotion, to call the deepest truths from the ocean.

My father—head lowered, arms raised, already battling the waves. My father—how I fight writing. How I fail to channel my energy and time to create a space for writing. He is the writer in me that doesn't understand that to write is to give.

My brother the manta ray. Ocean as homeland. Ocean as art. Ocean as family. To be ocean in its full power and expanse. In writing, to be inseparable from language. To be that connection of energy that lives between words. A pure conduit without boundaries. Lightning streaking through ocean water.

Me—treading water, surrounded by the ocean but separate from it, clinging to my finite human body. When the writing comes, where do I go? I begin to think that surrender is neither escape nor terror, but the freedom I have always hunted.

DARK WATER

I have always loved swimming. Swimming—like dancing, like singing, like writing—is most like flying. Tremendous effort transformed into beauty.

Tremendous effort expended to achieve velocity. Tremendous effort rewarded by freedom and the next challenge.

The last time I went swimming at night, naked in a dark lake—the starred night was moonless, the clouds purple on the horizon. The body suspended in water. In air. In music. In words.

And in that moment, I felt Lorca's words in my body, registering in my blood. In *Play and Theory of the Duende*, Lorca says, "The magic power of a poem consists in it always being filled with *duende*, in its baptizing all who gaze at it with dark water."

When I first read those words almost twenty years ago, I heard the directive: immerse them in dark waters. What I understood was that what I had to do in my writing was bring the reader to the dark water I lived in, to dissolve the separation between ourselves and our emotions.

And in the water that night, I heard Lorca, and it came to me—that the fear of writing and the fear of water intersect, that it was necessary to push through, casting oneself out of oneself to write things dark and to write them beautifully.

I want to be the river, the lake, the ocean. I want to write the mouth of the river and the ocean. The ocean without boundaries. Without lines. Without nations. Without fear. To go to the place where there are no boundaries.

DUENDE

What Lorca also said: "With idea, sound, gesture, the *duende* delights in struggling freely with the creator on the edge of the pit . . . the *duende* wounds, and in trying to heal that wound that never heals, lies the strangeness, the inventiveness of a man's work." Writing with duende is nothing like the talent gifted by angels or the capricious inspiration pricked by a muse. To write with duende is to struggle with your own soul and to birth words in the terrible aftermath. No superficial struggle will wrest out truth. Here, the twisted river. Here, our braided blood. Here, two nations, pulling and pushing on each other. Here, wound and not wound, line and not line, story and not story, silence and not silence. To live here strains the imagination, strains the heart. Pain may make us all recoil, but what is unique is how we resist, how we change to survive, what decades of struggle teach us about this strange work of healing and creation. How many years does it take to learn to see those possibilities?

THE BORDER

I was twenty-three the last time I left the border. Two years of silence had come to an end, and I was writing stories. Run, they told me, run. And I did, because I wanted them to breathe and grow. Because the box that defined me as daughter and sister and woman was becoming smaller and smaller, and soon it would have started deforming my bones.

What I didn't know was that when the border is in your blood, you take it everywhere you go. You take the wariness and the ever-alertness. You take that bordered vision, doubled and halved. You take the red mist of violence and the sun blasting down on you. And you also take the infinite horizons and a thousand shades of brown in all their faces and you take the sweetness of the orange groves in bloom. The roads live in you and the wind is always calling. The border was never all wound, and that is another medicine. *La herida abierta* holds its own healing.

HEALING THE WOUND

"We have said that the *duende* loves the edge, the wound, and draws close to places where forms fuse in a yearning beyond visible expression," Lorca said.

What more necessary work do we have to do but the wild work of healing? Healing that calls for tremendous effort and tremendous creativity? Work no one can do for us but that we must do for ourselves.

And yearning is what will take us there.

And though the wound may remain, may *la desembocada* live in us. Let us be the place where *la herida abierta* heals and heals and heals. Where saltwater and fresh water collide and meet and life flourishes. Where words and green leaves burst in profusion. A place where we all—the queer, the indigenous, the artist, the activist, the teacher, and the immigrant—are all one body.

Longing for a Language That Joins

Class Consciousness in Portuguese American Poetry

CARLO MATOS

I WAS FORTUNATE enough to grow up in a lively Portuguese community in Somerset, Massachusetts, and I felt very rooted in my ethnic heritage. What was not so clear was how to be an American, although I had always been one to some extent. These are not mutually exclusive drives, of course. To understand one is to understand the other. For those Portuguese American writers whose families were determined to leave Portugal behind for one reason or another, they often felt the significant loss of the living ethnic culture I took for granted. For example, Millicent Borges Accardi, who spent her summers in New Bedford not far from where I grew up, often describes in her poetry a desire for the traditions of the old country. In her poem "The Last Borges," she writes:

> As you grow older, papa,
> I long for a language that joins us,
> beyond our last name . . .
>
> Beyond linguiça,
> kale soup and sweet bread . . .
>
> But, the only Portuguese words
> you ever gave me do not stand for love. (2016a)

A longing is evident for what has been withheld—a piece of her that was present but shrouded in silence, leading to the desire for a language to speak the unspoken. A similar thing can be seen in her poem "Why Not the Irish?"

> It's always the "Portuguese!"
> Your questions about . . .
>
> How to cook kale or salted
> Fish, or malasadas . . .
>
> About times in our lives
> That your father would rather
> Not remember. (2010)

Her connection to her father is cleaved to a language that resists transmission, resists contextualizing the pieces of her ethnic identity she has been able to gather about her. Any reclaiming of the hyphenated experience requires a bifurcated approach because we are not just reclaiming Portugal, a place mostly fantastical for many Portuguese American authors because our parents lack the formal education necessary to provide access to larger intellectual and social narratives. The American part of the equation can be equally mysterious, a vague, formless space, present but unyielding. America is a place where the Portuguese have been smudged on the ledger and mostly erased. Or worse even, for those from Madeira or the Azores (as I am), to come from a place that might as well be Atlantis.

When I was a young man, I remember enjoying the coming-of-age shenanigans of the characters in the movie *Mystic Pizza*, starring Lili Taylor and Julia Roberts. I was drawn to Lili Taylor's trademark charm and Julia Roberts's wicked smile and 1980s hair-sprayed curls straight out of Bon Jovi's *Slippery when Wet*. But there was a key thing I did not notice, one crucial detail that I missed until I was much older and happened upon the movie again. The main characters were supposed to be Portuguese Americans. Good or bad, this movie should have left an indelible mark on me, because I was hungry for any kind of recognition that we existed as a part of American culture. *Mystic Pizza* is the kind of movie that viewers and critics alike seemed to enjoy despite themselves, and I, too, felt this way. But why? Was it simply Julia Roberts? Was it the lure of the coming-of-age story? Or could it be that the movie, with all its obvious nonsense, happened to address something essential in the hyphenated experience, some version of the American narrative that was an accurate representation of the lives of the people in my world? It occurred to me as an adult that what the movie got right was the working-class experience of many Portuguese Americans living on the East Coast. These experiences appear in many forms in my work and in many poems by important Portuguese American writers.

Millicent Borges Accardi, in personal correspondence, spoke about her experiences working in Connecticut:

> I was working for Pfizer in Groton, which is right next door to Mystic and probably where the characters would have really lived. My crappy Days Inn Hotel was steps away from the row of Portuguese working class bars and divey cafés. That period was one of the first serious forays into my heritage (on my own), sitting around having kale soup and linguiça and seeing PA folks who were not family. I wish they had not worked me like a dog so I could have seen more.

We live in a culture that refuses to acknowledge class distinctions. It may not be a surprise then that some Portuguese Americans have a tough time constructing a complete identity and that PA writers go searching in all directions for the missing pieces. Suppose we accept that Portuguese American identity is class bound, which only addresses a part of the overall problem. In that case, it may be no surprise that many Portuguese American writers struggling with how to capture their experience turn to typical first-gen themes, which tend to focus on things like food and fado music. It might also explain why these writers tend to focus on work, a set of experiences that are fundamentally class bound.

For instance, in Accardi's poetry, work is often a key factor in her self-conceptions of what it means to be Portuguese American. In her poem "The World in 2001" (2016b), she writes, "My Dad and me, we made fun of slackers . . .

> Workers who lost
> jobs. Girls who had babies out of wedlock.
> Folks who couldn't save.
> We thought those who failed just didn't . . .
> try hard enough, and that anything could be
> accomplished with a clean breath of ambition, care and love.

Her relationship with her father, always the locus of her cultural anxieties and desires, here manifests itself in the context of attitudes toward work. Work both joins and separates in the same way that many traditional ethnic experiences do. It joins her to her father, who is the symbol of her Portuguese heritage, and sets them both apart from those who have a different and maybe alien relationship to work.

In her poem "Angie Appropriates a Bar or Two" (2011), Nancy Vieira Couto describes a working world even more familiar to me, that of the mill worker. The slowly failing mills of the East Coast are powerful images in my first book, *A School for Fishermen*. They are the critical difference between the Portuguese American lived experience of the East Coast and that of the West Coast. For example, Couto writes,

> So they talked
> about the mill, about his five brothers
> and four sisters, mostly about how he
> was going to make it someday, make it
> big . . .
>
> as the textile
> industry moves south . . .
>
> and now here she is, a ma
> herself with a sinkful of greasy
> pots to scrub, a third-story tenement
> to mop and polish.

For me, Couto's poem captures many things that I consider part and parcel of the Portuguese American experience: the mills, the ambition, the tenements, and the disappointments. In some sense, Couto's poem is much more emblematic of the Portuguese American experience as I know it because it focuses explicitly on the significant role that class plays in identity construction.

Paula Neves, who grew up in New Jersey's Ironbound, in her poem "11th Birthday" (2018), describes a party where class and ethnic identity seamlessly merge:

> Apart from this, there are the staples:
> potatoes, rice, the deep-fried cod fritters
> they all call *bolas (balls)*, which, if I look
> at Diana now, would make me titter—
> understanding, as I am,
> how concerned they all are with *appearances* . . .

The first part of the poem is a list of ethnic foods—the same way Accardi establishes cultural difference in some of her poems—but the second half is something more complex. We go from food to a discussion of "appearances." These things are as often determined by class as they are by skin color, region, or country of origin. Neves, in her poem, is describing the appearances that set us apart from the Anglo-Saxon paradigm. She describes the girls deliberately singing off-key

> as small revenge for playing along with our mothers,
> who wouldn't want us to misrepresent
> why at other people's houses we get the stare of death
> if we dare to entertain a "yes"
> when we are offered
> anything.

I certainly remember getting the annual warning about accepting anything from the heavily laden tables of the families we were making *visitas* (literally "visits") to during the holidays. The tables were overburdened with delicious food, which was explicitly for guests, and yet we were not allowed to take any, because, as my mother said when we always balked, "They'll think we don't feed you, that we don't have enough to eat, that we didn't raise you right, *malcriado*." We were not allowed to partake of our own holiday spread either. This is not something I ever experienced in the homes of my non-Portuguese friends. To them, rooms were for living in—unlike the ubiquitous parlors full of sculpture, china, and chandeliers we all had in our homes. Food was for eating, and clothes were for getting dirty. They were not for the sake of appearances, and yet for all that, it only ever proved how much we did not belong.

However, this raises the question about what happens to those of us who make it out, who escape the sometimes severe class limitations placed on our lives. In *Late Rapturous*, Frank X. Gaspar, a native of Provincetown, Rhode Island, is faced with a different kind of erasure, the kind that comes at the expense of years of higher learning. As an older man, he remembers, in "The Marriage of Figaro," the working-class boy he used to be, who after years of schooling,

> still pronounced *Mozart* wrong. I can still be the boy now,
> even in those shameful moments when all I want to do is disavow him,
> the one with the holes in his shoes. (2012b)

These lines ring with irony and longing. By deliberately mispronouncing the name of the famous composer, some part of Gaspar can hold onto a self unmarred by the vast assimilative powers of the American educational system. His younger self haunts this book, haunts the successful man of letters that Gaspar has gone on to become. Like many of us, the more he belongs to the world of letters, the more he desires to coax that working-class boy outside himself, looking for a kind of authenticity defined mostly by class distinctions. In "All Dharmas Are Marked with Emptiness" (2012a), he describes a girl who works at the supermarket

> who printed an entire anthology of poems on a single eight-and-a-half-by-eleven sheet of Xerox paper and folded a hundred copies down to wallet size and passed them out to anyone who dared look her in the eye.

I knew many working-class folks, people who worked in supermarkets, gas stations, and convenient stores, who wanted so much to not only escape from our social class but to transcend it. And to us, there was nothing more transcendent and nothing more out of reach than the world of Art, with a capital "A."

In my most recent collection of poetry, *We Prefer the Damned*, this tension between social class and art making, between the high and the low, returns with a vengeance as I pay homage to the "paintings by all those working-class boys/[pseudo-bohemians who work too hard to count for the real thing]." And once again, it is work that, in my opinion, delineates a true bohemian—someone who by choice has decided to live outside the confines of the 9–5 world—from a pseudo-bohemian, who has no option but to work or perish.

Class in America has the strange quality of being invisible and yet completely restrictive. What this does for Portuguese American writers, I am suggesting, is erase large parts of our experience and yet limit our lives to mundane labor and mere survival. Our desire to create art or to live rather than to merely survive is never taken seriously, as if these enterprises are only for the children of privilege. In another poem from my new book, the speaker says, "We know about fighting but we can know about art too . . . They never tell us that" ("Who's the Boss?"). In the work of many Portuguese American poets, class plays a key role in identity construction, but attitudes toward work become more complex when we leave the safety of the working-class environment. As the children of immigrants and our children move beyond those jobs and begin accepting white-collar or creative jobs, there are a whole new set of issues to deal with. Like Gaspar, I too have become, for better or worse, a man of letters. In my heart, though, I am and always will be a working-class boy, but my living conditions no longer reflect that reality. I no longer live in a Portuguese community, because the type of work I do required that I move halfway across the country to a place with few Portuguese Americans. As we are pulled from our communities or as they disappear of their own accord, the threat of assimilation grows stronger because these jobs largely reflect an Anglo-Saxon worldview. What does it mean to be a teacher, a poet, a physicist, or a police detective for a Portuguese American? The poems reflecting this new world are being written, but there are not nearly enough of them. They are as essential to Portuguese American aesthetics as the first poems to introduce fados and *festas* and *malasadas*. There is still a great hunger by

Portuguese Americans to see representations of themselves on the big screen and TV, in music and novels. We need our celebrities, of which there are many, to own their heritage publicly, to provide for the next generation of young people alternative models for constructing the Portuguese American experience in the twenty-first century.

SOURCES

Accardi, Millicent Borges. 2010. "Why Not the Irish?" In *Injuring Eternity*, 35. Palo Verdes, CA: Mischievous Muse Press.

———. 2016a. "The Last Borges." In *Only More So*, 65. Ennistymon: Salmon Poetry.

———. 2016b. "The World in 2001." In *Only More So*, 51. Ennistymon: Salmon Poetry.

Couto, Nancy Vieira. 2011. "Angie Appropriates a Bar or Two." In *Carlyle & the Common Accident*, 230. Katona, NY: Foothills Publishing.

Gaspar, Frank X. 2012a. "All Dharmas Are Marked with Emptiness." In *Late Rapturous*, 11. Pittsburgh, PA: Autumn House Poetry.

———. 2012b. "The Marriage of Figaro." In *Late Rapturous*, 40. Pittsburgh, PA: Autumn House Poetry.

Matos, Carlos. 2021. *We Prefer the Damned*. London: Unbound Edition Press.

Neves, Paula. 2018. "11th Birthday." In *capricornicopia (the dream of goats)*, 9. Georgetown, KY: Finishing Line Press.

Let's Call the Whole Thing Off

Or, the Possibilities of a Contemporary US Latin@ Poetry

RAFAEL CAMPO

DURING A MORE memorable Associated Writing Programs conference not all that long ago in New York City, I participated in a reading of some two dozen fellow Latin@ poets, sponsored by a small community arts organization based in the South Bronx called Acentos. A rainstorm lashed Times Square that night—in Spanish, we would call it a *tormenta*, which appropriately sounds like *torment* in English and which is degrees of magnitude worse than the much more amiable *agaucero*. My Cuban-by-way-of-New-Jersey efforts to hail a cab so I could get to the venue on time, which were almost as comically maladroit as they were futile, seemed to underscore the fact that this reading, though featuring most of the best-known contemporary Latino poets, was an "off-site" event. Just when I thought it was utterly hopeless, a dignified white-haired couple pulled up to the curb in a cab right where I stood, and beneath their huge paisley umbrella, held open the door to the back seat for me so graciously that I felt as if I had been bequeathed a great fortune. When I finally arrived at the auditorium uptown, I was surprised to see it packed with over two hundred attendees, many of them with steaming cups of *café con leche* in hand and speaking so quickly and loudly to one another that for a moment, I flashed back to my grandparents' cramped apartment back in Elizabeth. Even the institutional fluorescent lights overhead seemed briefly as warm as strong, south-of-the-border sunshine.

No sooner had I arrived than I found myself being approached by

Francisco Aragón, who carried under his arm a copy of his recently published anthology of new Latino poetry. I knew Francisco's brother from my residency training years ago in primary-care medicine at the University of California–San Francisco; he had actually interviewed me for the program. First uncomfortable stereotype of the evening: that all Latinos who have been to college know each other. As I registered our tenuous connection, already he was asking me if I had seen the anthology, and then, in the next breath, whether I had been willing to review it. He handed me the thick, glossy volume just as it was being announced that the reading was about to begin and we should take our seats. I looked down at the book's title page as I found a place near the stage. *The Wind Shifts: New Latino Poetry* (University of Arizona Press, 2007). Before the room quieted down for the first introduction, there was a spontaneous burst of thunderous applause.

Fast forward seven years, and another new anthology has just appeared, with the latest designation of the same community of writers proudly featured in its title: *Angels of the Americlypse: New Latin@ Literature* (Counterpath, 2014), edited by John Chávez and Carmen Giménez Smith. Despite its promise of the same kind of exuberance produced at that off-site AWP reading on a cold and dreary night—its cover pulsates with pinks and reds as vibrant as the flesh of a ripe guava—no one has yet asked me to review it. I realize, as I begin to think about the state of "Latin@" poetry today, that though I did write a review of that earlier anthology, I was unable to publish it; though I had focused much of my enthusiastic response on the poems it contained by Richard Blanco, who a few years later would go on to read a poem at President Barack Obama's second inauguration, back then no book-review editor was interested in my three thousand words on American Latino poetry.

Both these anthologies and the peculiarly American love-hate relationship with all things Latin@ that they seem to represent have inspired in me, too, a number of conflicting feelings and thoughts. Perhaps it is a kind of reflex to think in hyphenations when considering anything to do with our particular position in the United States. So here is a list of these inescapable archetypal tensions:

> Histories: Hispanic versus Latino/a (versus Latin@)
> Gender: Latino/a (machismo) versus Latin@
> Sexuality: "gay" claimed versus imported as a Spanish word (machismo, again)
> National identity: the Spanish language diaspora
> Borders: the deliberateness of being fenced out
> Language: bilingual/bicultural, "speaking the language"
> Class: politics of oppression, diversity/polarization of beliefs
> Race: mestizo/mulatto/zambo, obsession with "the taint"/ "one-drop rule."

Where does one begin to define the territory of any attempt to speak of a Latino aesthetic? Hispaniola seems so utterly distant, yet in some fundamental sense still embraces us all. But even before running down the list further, the whole notion of tensions seems characteristically Latin@—we are at once inside the border and fenced out; we speak Spanish and/or English, and/or Spanglish; we are the children of landowners and of migrant workers; we read Neruda and Vargas Llosa; we are every gradation of skin color in the spectrum of what is humanly possible. Perhaps such a list paradoxically reveals just one foundational truth: we are both blessed and vexed by our contradictions. Perhaps such a list demands only that we complicate ourselves more profoundly.

Part of me has never felt so at home as when among the myriad voices of fellow Latin@ poets who have become a kind of familiar chorus singing of exile, of oppression and social justice, and ultimately of heartbreak, with an innate musicality that, since it is not present in English, must somehow have its origins in Spanish. Yet part of me has recoiled at the feeling of being summed up, like the way I would cringe when my grandparents would try to speak Spanish in the American supermarket, wishing they could master English, wishing they were more respectable, wishing we were as mainstream as the bespectacled lady at the register who scowled at us. Part of me has rejoiced in the collective refusal to be marginalized or silenced that anthologies like these present, that even in a larger American culture that so disdains poetry, a wellspring of the Latino reverence for expressive language can still sustain and delight, the way singing to myself those old Cuban songs I learned from my *tía* somehow kept me alive during the long winters of my adolescence. Yet part of me has stubbornly resisted the blatant rage voiced in the heat of "spoken word" poetry, even though it is the same rage I myself felt as I studied Robert Frost and Emily Dickinson twice as hard, as if in response to the crusty old white pre-med advisor at Amherst College who once told me I would never get in to medical school.

Part of me has wondered at the sheer diversity of poetry being written by Latinos, from the elegantly formal quatrains of Julia Alvarez to the fiercely intelligent, full-bodied free verse of Martín Espada (and yes, of L=A=N=G=U=A=G=E poetry and spoken word, too), the uninformed application of this ethnic category thus immediately dooming any attempt to unify the writing under a single structural impulse or prevailing aesthetic. Another part of me has bristled at the assumptions made about the same writers in a similarly vain attempt to unify us thematically, as if we must all write the same poem and that it is a poem about exile, or immigration, or chocolate and sex, or swaying palm trees, or noble grandparents, or oppression. In the post-identity politics world, part of me has thrilled to the call to action that such readings and anthologies perform, providing an outlet for work that still rarely graces the pages of mainstream literary journals, and refuting the concatenating notions that Latinos don't read/are illiterate/can't speak English. Yet part of me has been vexed by our failure as a poetry to claim (and to challenge, and even to critique) all the various influences we embody—not only that of Eastern European magical realism (Brodsky, Miłosz, Szymborska, their fantastical post-totalitarianism narrative somehow always out-haunting the worlds of Allende, Borges, and Neruda, at least in the view of many critics) but also the now haute hip-hop culture that is African American *and* Latino (and like its predecessor jazz, frequently viewed monochromatically).

Part of me has marveled at the mindless enthusiasm these days for all things nominally Latin@, from chips and salsa and Che Guevara T-shirts and mojitos to cilantro and Frida Kahlo refrigerator magnets and Buena Vista Social Club CDs, and the concomitant attempts to brand Latino writing, which has led to the marketing of big names like Sandra Cisneros and Oscar Hijuelos as suitable to point to in one's library. Part of me has reviled the facile assumptions that lump us all together, so that the reason Latin@ writing never receives much review attention (never mind major literary prizes) is because there aren't enough qualified Latinos to write book reviews (the "only Latinos can review Latino writing" rule) or because each category is only allowed a few notables, no matter how different the actual writing, who are all we can talk about (Edwidge Danticat, Jamaica Kincaid, Derek Walcott; Gish Jen, Ha Jin, Amy Tan; Terry Macmillan, Toni Morrison, Alice Walker; Jhumpa Lahiri, V. S. Naipaul, Vikram Seth). (These "rules" are magnified one thousand fold for poetry in particular, for which there is so little attention to begin with.)

Part of me has embraced a vision of Latino writing that is actually without boundaries, where feminist, Afro-Latino, and queer voices challenge the stale old racist machismo, where *Latino* is taken to mean not exclusively Chicano and Boricua (Mexican Americans and Puerto Ricans being traditionally the largest US Latino subpopulations) but also Chilean, Guatemalan, Dominican, Salvadoran, Cuban, Nicaraguan, Argentine, Venezuelan, and the many other national identities comprising us. Yet part of me has been dismayed of the kind of clubbiness among Latino poets that still persists, aping what we see in the white literary world, which results in anthologies that seem to be full of work by the editors' friends and ex-students, and in general what seems at times an overly deferential fawning over those same majority-approved big names.

All of these internal divisions should, of course, be interpreted as themselves distinctly Latin@; the inescapable metaphor of the border looms ever large in the Latino consciousness and is all the more magnified these days in the context of the current mean-spirited American debate over immigration. Yet what about them is also indelibly American? Writers like Gloria Anzaldúa have rightly and incisively addressed the electrified fence that intimidates, while beckoning to, the Latino imagination; it is a border that can never be surmounted and whose power to keep out "the other" only grows as more and more try to gain entrance. More recently, Ilan Stavans and other critics have questioned its paramount significance and have begun to see such innovations as Spanglish and Tejano music as fruitful expressions of an American-inspired fusion of identities that transcends the border. In the postcolonial, post-identity-politics, brave new globalizing world, the border has lost its relevance, unable to stand in the way of a Pan- American utopia where one can microwave a frozen burrito in Toronto or where a Nuyorican poetry slam can be enjoyed via podcast in old San Juan.

Richard Blanco's poems are among the most admirable written by the younger generation of Latin@ poets, enacting some of these concerns without fatally over-explicating or over-dramatizing them. In addition to reading at the second Obama inauguration, Blanco has published two volumes of poetry, *City of a Hundred Fires* and *Directions to the Beach of the Dead*, which recently won the PEN/Beyond Margins Award. One sees Blanco struggling repeatedly with how to position himself in relation to his Cuban heritage and his American future. The speaker in his poems is often in the midst of a journey, as in "Crossing Boston Harbor" (2007b), which concludes:

> So much of my life is spent like this—suspended,
> moving toward unknown places and names or
>
> returning to those I know, corresponding with
> the paradox of crossing, being nowhere yet here,
>
> leaning into the wind and light, uncertain of what
> I might answer the woman to my right, anchored
>
> in a flutter of cottons and leaning over the stern,
> should she lift her eyes from the sea toward me
>
> and ask: So, where are you from?

The unrhymed couplets in the poem seem an expression of the speaker's unfulfilled wish to be joined to a single place, to be from somewhere, to be able to complete that provocatively unfinished last couplet. The oxymoronic images in these last lines underscore this perpetually divided state: the speaker "being nowhere and here," the otherwise nondescript woman at once fluttering and anchored.

Elsewhere, Blanco admirably embraces sentiment without veering into the utterly sappy, as in "Chilo's Daughters Sing for Me in Cuba" (2007a). In my Cuban family, we used to joke that if you weren't yelling or crying when you said something, you didn't really *mean* it; translating this cultural imperative into an American poetics that values icy, oftentimes neurotic detachment above all else is a formidable obstacle to any Latino poet. Yet Blanco accomplishes this alchemy, indulging in his aunts' and cousins' calloused fingers and the "typical" delicacies they create all the while insisting on the specificity of their evocative names, and those romantic old Cuban songs:

> . . . Rosita sings old boleros,
> for our *tíos* and *tías* still in love with love.
> Nivia sings *danzones* to honor our grandfathers
> who'll be buried in the same ground they tilled.
> Delia sings the old *décima* verses of *guajiros*
> who made poetry out of cutting sugarcane.
> And we all sing *Guantanamera*, over and over
> again—*Guantanamera*, because today the food
> is plentiful, *Guantanamera* for the lyrics that praise
> the good people of this country
> where the palms grow, *guajira Guantanamera*
> because the revolution that never ends will
> never change them, their stories, this land.

The attenuation of family bonds across generations is deftly suggested by the humble poetic device of list-making, which in turn echoes the distance from his homeland this poet of exile recreates here. Yes, we feel the familiar heartbreak, but it is yet made fresh by the ironic comment on the ubiquity of "Guantanamera" for Cubans in the repetition of the song's title, and the voice-catching, awkward enjambment of the lines.

Equally impressive and a newer discovery for me is Sheryl Luna, whose *Pity the Drowned Horses* (2005a) won the inaugural Andrés Montoya Poetry Prize for the best first book by a Latin@ author. Luna's poems similarly recognize the opportunities for making meaning using the unique resources in poetry; they are specifically American poems in their distinctly hybridized yet plain diction. In her poem "Two Girls from Juárez" (2005b), for example, through a jolting allusion to the poet Sylvia Plath, she shows us how utterly daunting the estrangement of cultures across borders can become:

Let's Call the Whole Thing Off

Two girls from Juárez hesitantly step toward my desk.
"Ms.," one says with a paperback of Plath's *Ariel*

corners folded and coffee-stained. "Was she white
or black?" One with over-dyed red hair and black

roots announces, "She was prejudiced!"
I am now questioning my life in the desert, questioning

as lightning rips the sky like an instant of daylight
in the hard black lake of night. In Plath's "Daddy"

a black man bites a woman's heart, and all the wit
and the wordplay between darkness and light shrugs.

I am bitten. The girls want to know
about Plath's gasps, about her white
eyes in the darkness. One wears an electronic
bracelet around her ankle.

The other's cheeks are red with too much rouge.
I imagine they live nights dangerously

in an Oldsmobile by the Río Grande,
that they love for real and that they love to love.

I smile at them with no answers. I lost answers
long ago and the faces of my colleagues grew ghost-like

and words fell away and the poetry cancer came
like a priest for the sacrifice.

What is remarkable about this poem is how it at once critiques Plath and itself as a reading of Plath. The standard feminist interpretation, as laid bare by the grim reality of these two girls from a poor Mexican border town, becomes richly complicated. The poet at once recognizes the raw sensuality of her interlocutors, seeing them as more genuinely living the dangers of their desires—"they love for real and they love to love"—in an implied comparison to the brainily unsexy Plath, and yet almost comes to pity them in their ignorance. Yet the truth of their experience, she suggests, is ironically consequent to the oppression of women that Plath is at least privileged enough to denounce. The speaker's identification with Plath is a fraught one, because she also sees elements of herself in the girls; again, we are at crossroads here, Latino pulling us in toward the deprivations and exaggerated colors of Juárez, and poetry pulling us out toward Plath's imperfect, entitled, white, education-enabled feminism. As with Blanco's poetry, what is ostensibly Latin@ here is ultimately, and ironically, also a familiarly "white/or black" American problem: With whom is the speaker most aligned? The soul and its uncouth longings or the intellect and its enticing sophistries?

Here in Boston, not far from where Plath studied and wrote and where now a gay, bilingual, Cuban American physician-poet can eat a pizza ordered from a Brazilian restaurant smothered in chiles, chorizo, and *queso blanco* while reading Blanco and Luna, Espada and Alvarez, and a whole host of other extraordinary Latin@ poets, perhaps it is too easy to become dyspeptic. Perhaps one of the downsides of globalization is the diluting of whatever it is that is authentically Latino—the piquant mojito that drenches Richard Blanco's boiled yucca, the caked-on rouge accentuating the broad cheekbones of Sheryl Luna's girls from across the border—as it yet fails to tear down that electrified fence. Alas, too many of our merely good poems lack this gripping authenticity, trading ambition to become the next American Idol for the kind of attention to craft that makes any poem poetry first, before it can become an organ of success, or assimilation—or a protest against such success or assimilation. Some of our poetry is starting to feel "schooled," but in the glibly American-style, one-dimensionally confessional, workshopped-to-death way; others are too defiantly enraged, so intent on rejecting some version of "the establishment" that they make themselves deaf to their own rich literary heritage (which, whether we like it or not, must include Frost and Dickinson as much as it does Lorca and Paz).

On the other hand, the best poems in our idiom—alongside those of Blanco and Luna, I would place Rosa Alcalá's duende-infused *cantes* and

Kevin González's Antillean formal experiments, as well as the work of Lucia Perillo, Rigoberto González, and Ada Limón—enact what I might propose as a loose definition of a new Latino poetry; through brilliantly crafted language, in which the inherent rhythm and rhyme of Spanish revises the unmusical awkwardness of English, they evoke an empathic response in their audience that situates us at the border itself, allowing us to straddle it, feeling intensely its paradoxical impermeability and porosity. They are neither crude *gritos*, nor are they manicured Americanization; they are unafraid to showcase the quintessentially Latin@ penchant for sentiment, the wailing mariachi and the melodramatic tango always unforgettably in their consciousness, but they are never merely tragically banal.

Finally, and perhaps most importantly, they are true to revealing the US Latin@ condition of marginalization, poverty, exclusion, exile, and oppression with a generous restraint—be it in the guise of a struggle with rules of the sestina, or a dialogue with the great tradition of our political poets—that engages and provokes readers, that even enrages and wounds us, but without alienating us in the end. Ultimately, they are as American as that democratic dream of something better, of a culture in which colors and spices and languages mix without melting away, of an indomitably plural society in which we are all welcome to speak and are heard.

SOURCES

Blanco, Richard. 1997. *City of a Hundred Fires*. Pittsburgh, PA: University of Pittsburgh Press.

———. 2007a. "Chilo's Daughters Sing for Me in Cuba." In *The Wind Shifts: New Latino Poetry*, edited by Francisco Aragón, 45. Tucson: University of Arizona Press.

———. 2007b. "Crossing Boston Harbor." In *The Wind Shifts: New Latino Poetry*, edited by Francisco Aragón, 46. Tucson: University of Arizona Press.

Luna, Sheryl. 2005a. *Pity the Drowned Horses*. Notre Dame, IN: University of Notre Dame Press.

———. 2005b. "Two Girls from Juárez." In *Pity the Drowned Horses*, 41. Notre Dame, IN: University of Notre Dame Press.

How I Came to Identify as a Latina Writer

ADELA NAJARRO

AS A LITTLE girl, I always had my nose in a book. I remember my mother sending me off to bed and halfway through the corridor sliding down the wall to finish the last paragraph on the last page I would read that night. I read on the school bus. I read in the library. On the living room couch as I waited for my mother to come home, I read from the set of encyclopedias she had bought the year of my brother's birth. Though I did not understand everything I read, I tried to read a bit of it all. Through fairy tales I began to envision Europe and its forests, the woodcutters, cottages, gray wolves, black bears, and the concept of snow. Through the biographies of Daniel Boone, Abraham Lincoln, and Laura Ingalls Wilder I envisioned a United States frontier where pioneers constructed log cabins in Kentucky and learned to walk through forests with the stealth of Indians. I was fascinated with the solar system, rockets, and walking on the moon. Eventually I hit upon the Harlequin Romances and Marx's *Communist Manifesto*, of which I understood not a word. In books I found possibility: men, mostly men and boys, sometimes women or girls, who were brave and made it on through. I would be brave. I could make it on through.

I have made it through trying times. Now I write stories for others to read. Even though I compose poems, essays, emails, and myriad other forms of written communication, I call them all stories, since the word *story* acknowledges the indeterminate status of language, that writing is imaginative, constructed, only one version of many possibilities and that even my one version on this page will change each time it is read. Though I can separate personal experience from language, literature, and the making of culture, I choose not to. I have a story to tell: a reconfiguration of how I came to identify as a Latina poet. The story ends with Spanglish as part of my poetic toolbox and begins with a little girl riding along with her dad doing *mandados* during Easter break when that much needed repose in the second half of the school year was still acknowledged by its religious signification.

Let's say it's 1971, Easter vacation, and I am visiting my father in San Francisco. I'm in the passenger's seat of his truck. Let's say a blue Ford pickup and, as mentioned earlier, I'm tagging along with my father on one of his many *mandados*, the errands here and there that he needs to accomplish, and that this time they are of no great significance and can be interrupted by the chatter of his little girl. Maybe we go to a hardware store, and I stare at the rows and boxes filled with progressively sized screws, bolts, and nails. There are power tools. The store is crammed from ceiling to floor with everything needed to fix up this house or that apartment my father is currently renovating. He chats at the counter while I stare at the back of the cash register. Then we get back into the truck and drive through the Mission District taking side streets to avoid the traffic of the main thoroughfares. At a stop sign, my father tells me to duck, to duck under the dashboard and hide. I feel his hand rest between my shoulders. Perhaps I am something special, a surprise kept under wraps and blue ribbons, but no, I am something to be hidden—his illegitimate daughter. My father has spotted his wife's car at a stop sign or perhaps pulling out from a driveway, and he wants to avoid any problems, so he explains. She doesn't know I'm in town, that he sent the money for the plane ticket, or that I'm sleeping in the rollaway bed next to my grandmother. He explains that it is necessary for me to disappear under the dash for only a moment, and for a moment, I no longer exist, my presence erased.

I have known firsthand the power of setting aside that which is problematic and how we can clean up a story into a more streamlined version. Denial, erasure, forgetting can be put to good use as we construct the stories of our lives, not only for the individual but perhaps also for society as a whole. The personal and the cultural at times seem to work in the same fashion.

There are stories that we remember and stories that we forget about American history and our personal pasts. Usually the ones forgotten are alternative versions of what happened where, when, and why. I have never spoken to my father about the dashboard incident, and perhaps I should. But I don't want to hear it. I don't want to listen to his denial and then his acquiescence that maybe something similar might have occurred, followed by that hoped for apology. This process would take too much work on my part, and at times that is how I feel when telling and retelling the story of Latina literature, culture, and history. The Latina/o story has so often not been told within United States history. Forgotten or ignored are the effects on Chicanos living in the States of the Mexican war and the annexation of Mexican territories.

Forgotten or ignored are the land-grabbing schemes after the Treaty of Guadalupe Hidalgo and the consequent loss of Mexican land ownership. Forgotten or ignored are the effects of Manifest Destiny throughout Latin America. The stories are out there—at the university, on public radio and television, in books and novels—but they are not the dominant versions, and they are not the ones that influenced thirty-one states to pass English-only legislation. Our history may be the story of what best fits at a certain point in time, a convenient story, a story that allows those in power to continue in their roles of obscuring the inconvenient, whether that be a father or the Anglo culture of the United States.

At the end of this story, the personal, cultural, and political intertwine, but for now, I am still in the past reconstructing the events that led me to identify as a writer, as a Latina poet. During my childhood, the big secret was that my brother and I were my father's second *familia*, the other ones, and this was not a good thing to be. However, living in the United States offered an option that could sanctify our existence; my mother, brother, and I would simply disguise ourselves as one of the many recently divorced and single-parent homes, and from there I learned the power of language. Instead of stating that my parents were not married, I could state that they were not together or that they lived apart or that they were separated. Separated was my favorite way to describe the situation because I knew that whoever I was talking to would assume "separated" as in the first stage to divorce rather than a literal meaning of the word. Perhaps this is where I first learned the power of words, about how language can be manipulated to create an illusion, the illusion we sometimes call poetry, the illusion we sometimes call art.

I always sensed that there was something up with my parents, though until the sixth grade, when my mother thought it was time or that I was ready, no one ever spoke that one version of the story where the absence of wedding vows came into play. Perhaps I had been making roundabout accusations, such as questioning her when she signed school notes with Mrs. Najarro. On a Saturday afternoon in the quiet of her bedroom, she told her version of the story, a story I knew, a story central to my understanding but one that I really could not understand. All I felt was my mother's overwhelming pain, her bravery, her anguish, and as emotions took over the room, words stopped. We held each other, a flood of love commingling with sadness. I now understood why the Mrs. Najarros and the separated terminology were necessary: that amount of pain had to be hidden, and some versions of the story cannot be told.

At times I think that is why as a society we wish to put aside the horrors of slavery, the second-class status of Mexicans in the Southwest, the genocide of Native Americans. These stories are just too painful to dwell on, and as a society it is simply easier to believe the Hollywood version of the Wild Wild West and David O. Selznick's version of the South in *Gone with the Wind*. Though we know these films veil truths of the past, they offer versions of the story that we can live with. My family took on the same approach; all of them—my father, my mother, both sides of the entire family—were in collusion to forget, to ignore, to let the past be the past, and to stick with a version that would work in society. We were in the States after all, and here you could be whoever you wanted to be.

In this way, my upbringing prepared me to become a writer. I understood the power of multiple connotations within a word, how truth or meaning is indeterminate, how one story can have multiple versions, versions we choose to accept or ignore depending on what we need in order to continue in this grand project of the United States and the eternal pursuit of happiness. But these are all conclusions after the fact, what I have learned at the end of this story here presented in the middle of the telling. Though I had an intricate relationship with language from reading extensively as a child and from the manipulation of my birth story, ultimately, when I began writing in earnest, I wrote to prove that I existed, that I was something, that I was here.

During my MFA, I wrote poems carving out who I was and how I had become, and still to this day some poems take on that necessity. There was a time when I actually thought that if I could get the words just right, then the reader would understand, not only the poem but me, Adela Josefina Najarro. I was willing to work toward clarity. I was willing to open all the closet doors of hidden secrets. I would tell all, and in so doing I would rebel against my family's collusion to tell the cleaned-up version of the story. As an added benefit, perfect strangers would sympathize with my plight, my worries, and the injustices placed on my soul. A grand project for poetry, and ultimately a futile one.

How Spanglish enters my poems is at the end of this story, and now in the middle is the beginning of how I began to change as a writer, how my understanding of the possibilities of poetry and of the written word began to alter. For my last MFA workshop, I finally put up for public inspection poems that I had been working on for nearly a year, poems that through their language I knew captured my tormented soul. I expected the readers in the class to understand, that through the language of the poems they could actually come to rest in my experience, literally know what I know. However, that didn't happen. In that towered room with many windows and the comfy chairs arranged in a circle, as I listened to the workshop paraphrase my heart, I began to realize that there was something more at stake. I could rearrange the words on the page in twenty million different ways, and no one would ever know what I know. Language cannot capture my experience verbatim, and language does not reveal the "truth" of the situation. Barriers exist between the author, the text, and the reader. I did not behave very well at the end of this workshop. I accused the class of not being good readers. I left at break. I was stunned into silence.

However, this silence was not a silence of erasure but one of solitude, perhaps meditation, a downtime to let personal experience and the possibilities of language find a new relationship. What was the purpose of poetry if not to cross the boundary of my own isolation? I did not arrive at an answer to this question immediately, and I wonder even now how much this internal desire to be heard and acknowledged drives my obsession to write. However, from that moment on, I stopped trying to capture my own experience verbatim through words on a page. I often still write from an autobiographical perspective in my poems, but I view the autobiographical not as concrete truth but as another tool to construct a collage of language. The autobiographical can lend authenticity to a piece of writing. The autobiographical can pull on the heart strings of an absent reader. The autobiographical can be manipulated just as any other form of language.

But again, these are conclusions after the fact, conclusions arrived at the end of the story. My reflection on language and literature comes together with the personal, in that my experience as a child manipulating the language of my parents' relationship equates to the process by which we create imaginative literature: threads of what happened where, when, and why woven together to present one version of one of many possible stories. The story here of how I came to identify as a Latina writer continues from my MFA to my doctoral studies at Western Michigan University, where I ran across for the first time, or once again, Plato, Wordsworth, Keats, Saussure, Eliot, and dear Mr. Harold Bloom, all the voices through time discussing the dos and don'ts of the possibility of literature, that transient entity that I was trying to create.

I read these authors not out of respect or a desire to understand the history of poetics but out of a need to find a new direction for my own writing. I let go and stopped forcing words into meaning. Instead, I began to play with language and allow memory, words, and images to collide, the writer as orchestra leader. A little more trumpet of childhood, a muting flute of snow, a violin chorus of nouns. Amazingly, in letting go of the preordained idea for a poem and its purpose, my central concerns nonetheless emerged. Some might say that perhaps a muse had found me or that I had tapped into the subconscious, but I say I had found magic. Magic as the unexplained and that which cannot be explained. I learned to trust the power within the written word and let it go at that.

In Eliot and Bloom I found the idea of influence and tradition and that as a writer I was in conversation with writers who had come before. Though my original impetus for creating poems had been to escape the isolation of the self by attempting to create poetry that equated my personal experience, a trajectory that I eventually realized as impossible, the idea of literary tradition filled my basic need to conquer isolation. It was not only me writing in front of my computer, but I was writing in the company of Elizabeth Bishop, Sylvia Plath, César Vallejo, Rubén Darío, Coleridge, Wordsworth, and Whitman. Every time I read, I was in conversation with the author, and every time I wrote I was talking back. The fact that most of the authors I read were dead and unable to join me at the local coffeehouse for a double espresso mocha was a bit of reality that I could live with.

However, I did not take on straight the idea of literary influence as proposed by Eliot and Bloom. For one, I am female, and throughout the history of Western letters, women authors are not proportionately represented. And then, as I began to identify as a Latina writer while in the midst of studying for my doctoral exams, I began to wonder, Where was my influence, and where was my tradition? When I fell in love with the work of Blake, Wordsworth, Coleridge, and Keats while studying Romantic poetry, I daydreamed about nineteenth-century Britain. I envisioned an emerging industrial London with smokestacks and chimney sweepers and Blake's little boy with soot on his face crying himself to sleep at night. I began to wonder where my family was at that time. They were certainly not in London, but in Nicaragua, in the tropics, where there were no downy green hills and little lambs, much less a nightingale. Without a direct, personal connection to Britain, I began to question my relation to the Romantic poets. How could a group so different from my own situation in terms of gender, ethnicity, and time influence my own work? Wasn't there too much distance between the Romantic poets and me? Perhaps all writers address similar questions, but as I was thinking over the problem, I began to realize that influence on one's own work is not a conscious process but arises through the cumulative effect of all that one has read. I had only read American and British authors, mostly men.

And so I began to consciously expand my reading to include women, Latino/a and Latin American writers. As a Latina writer, I began to claim the legacy of two literary histories, that of the American/British canon and that of Latin American literary production. But more specifically, I began to search for Latino/a literature, not only Latin American literature but also works by others who were writing in the United States who did not fit into the American British trajectory of history and culture. And now we're back full circle to the original father dashboard story of my erasure as a child. When looking for Latino/a literary influence, I once again came upon erasure, not the erasure of the individual but of entire cultures and history.

My personal feeling of erasure expanded to an acknowledgment of the erasure of the history of Nicaragua, Mexico, Cuba, Puerto Rico, the rest of the Caribbean and Latin America in the United States. I found that the history of Nicaragua was inexorably tied to United States Manifest Destiny ideology and that the history of my family's personal stories was a microcosm of the economic and political interrelation between the United States and Central America. As I looked to my own poems, if I did not mention the details of my Nicaraguan bilingual self, I was contributing not only to my personal erasure but to the erasure of the entire Latino/a community in the United States. Ignoring my *Latinidad* would entail letting go the details and stories that did not fit the conception of the United States as one nation under God, with justice and liberty for all, and would add to the creation myth of the United States as a land of opportunity, open, free and culturally unrestricted. At the same time, I was not about to lose sight of what I had come to understand about creating poetry as art. A poem cannot be written from an intention, is not created to educate, can never capture the suffering of an entire group of people; a poem has to focus on its language, and at times this language does educate and does capture the injustices of the world. It is a mysterious process, again a letting go, a bit of magic.

In the middle of graduate school, I began to realize the importance of accepting my *Latinidad*, of allowing my *Latinidad* into my poetry, but the question of "how" still remained. I never forgot that workshop where I thought that through writing, I could directly lead the reader into jumping into my experience. It feels the same if I start to write about Latino/a subjects beforehand. Through my own experience with poetry, I have realized that a poem cannot arise from a preordained agenda, whether that be the desire to break the binds of my own isolation or the desire to voice the history of Nicaraguans in the United States.

Ultimately there is only the language in which we write, but language is always culturally charged, and poems cannot escape their cultural consciousness. It might be argued, for example, that a lyric poem about a dandelion would not be culturally charged, since it is only a poem about a flowering weed. But whatever flower we choose to write about is a flower in our culture. The dandelion might capture a poet's imagination because it is a central artifact of suburban life in the United States. Is there any detail that is not a detail expressing our current cultural configurations?

As a writer, I have a choice between the details I allow into my writing. If I begin a poem about my family, I could relate the details in an Anglo suburban discourse by replacing each *tías* and *tíos* with aunt and uncle, by replacing Managua, Nicaragua, with Springfield, Illinois, and replacing *carne asada* with burgers on the barbecue, or I can choose not to. By allowing my *Latinidad* into my poems, I allow myself to speak and break with the silence imposed on women and Latinas. Latinas can and should write in the details and language of their experience and in so doing perhaps expand what is conceived as American experience, but from an interior necessity not a preordained agenda. Finding this interior necessity and how it manifests in words on a page is a subjective process, one that I have attempted to recreate by sharing parts of my family history as vibrations throughout this fluctuating narrative.

T. S. Eliot's essay "Tradition and the Individual Talent" articulates the writer's obligation to cultivate a historical sense, a historical sense that I interpret to include all history, the personal, the political, the cultural, and the literary. Experience is what cultivates the creative imagination, the experience of a life lived, the experience of arguing with dead white men, the experience of being politically and culturally aware, the experience of everything that one can get her hands on. As a Latina writer, I have found the necessity to move beyond US American intellectual borders by looking to Latina and Latin American authors for inspiration.

I have already related one story about driving around with my father on his route of *mandados*. There are many more. During elementary school, when spring break was still Easter vacation, I would take a fifty-minute flight from LAX to San Francisco and spend time with my father, grandmother, and the paternal side of the extended family. Perhaps it was on a Wednesday, and we were once again completing errands from here to there on Mission Street.

We passed by a bakery, Adelita's Pasteles. There, my name written on a storefront for all to see, in San Francisco, that city that is now one of the many locales in the States for Central American immigrants and refugees; my name, myself, etched as part of US Latino/a landscape. Viewing that sign, I began to learn that I did belong to my father, to the Mission, to the United States , and I have kept looking for community and connection ever since. I have found a *Latinidad* that I can claim as my own within the literature of Latina writers in the United States. Our stories are different. The country of origin, the reasons for immigration, the experience of growing up in this country all lead to various tales, trials, and triumphs, but what we have in common is that feeling of standing on a figurative border where the past, the family, is over there, while the present life in the States is here, now. Navigating this figurative borderline, to use Gloria Anzaldúa's metaphor, is a central concern for Latina writers.

Now heading toward the end of this indeterminate narrative, Gloria

Anzaldúa's seminal work *Borderlands/La Frontera* comes into play since she places the Chicana woman on a literal and figurative borderland, a creviced canyon between the United States and Mexico, a line straight down the middle of the body between two seemingly divergent cultures. Anzaldúa insists that this location of rupture is not one of victimization but the locale from which a new consciousness emerges, that of the mestiza who "copes by developing a tolerance for contradictions, a tolerance for ambiguity.... She learns to juggle cultures" (1999, 101). The Latina poet stands on a figurative borderland and juggles US Anglo culture with the culture of whichever Latin American nation she claims as the homeland.

At the center of the pull between two cultures is the pull between two languages, Spanish and English. As an emerging writer, I had questions. Is there a "right way" to create Spanish poetry? What are the rules for using Spanglish? So many times, teachers, tutors, and other writers had felt the need to correct my use of language, since my writing and speech carried its own rhythms. I have now come to understand that my use of language has never been incorrect—well, except for those occasional comma splices. Instead, my use of language is permanently marked by my linguistic and cultural duality, and that is not a mistake, an error, or wrong. The concept of a "right way" and "rules" reflect how my own thinking about language had been formed as part of our cultural dynamics. So called "right ways" to speak and write are not verifiable concrete truths but are instead cultural formulations that value certain linguistic performances over others. For example, what is referred to as standard English is in actuality the English spoken by the college-educated middle class, regional dialects deleted. This standard English is viewed as "good" English since it replicates the idea of what the United States should be and sound like: middle-class America. But there is more to the United States than cookie-cutter suburbs and multiplex movie theaters at the mall. Throughout my experience as a Latina woman in United States society, my use of Spanish, and especially my use of Spanglish, has been silenced. My desire to find the "right way" has been a desire to validate my bilingual linguistic repertoire in a society that I perceived as continuously demanding English-only, and in appropriate situations, Spanish-only. I have given up the idea of a "right way," and I now accept that at times, my English is Spanish influenced and that my Spanish is English influenced, and that's just the way it is. Even though I no longer feel the need to adjust my language to fit the "rules" of whatever discourse I encounter, it is impossible not to negotiate language as we write and proceed in our daily lives. I have been trying to allow the use of language that arises in my head to come out in my poems, in this essay, in the very way I speak, but this process is one of continuous negotiation between what I want to say, how I want to say it, and society's expectations.

However, now with a doctorate in English literature, *el título* that signifies that I put in the necessary time and work to make unverifiable statements, I find that the universal can be understood only through particulars. I understand Keats's obsession with the cycle of life and death precisely because of the pumpkin gourds, the poppies and full-grown lambs of "To Autumn." I understand Li-Young Lee's relationship with his culture and father precisely because of the persimmons in the poem by the same name. And where would W. C. Williams be without that wheelbarrow and those ice-cold plums? It is the details that cross intellectual, emotional, and cultural boundaries. It is through details that we communicate with one another and come to understand ourselves. Being Latina, my details incorporate red chili, a macho dad, and my grandmother's votive candles at the feet of Catholic saints in her bedroom altar. The universal comes by way of the specifics of everyday life as put forth by each author's creative play with language. There is certainly one thing I will continue to do, and that is read Latino/a and Latin American authors and allow the influence of the excluded in American letters to enter my work. I have seen Borges lurking around the corner, and Vallejo won't stop crying in my bathroom.

Right now, Alfonsina Storni is lighting a smoke on my living room couch.

SOURCES

Anzaldúa, Gloria. 1999. *Borderlands/La Frontera: The New Mestiza*. 2nd ed. San Francisco: Aunt Lute Books.

Bloom, Harold. 1997. *The Anxiety of Influence*. 2nd ed. New York: Oxford University Press.

Eliot, T. S. (1919) 1991. "Tradition and the Individual Talent." In *Critical Theory since Plato*, edited by Hazard Adams, 760–66. Orlando, FL: Harcourt Brace Jovanovich.

A Graffiti Artist in Academia

MICHAEL TORRES

GET UP

I GET MY work ethic from a sixteen-year-old me who spent hours a day sketching his tag on anything with a blank surface. I always practiced, always wanted to get better, and I don't think it's a coincidence that I look to those years for discipline when I write now.

◆ ◆

Before poetry there was graffiti. In 2000, my parents had me enrolled in Diamond Ranch High, a shiny new school built on top of a hill, instead of sending me to Garey, where all my friends were headed. My parents wanted their son to get a better education. What they got was a graffiti artist. For two years, I was a skater—spiked hair, talking new tricks with my friends. This to say: I blended in with the white kids' uniform of loose T-shirts and tattered shoes. Halfway through that second year, though, all those school friends were getting driver's licenses, trading in skateboards for their fathers' Beamers. They began wearing Abercrombie and Fitch. No one wanted to be a skater anymore, because they wanted to be men. Eventually, they dated the cheerleaders and rode off to winter formals in limos. I shied away, developed acne, bad acne; I spent mornings finding ways to make new outfits out of the two sweatshirts and three T-shirts I had. At some point, I realized that the former skaters and I were no longer friends and that we were not going to be friends anymore.

There was no Latino Club, and I would not learn about MEChA—the Movimiento Estudiantil Chicanx Aztlán—until college. There was, if only, a Spanish club, which I joined for one semester just to talk to a girl who would never be interested. During this semester, I went on a field trip to Olvera Street in Los Angeles, the oldest monument of Spanish settlers now turned tourist attraction. (You can get your picture taken on a fake donkey and sport a sombrero!). I remember two things about that day. The first was the collect call I received from my best friend Miguel, who was serving time in YA for breaking another boy's jaw with his fist. I remember a distinct feeling of loneliness out of separation and the sadness I felt for both of us because he wasn't here with me, because I wasn't there with him. The second was wandering away from Olvera Street after an hour and finding myself in Chinatown for fried rice and teriyaki chicken.

I didn't belong anywhere.

◆ ◆

In the summer after sophomore year, I found the only people like me, which in high school meant the people who looked like me: the other Mexicans. Dark young men, short in stature but muscular, young men with black mustaches already coming in to match their thick black hair. These were the graffiti artists. I came back that junior year bald headed and baggy jeaned, my skateboard somewhere in a corner of my bedroom.

◆ ◆

2003. Pomona, CA. I'm waiting for it to get late enough to pop the screen off my bedroom window and climb out onto the wet grass. I'm trying not to make too much noise with the JanSport I've packed with flat black Krylons and silvers from the 99 cent store. I'm sixteen and ambitious, a graffiti artist now. My homies call me REMEK, a name that means nothing but what I will make of it. REMEK was unavoidable: A Mexican American teen rebelling for sake of identity: I am REMEK, and REMEK was inevitable.

◆ ◆

What attracted me to the other Mexicans was that they didn't seem to care about the affairs of anyone else on campus. They walked with their chins up, a stride led with intent, the intent to intimidate. They were fearless in a way I wanted to be. There was no school spirit in them, and this indifference was captivating. I, too, wanted to not give a fuck. I learned, however, that they did care about something. They each wanted to "get up."

"Getting up" or "to get up" meant making sure your tag was written on as many spots as possible. It meant consistency. It meant fucking up the city: freeway walls and rooftops colored-in. Getting up equaled infamy and notoriety; it meant establishing a name for yourself and building that reputation. Getting up was how we each individually, but collectively, created an identity for ourselves. We were being left out at that school; as clichéd as "the poor kids from the other side of the tracks" sounds, it was true. But with graffiti, we named our anger. No one saw us, but we made sure we were seen.

Those years were the most formative of my adolescence. I didn't want to play football for the team; I didn't want to join the Associated Student Body. I didn't have to. Being known as someone who "gets up" was one of the highest compliments that can be paid to a young Mexican boy finding himself in a world that didn't seem to want to offer him anything more.

For the next few years, I dismissed homework assignments to practice writing my name. I didn't realize then, but my obsession with my name and how it was displayed was how I picked up discipline for studying craft with poetry later on. I didn't want to just "get up." I wanted to get up and be damn good at it. I mimicked those graffiti artists who were greater than I. I studied their approach. I took their style and developed my own, learned about shading, direction of light source, dimensions and perspective. I became a student of graffiti art.

◆ ◆

Juan Felipe Herrera once told me, "You always want to be the student. That way, there's always something to learn."

♦ ♦

2014. I get up early. Or late. I sit and I write. Or stare at the blank page. I get up, I make toast. I wash dishes. I think. I go for a run. I wish I had a pen and paper. I grab a rock and jot notes on a wall at the park. I go back later to write down what I've scratched into a wall on a mini notepad. The mini notepad comes with me to work. My bosses all know what I'm doing. I begin poems. Many. Finish some. Forget others. Send them out. Get rejections. An acceptance here and there. I get up. I am the student. I read poetry. Lit mags. Online and print. National Book Award winners and first books that friends tell me I should check out because they will shake my foundation. I read other genres. Fiction and creative nonfiction. Especially creative nonfiction. I peruse JSTOR. I rest. I watch *Mad Men* or movies—most recently, and for the first time, *Harry Potter* (sorry it took me so long). I seek the inciting incident, the controlling image of the narrative. I sleep some. I get up. In twenty or thirty years, if I'm still a student, still growing, I'll be happy.

♦ ♦

At sixteen, my fellow graffiti artists and I spent our afternoons driving around Pomona and neighboring cities looking for blank walls to return to at night, places where our names would be seen. I was obsessed with being known, with being accepted. Years later, I wondered why, why this desire took over my adolescence. It wasn't until a community college Chicano studies course that I realized the history I had learned (or heard but not really paid attention to) in high school did not include me or anyone like me and the graffiti artists.

Artists—graffiti and poetry—are historians as well. Back in high school, I thought that what was happening with losing those skater friends and making new ones was just part of life. I think now I was wrong. *Where were the Mexicans on the homecoming court and in textbooks?* Graffiti was not only where I began to take myself seriously as an artist who minded craft; it was where I began to record history, the way I saw it. We want not to be seen doing what we did, but we wanted everyone to see what we had done. I was writing my name, not in stone but on cinderblock wall.

Stay Up

◆ ◆

I would love to take full credit for becoming who I have become, that Michael Torres made Michael Torres the way REMEK made REMEK. I wish I could say I got myself here because I worked for it all alone, hours into days of little sunlight through a window that reached my desk. But truthfully, whoever I have become as an artist and a person and whoever I will be in the future is a direct result of a community, a community of writers much like the community of graffiti artists I came up with.

◆ ◆

After fully embracing the graffiti life, those friends and I assembled a collective, a group who shared the same mission to "get up." We made a crew.

Every month or so we held meetings. We were *that* organized. Once or twice, meetings took place in the front yard of my parents' house. Imagine twenty-plus young Mexican men with bald heads, milling about in sagging pants and black hoodies going through a list of topics to discuss.

- Where should we and where shouldn't we paint now?
- What do we do about the beef we have with [insert crew name here]?
- Should we let [insert graffiti artist name here] into the crew?
  - If so, how many spots must they paint to attain membership?
  - If not, how should we reject their proposal?
- When is our next trip to the beach?
  - Which beach?
  - Who's bringing what?
- Should we go buy more paint?
  - Who's driving to Walmart?

My mom must have just thought her son was very popular. Those meetings weren't just a thing we thought we needed to do. They were reassurances for me. I see that now. It was something to let me know that what I was doing mattered. They meant I meant something. Whenever each came to a close—any time we departed, actually—we would bid our farewells by telling each other to "stay up."

"See you tomorrow."

"Laters."

"Stay up, homie."

◆ ◆

It was recognition. Solidarity and admiration. An equivalent would be saying, "What you're doing is great. Keep it up. Don't let anyone tell you any different."

Stay up.

◆ ◆

I might have all but failed a few classes that final year at Diamond Ranch High, but I was doing something I felt was important.

I wanted to be something greater than I was at the time, so I practiced. A lot. But now I wonder: Who did I think I was? Or a better question: Who did I think I was not as a boy walking with his head down, connecting the dots of black scabs of gum stuck in the hallways between Math and US History? Why did I desire acceptance to the extent that I drew REMEK on my backpack, full color, that I painted it on walls all over town. And why do those years so long ago now serve as a point of reference, in academia, in a master's program, when I begin to question my own work ethic?

◆ ◆

I remember walking around in our large group of Mexicans during those school lunches and having people excuse themselves or stand aside, running their backs along the wall. They would part. For the Mexicans. It was biblical. And for a moment, we literally marginalized them. We lit the walkway up, and they stood in the shadows. I loved this power. I'm not ashamed to say it now, and though none of us said it then, I know they loved it, too. We just kept walking, discussing our business like it was nothing special, like it was how things were supposed to be.

When people noticed us, we were thugs to them, knuckleheads, troublemakers, kids they didn't want to deal with. School administrators, teachers, the student body. All of them. Maybe this is why we pushed each other to be great at what we did. If we were not going to be the best of the bottom, who would notice us, why do it at all? Maybe somewhere in our unconscious we knew the world didn't see us but left us to our own undoing of clichéd scenarios of gangs and drugs. Maybe this is why we worked on craft, why we put our names in more and more places.

We demanded to be noticed. I was the most disciplined when it mattered, when my existence was on the line. I am the most disciplined nowadays when I think of poetry in those terms.

◆ ◆

The first time a printed publication containing my poem arrived in the mail, my mom told me that my dad got a hold of it and smiled at the fact that his last name was there on the back cover. Who of us hasn't looked for last names like our own in lit mags, on bookshelves, to open up and read something we can, in some way, find familiar? If we're not writing down our history, who is?

◆ ◆

When my first chapbook was published, I got a call from my best friend, Miguel. By this time, we were in our mid-twenties and he had moved up to northern California with his girlfriend and two kids. He called to tell me he had gotten his copy. I told him I would write a full-length book one day. He said, "Good. You have to write about us so they know who we are."

◆ ◆

As graffiti artists, we weren't team captains, didn't even show up for tryouts. We weren't class presidents or leaders of the class of whatever year. During rallies, we were the ones in bleachers leaning away, elbows against the row behind us. Around campus, we slipped into the shadows to record the brief history of our lives in paint markers. While everyone had their backs turned and their hands up cheering for Diamond Ranch Panther football, we took drill bits to surfaces and inscribed our names for the rest of eternity to find after everyone went off to the vast green quads of universities. We pulled our hoodies over our bald heads and walked into the obscurity of our own futures knowing our new names were ours to pronounce and define.

I think now that my indifference saved me from hating them and that my desire for attention and acceptance made me an artist. For me, poetry is nothing short of the same reasoning. I want someone to read my work and say, "Yes, he knows how I feel." I yearn for that.

I wanted the legacy of REMEK—until the end of time or until the school district remodeled the gymnasium, whichever came the latter. So it's no wonder we "got up" as much as we did; it's no wonder we told each other to "stay up," to keep the pushing forward, keep working on that new piece. This kept us from being engulfed by inexistence, by the margin coming at us like a patrol car's headlights. This world we were entering after high school was a system that shut down our grandfathers, the pachucos, that shut down our fathers, the overtime workers coming home proud but tired, still broke, with sweat stains on their collars. This system called our *tíos* over and called them *braceros*, then told them to go back home. Some went; others found a place in Santa Ana, a wife, a family. This world took our brothers and our *primos*. It left our mothers with little choice but to pray for us all, to light a candle in the street and hold their hands near the flame to keep it from going out.

Puerto Rican Poetry and a State of Independence
A Family Affair

BLAS FALCONER

ALTHOUGH I GREW up in the suburbs of Washington, DC, removed from any Latina/o community, I spent many summers with my grandmother in Salinas, Puerto Rico, where everyone seemed related, somehow, and probably was, considering how many generations my mother's family lived in this small town. Free to do what we wanted, my sister, my brother, my cousins, and I spent our days galivanting in the streets. We palmed quarters from my grandmother's dresser to play pinball in the local bar, where older gentlemen sat at dominoes for hours. We bought *pan de agua* at the bakery around the corner or went to the theater to watch karate films or skated around the town center.

Most days, we hitched rides to the beach in the beds of trucks. There, we lounged in the hammock telling stories, went swimming or sailing, watched fishermen on the pier. We picked passion fruit from my uncle's roof or begged one of the older boys to climb the great tree and collect *quenepas*, Spanish limes, our favorite. At dusk, we wandered into the kitchen of my grandmother's restaurant, where we always found her with her sister and the other women preparing orders onto large silver trays, plate after plate: *pescado al mojo, arroz con gandules, pastelles, mofongo, tembleque, flan*.

My grandmother and great-aunt, who put their brothers through medical school by working in that kitchen, welcomed us, their hands and faces slick with sweat and oil. The waiters would pull several tables together on the patio, where we could see the ocean, the pier, and on clear nights, the lights of Ponce—all the cousins sitting together, famished from a day of being in our bodies entirely. At night we took showers, rinsing the salt from our hair, our skin tight and slightly burned, before going to sleep, sometimes four to a bed.

◆ ◆

When my grandmother locked the restaurant doors each night, she came home, got in bed, and spent her last waking minutes reading from one of several books on her side table.

Thumbing through them, I was always curious by the range of subject, genre, and language, though I had only ever heard her speak Spanish with any fluency. Some nights, I would knock on her door, and she would invite me onto the bed to talk about the day. If she liked what she was reading, she would become animated, again, despite the many hours on her feet, and go into great detail about the author and the work itself.

On one memorable occasion, my grandmother was reading *Yerba bruja*, a book of poems by the Puerto Rican activist Juan Antonio Corretjer. Born in 1908, Corretjer was raised within a pro-independence family. As he grew up, he attended rallies, joined political youth organizations, and wrote poetry, essays, and pamphlets on behalf of the cause, a cause that my grandmother, born nine years after Corretjer, also supported. *Yerba bruja*, which has been translated as "bewitched grass," is also the Spanish name for a plant (*Kalanchoe pinnata*) with several medicinal uses.

Sitting up in bed, my grandmother explained that in the 1957 publication of this poetry collection, Corretjer uses the plant leaf as a metaphor. The poet had opened a book, she said slowly in a Spanish that I could understand, and found a leaf that had been used to mark the page. Corretjer was surprised to see that the leaf had continued to grow after it was pulled from the stem, just as Puerto Rico would grow after ties with the United States were broken. Puerto Rico would grow, overcoming adversities. In this way, *yerba bruja* became a patriotic symbol for Puerto Ricans.

◆ ◆

In those early years, before the highway made trips from the airport in San Juan to Salinas comparatively easy, I would go weeks without ever hearing

English spoken by someone other than my siblings or cousins. But as I grew older, the presence of American commercialism grew stronger. One year, on the way to Salinas, we stopped at a Burger King, which seemed to me odd and foreign within this context. As I grew older, I could see more advertisements for American products. On the radio, more American music was being played. And each year, my grandmother seemed more frustrated with the assimilation, even in her small town, which for so long seemed relatively unaffected by the greater cultural influences of the United States.

It isn't difficult to understand my grandmother's hostility toward the United States. Born in 1919, merely twenty-one years after the Spanish-American War, when the United States annexed Puerto Rico, my grandmother must have bristled with distrust. In 1917, as a result of the Jones-Shafroth Act, Puerto Ricans were granted citizenship, so two months after the act was passed into law, when the United States issued a draft for World War I, these newly named citizens were expected to serve.

Coincidentally, the first Puerto Rican to be drafted was Eustaquio Correa, who shared my grandmother's last name.

Moreover, despite American success in promoting health and sanitation on the island, the United States did little to stabilize the economy or promote fair wages, particularly among sugar cane and tobacco workers, so the booming population had few resources. These, among many other issues, led to the formation of the Independent Party. For my grandmother, poetry was a means of promoting a particular political agenda, its aim to speak for the people, to instill pride in a community, to bring them together in resistance to American rule and assimilation.

◆ ◆

My grandmother's insistence on the relationship between art and politics must have been influenced, in part, by the emergence of another politically charged art form: the *plena*. The *plena* is a musical genre that began in the sugar growing regions of Puerto Rico's southern coast around the late nineteenth century. Influenced by immigrants from the Virgin Islands, early *plena* blended both African and Spanish musical traditions. In the early twentieth century, musicians began to compose lyrics. The songs covered various topics, humorous and profound, but the *plena* is referred to as "*periodico canto* (the sung newspaper) because the songs often deal with important current events" (Anderson 55).

One famous song tells the story of a woman who has been stabbed by her abusive boyfriend. But it moves beyond the personal tragedy to implicate the community, which knew about the abuse and did nothing to stop it. "Temporal," a song about San Felipe, a hurricane that walloped the island, expresses concern for the fate of its people. Another song tells the story of an American attorney who came to the island to challenge the agricultural system that was in place. In the lyrics, a shark, meant to represent Puerto Rico, eats the lawyer who threatens the livelihood of local farmers.

As a young boy, strolling the sidewalks, I heard this music blaring from cars, from bars, from the record store. The fast finger work on the guitar. The scratch of the metal comb along the husk of the dried gourd. The fingers slapping the tambourine-like percussion. The men's imperfect voices wailing, lamenting, it seemed. One of my earliest and most vivid memories is from one of my grandmother's parties, where a band of men dressed in crisp white shirts played late into the night, and we danced well beyond my bedtime. This music, born in Ponce, Guayama, and Salinas, must have had a profound impact on my grandmother, shaping who she would become, her relationship to art and its role in the community.

◆ ◆

Another Puerto Rican poet who spoke out against colonial power and influence was Julia de Burgos, and my grandmother introduced me to her work as well. One summer evening, after closing the restaurant early, we went to a small video store to pick out a movie. As I was scanning the shelves in the small room for an American film, my grandmother spotted a documentary on de Burgos. That night, we sat close to my grandmother's small television to listen to poetry, as various grainy images of town plazas and landscapes flashed on the screen. According to my grandmother, de Burgos as a young adult lived not only in the small town of Salinas, where she briefly taught, but in the very apartment in which we were sitting. According to my grandmother, who was only five years younger, the two women were friends.

Born in 1915, Julia de Burgos was the oldest of thirteen children. As a young adult, she became more politically active, abandoning her earlier aspirations to become a teacher. In 1936, she joined the Puerto Rican Nationalist Party and was elected secretary general to The Daughters of Freedom, a women's organization within the party. De Burgos wrote three books of poetry, the last of which was published posthumously. Her lyric poems often addressed her personal life, but she also wrote politically driven poetry. At the young age of thirty-nine, Julia de Burgos died of pneumonia in Spanish Harlem.

As with much of Corretjer's poetry, de Burgos often turned to the landscape to convey a sense of national pride. "Flood my spirit," she writes in "The Great River Loiza," one of her most famous poems. As Edward Hirsch explains, the poet "links her childhood river ('my well-spring, my river/since the maternal petal lifted me to the world') to the source of her art ('and my childhood was all a poem in the river/ and a river in the poem of my first dreams'), and the grief of her native island" (2006, 183). The poem ends:

> Great river. Great flood of tears.
> The greatest of all our island's tears
> save those greater that come from the eyes
> of my soul for my enslaved people. (2006, 41–44)

As I recall, this poem, in particular, spoke to my grandmother, who was less taken by personal narratives or issues of race and gender. She dismissed stories of racism and sexism with a wave of her hand, so I imagine the idea of writing about the LGBTQ experience would have seemed outrageous to her, if not downright shameful.

◆ ◆

By the time I turned fourteen, my grandmother was asking—and often—how many girls I was dating—"Why only one?"—and if I had lost my virginity. Over the next few years, the questions became more personal, more inappropriate. What I gathered from her questions, from the way she beamed over my uncle, my older male cousins, was that men were not only free but were encouraged to "conquer" women. Then, one morning, as I was walking from the shower to my room in nothing more than a towel, my grandmother stopped me in the narrow hallway.

"Are you gay?"

Half-naked, water dripping onto the tiles, I paused. She had never—no one had ever—asked, and I wondered for a moment if she was inviting me to confide in her this secret that I had been carrying around most of my life.

Then, her open hand rose up over her head. "Because if you are, I'll beat you."

What I understood in that moment was that she wasn't asking me if I was gay. She knew that I was. What she was telling me was that, under no circumstances, was I to admit it. That admission would bring shame upon her, upon the family. In her eyes, my own particular identity was in direct conflict with the identity of the larger family. So I kept the secret for ten years, bearing my own shame, doing my best to navigate the increasing hostility from my grandmother, my mother, and later, several of those beloved cousins, until ultimately, I felt that I could no longer visit this place, these people, I had once loved more than any other.

◆ ◆

I always admired my grandmother's independent spirit, but as I grew older, I saw that her politics were more complicated than I had originally thought. There is no question that she rejected the United States' presence on the island, but did she really want independence?

Alongside her books of fiction, poetry, and history, one could always find tabloid magazines from Spain. She seemed particularly eager to see photos of the king, of his children. She wanted to know the latest rumors, and she became downright giddy at the thought of a royal European wedding.

My grandmother was obsessed not only with Spain but with Italy as well. My grandfather's parents had immigrated from Italy, and I assumed at first that her fascination and romanticization of the country came from a longing for her husband, who died the year I was born. To say something was Italian—or European, for that matter—was another way of saying that something was the best. This was often expressed in her aesthetics, whether considering fashion, food, furniture, art, or architecture. In regard to beauty, pale skin, bright eyes, light hair were the things to look for. I remember one day, looking at family photos with my grandmother. She gently took one in her hands.

"You see," she said, "your mother was an unattractive young woman because of her coloring."

I was shocked to hear her say this about my mother, who I had always thought beautiful, but I was also surprised because my grandmother had a darker complexion, dark hair and dark eyes, like my mother. Almost all the women in the family did, and they were all considered unattractive by my grandmother's standards.

My grandmother often claimed that her complexion was a result of too much time in the sun as a child, but once, at dinner, when my brother innocently asked about my grandmother's father—someone we knew nothing about—my grandmother became tight lipped and defensive. My aunt leaned over to me and whispered, "To learn about his family, we'd have to go to Africa." As I grew older, it became clear that my grandmother felt shame as a woman of color. It seemed that she had internalized an awful myth about beauty and race. The irony, for me, at least, was that politically, as an Independent, she seemed to reject colonialism, but as an individual, her own psyche had been overcome by these Eurocentric ideals that neither she nor her daughter, my mother, could ever live up to.

◆ ◆

My grandmother's love of poetry ignited my own. I have always known that, but it is only recently that I have come to see how much she has shaped my understanding of poetry and its function for me as a gay Latino man. When I began, I did not write to or for a community, as Corretjer did, as de Burgos did, as my grandmother would have had it. The first poems did not come from looking outward but from a turning inward. My voice came out of a deep and painful silence, held years long, the written page a space in which I could openly acknowledge, for the first time in my life, my own fear, confusion, and desire. But implicit in that acknowledgment was a rejection of who I was supposed to be, a questioning of power systems, a renunciation of the cultural norms that had been imposed on me by my own family. If my grandmother had internalized a racism associated with Eurocentric ideas of beauty, I internalized the notion that I was shameful because of my sexual orientation. To listen to my own voice, to turn to the written word, was the beginning of my own war, my own independence. In that way, Corretjer and de Burgos, even the *plenas* I heard growing up, remain models, as my grandmother always intended.

SOURCES

Anderson, Thomas F., and Marisel C. Moreno, eds. 2012. *Art at the Service of the People: Posters and Books from Puerto Rico's Division of Community Education (DIVEDCO)*. Notre Dame, IN: Snite Museum of Art.

Burgos, Julia de. 1995. *Song of the Simple Truth: The Complete Poems of Julia de Burgos*. Edited by Jack Agüeros. Willimantic, CT: Curbstone.

Corretjer, Juan Antonio. 1957. *Yerba bruja: Portada de Rafael Tufiño*. Guaynabo: publisher not identified.

Fernandez, Ronald. 1992. *The Disenchanted Island: Puerto Rico and the United States in the Twentieth Century*. New York: Praeger.

Hirsch, Edward. 2006. *Poet's Choice*. Orlando, FL: Harcourt.

La Plena. 1967. Departmento de Instruccion Publica, Division de Educacion de la Comunidad. https://www.youtube.com/watch?v=vjQfgbAmozQ.

Notes on Teaching and Learning the Mother Tongue

JUAN J. MORALES

GROWING UP, I was so used to my parents' accents that I didn't know they had them. I didn't realize they had accents until I was twenty and someone asked if it was hard for me to understand. I'm still confused because I'm a strange combination of Latinx at some dinner parties and a gringo whenever I enter the *carniceria*. The confusion is the language of who I am.

◆ ◆

When my parents decided not to teach me Spanish, there wasn't a discussion. It just happened, and I felt relief. I had plenty to do growing up and knew enough to ask for a glass of milk or to ask where I left my favorite hoodie. I passed the phone to my mom without saying anything when I heard the Spanish greetings. I coasted through Spanish class well into college relying on what I overheard at home between watching *Primer Impacto* and dubbed versions of *E.T.* and *Twister*. I filled in the right conjugations on tests and never spoke it out loud. My confidence grew and got knocked back down in college when our teacher reminded us that we only had the proficiency of fourth or fifth graders. I pretended not to accept the insult and passed with my B. All of this didn't feel like I was cheated until my niece moved in with us. I watched her grow up in a bilingual household and use her Spanish on the playground whenever a new student arrived from Mexico, Venezuela, or Costa Rica. Even though she had blonde hair and blue eyes, she acted as the bilingual guide. Listening to her stories of playing in two languages, I could feel envy brew inside and regretted that I had decided not to learn on my own. Years later, in my twenties, when I asked my mom about when she decided to address me only in Spanish, she could only answer, "I guess we could have done better." I didn't press her, but it took time to realize that they came from a generation punished for speaking Spanish. They were also taught to deny their indigenous roots. The United States was not always her home. Back then, I thought she spoke about their regret, but now I include myself in that answer with the awakening I never pursued until now.

I currently live in Pueblo, Colorado, a small working-class town forty minutes south of my hometown, Colorado Springs. I hear Spanish here and dine on Mexican food regularly, but I can feel isolated by my Ecuadorian/Puerto Rican heritage, the same way I feel excluded in the ruckus of Spanish conversations with my family. During a trip to Puerto Rico in 2014, the last one my father would take before he passed away, I expected to find closure and connection somewhere on the island, either on a wrong turn lost in the rental car or partially buried on the beach.

Instead, I came back with the hunger for the native tongue, to return to the search for the words that still elude me.

◆ ◆

Ever since I started teaching at my university, I have always done my best to teach as many BIPOC poets as possible. I used the memory of my undergrad Chicano Studies and Multi- American Ethnic Lit courses to intersect the lesser-known parts of American history with the literature we have yet to read. My role became, and still remains, one of exposure to new cultures and writers, with my students telling me, "I didn't know these writers were out there." They say it with hope and delight in their voices. I was in the same place, sitting in workshops, writing and reading poems about uninspired college students being struck by inspiration the night before the story is due, the "he said, and she said" story, and the ones where characters died in horrific car crashes. I kept asking myself, "Am I just writing wrong?," until my teacher gave me a copy of some Martin Espáda poems from the anthology, *Poetry like Bread,* and I found a copy of Pablo Neruda's *Residencia en la tierra* in my parents' garage after my brother moved out of the country. Inspired to contemplate the bilingual world by Neruda's "Walking Around" and "Ars Poetica" and nodding in solidarity with Espada's "Federico's Ghost" and "Jorge the Church Janitor Finally Quits," I suddenly saw how a poem can protest the injustices around us by just using our daily language, without apology or hesitation. I failed to recognize I was another victim of the US high school textbook industry and an exclusive literary canon until these poems opened doors to finding more Latinx writers that continues for me today in moments of embarrassment with my fellow writers, who speak of influences and heroes I have never heard of.

I think about the story of Gabriel García Márquez on his pilgrimage to visit Faulkner's South and how they forced him to ride in the back of the bus. Then, I think about how I could pass with my lighter complexion and maybe sit in the middle. Because I grew up with such light skin and eyes, some people are surprised I am Latinx at all.

◆ ◆

I used to know a guy who had a grandma who hated me with an intensity I could not understand. She was an old southerner who told me to leave the dog alone when another friend provoked it, made me wash dishes I hadn't used, called me a "kiss ass" when I answered her questions politely, and always tried to get me to leave their house the minute I arrived. A few years later, my friends pranked me good and told me that our friend's racist grandma had died. I couldn't contain my smile when I said, "Really?" They answered, "Oh my God, no! You're going to hell for wishing that!" I know I should have felt guilt, but instead I wondered if she had passed any of this bigotry along to anyone else.

My last time in Puerto Rico, everyone spoke English and spotted us as tourists immediately. Maybe we were the whitest ones around or we were too far from San Juan, but they spoke with kindness. Maybe they wanted to practice English, assumed as an act of kindness instead of a doubt of our abilities. I got cocky at a movie theater in Mayagüez, trying to buy two sodas and a large popcorn, when the cashier finally lost her patience and said, "You know, we can do this in English." We laughed it off, but afterward, I was bitter about the Spanish words stuck in my throat. I slowed down to translate the words I knew, to sniff out the cognates, to see the shape of the sentence scrambled somewhere between Spanish and English. I forgot I had to get momentum back and feel the rhythm of Spanish, that fluid feeling of the next word finding me, escaping my mouth, and free to fly.

◆ ◆

Strange when it became routine for everyone to ask me, "How was prison?" For a six-month period, every two weeks, I took my beat-up Spanish-English dictionary, photocopies of poems, and a pen and accompanied fellow volunteers to the El Paso County Jail. With the IDEA Project, based in Colorado College, we read and wrote with the inmates, all in the Spanish I was struggling to master. After my first session, I drove home exhausted by adrenaline, a full day of teaching, and a wicked cold. I smiled about limping through in Spanish and teaching a Neruda poem. I even coaxed inmates to write a poem. As the sessions went on, the inmates would first resist but loosen up to write honestly toward the end of the session—drift of perfume, clearing the table after their last family meal—staring at ID bracelets they could not remove. Memories pressed into bilingual haiku, sonnets, odes, and free writes. Their status as ICE detainees made them here one minute and deported the next. They understood the life they lived and the pain of being separated from their families who could not come to visit. The men's group dwindled down to one, and on our last visit with him, we gave him the prompt, "What do you miss most on the outside?" His poem flowed slowly, and we wrote one word at a time together for his poem to emerge. The poem he wrote vanished into the project's archives, a file somewhere full of handwritten prose and poems, so I wrote to preserve his poem.

Perfume

When the inmate answers us with "perfume," I assume
he misses the beauty of a specific woman he lost,
bathed in her subtle scent, a droplet of delicate.
I translate it wrong but he is patient to point out

the correct word in the Spanish-English dictionary.
Not perfume, cologne.

We negotiate the mislaid words between us. We write
in the D Block lounge about how he misses
the bottles of cologne that lined his bathroom window,
how he shaved and then smiled in the struggle
to pick the right essence for the day.

He's soft spoken but tells me the inside is absent
of smell. He would accept the bad ones over nothing.
When we finish our session, he returns to his cell
and I am left with a spare poem by an accused killer,
charges that hang over me like a mist.

We sat in the small break room in silence, impressed with the poem. After this session with the male inmate, he was deported or transferred, and our work with the men's side ended. We continued to work with the women inmates for another three or four months until the program shut down. My Spanish words became phrases and sentences and paragraphs in this time, and I am grateful for their patience with us. The IDEA Project concluded on a regular day when our organizers butted heads with the prison administration over the inmates' writings, an article in the local paper, and the handmade chapbooks that the prison ultimately labeled "contraband." We teachers found ourselves stuck between censorship and the protest of prison policy. It is important to support beliefs, but what about the inmates? We just wanted our badges back so we could teach.

◆ ◆

At the bar, my friend introduced me as his Ecuadorian friend. The stranger and I swapped names, and he asked if I spoke Spanish. I answered, "*Un poquito*," and he replied, "Sounds like you're not really Ecuadorian." He could tell I was pissed when I answered, "I do fine. I was being polite." The conversation disappeared into the bottom of my drink.

Growing up, my dad and I always caught each other in small windows of hours because he worked a late shift, asleep before I went to school and coming home after I went to bed. I admired him so much for how hard he worked and his no bullshit attitude. My mother was quieter than he and anchored us by keeping the bills paid and keeping our house afloat. I once told someone that I admired my father more than my mother. As soon as I spoke these words, I knew they were wrong, and the guilt of machismo still lingers in my DNA. At the time, I was blind to the sacrifices my mother made on my behalf—taking me to every practice and rehearsal, mending my clothes to last a little longer, talking me through my teenage heartbreaks—and I am still working to atone for them with words. To restore the balance of yin and yang, masculine and feminine, that I carry forward inside, on a similar axis as Puerto Rican and Ecuadorian.

The transformation from my first poetry collection to my second challenged me to change from observer to participant, making sure the storytelling always remained intact. As I thought of my poems beyond my first two books, I pursued the need to expose the personal gaps I had not covered yet. When I write comments on my students' poems, I will write CHALLENGE, in all caps, followed by a specified task. It could be cutting the poem in half, adding three stanzas, abandoning the rhyme scheme, or flipping the poem's order. Subtly, I am hoping that the challenge lets me discover where the form and content meet, allowing the emotional intensity to follow. These challenges invite me to inject humor into a break-up poem, to write about my blue-collar town, to stare at an ocean while grieving my father, to politicize zombies, home improvement, or a sport I have always loved.

"Inside an hour"

I can figure out which guys on the pitch are assholes on and off the field, like the one *vato* with the neck tattoos who drives a different sports car to the field each week, who talks shit to his teammates when they don't pass to him, who can place a precise cross when he shuts his damn mouth, who always mooches water, who gives me a polite head nod at the same Mexican restaurant every time I see him, who pouts during a game and won't chase the ball when his team is down by three or more goals, who searches behind the trees on the far side of the soccer field and deflates the *pelotas* he finds and stuffs them in a suitcase bound for a Chilean orphanage, who once called my team captain a motherfucker after scoring a hat trick and almost sparked a brawl. He's still an asshole, but I learn each Sunday playing pickup soccer how he favors his right ankle, like me, inside an hour, and slowly I discover that maybe I'm an asshole too.

My challenge for the poem was to complicate this other soccer player but to also avoid the joke or anecdote. I had to get to know someone I didn't know and to think about the connections I had overlooked. Putting aside the anxiety of this becoming an obligatory Latinx poem because it dealt with *futból*, I shaped it into a prose poem to celebrate compressed time and also the shape of the pitch, somewhere I regularly play. There is definitely poetry to our games and plenty of changes, inspired by unpredictable bounces, kicks, and shots.

◆ ◆

I never meant to be a writer and never declared it as a child. I look back to see journals of all shapes and sizes packed together in a basement box. Some are large notebooks with gridded math paper, a happy orange carnival scene, and a black one with Sex Pistols and Pink Floyd stickers that contain my thoughts through most of my life. Today, I still carry a notebook with me everywhere and also make time to write with my students in class. That habit kicked in somewhere and it stuck, helping me stumble into being a poet and a writer. I spent ample time on trips to the British Isles, Ecuador, the Yucatan, Oahu, the Pacific Northwest, Italy, the Midwest, Ireland, France, Switzerland, and even in my home state just writing what surrounded me even if I didn't understand how collecting the words shaped my poetics and language. I disappeared on stoops, kitchen tables, and parks just getting it down without worrying about getting it right. The journals filled with failed poems, hauntings, my attempts at clever observations, surreal dreamscapes, and handwriting even I couldn't read. Now I tell my students, this is where your poems begin.

After a poetry reading, a famous poet congratulated me and then asked me if I was open to feedback. After coaxing it out of him, he implied that what I was doing was a gimmick: "I know you're writing and reading as the Puerto Rican-Ecuadorian poet born in America. It's just that"—he paused to find the right words and shifted his point into a compliment about my poetic skill and abilities—"there's scansion, meter, and talent in these poems. You don't need to rely so much on the cultural part." Of course, I boiled inside, but I didn't argue. I decided against making a scene and spoiling the evening. I couldn't help feeling defensive, but I didn't want any scrap of it to show, thinking about how these poems about my parents, my geography, and the mix of English and my adequate use of Spanish are my voice. That was never a choice. The poems still come from a place of insecurity, of being the gringo tourist when I visit my extended family, and the parade of names I get called when people first meet me. Jose, Pedro, Juan Pedro, Carlos, Juan Carlos, and others.

What I Said One Time When a Woman Called Me Jose

> "Not all Mexicans are named Jose
> and not all Mexicans are Mexican, and,
> in fact, there are other countries
> where they also speak Spanish,
> and I am actually a U.S. citizen born in this country
> and English is my first language."
> I stopped when she apologized for being
> inconsiderate, said it was an honest mistake,
> and my mean streak kicked in to convert
> her guilt into a seething sun's glare when I told her,
> "That's okay, my middle name is Jose."

I can laugh now when it happens, but it still connects to the anxieties of not being proficient enough in Spanish, like the embarrassing typo of a Spanish word in my first book, those discriminating moments someone slips in before they realize I'm Latinx, the discomfort of not knowing a famous Chicanx writer at a conference bar, and the reminder that I am American. Can't debate that. Can't debate the fact I was born in Iowa and grew up in Colorado with this voice.

My parents, as the mountain and the island, work as a metaphor, but how about the rest of the family and friends who also helped shape the crude Spanish in my mouth—my trilingual sister who grew up being called a spic in one place and a kraut in others, my quiet sister who answers in English and knows more than she lets on, my brother who left the United States and forged his gringo accent into damn fine Spanish, his wife and my sister-in-law, who speaks English but only uses it sparingly, the inmates who spoke English when the guards weren't around that have since been deported from the El Paso County Jail, and my students in Pueblo. Without them, I would have given up and stopped reaching out for the words that flit around me, like the hummingbirds both of my parents describe from their childhoods even though they grew up in two different countries.

◆ ◆

At an early age, my family moved to the south side of Colorado Springs, just outside of the military base, Fort Carson. Throughout my life, Cheyenne Mountain and Pikes Peak remained in my line of sight: Pikes Peak, a famous fourteener with rugged beauty and unpredictable weather next to Cheyenne Mountain, which housed NORAD, a cluster of blinking antennas at its top, and real estate creeping farther up the mountain's face. Both have become symbols I pondered on a daily basis. Along the Front Range, the mountains remained our daily compass, always helping me know which way was west. It also led me geographically south to where the Andes rise along the west coast, cutting through Ecuador and Perú. This also took me to the obsessions that shaped the first drafts of my second poetry collection, *The Siren World*. By reaching back, I hoped to stumble upon the language and history of my mother's patria, depicting how my poems gravitate toward a place frozen in lost time, remaining etched in the stones that are overgrowth, refusing to be specifically marked. The manuscript was close, but something was still missing. I felt a drastic need to cut back the Incan poems, the poems that turned into pieces that would make the strongest Latin American historians nod. The problem was that they were historical reenactments without connection to me or the present. When I finished slashing, the book wasn't a book anymore. I fell into panic mode before looking over at the piles of poems about Puerto Rico, my father's home. I suddenly wondered if the two could come together the way my parents did so many years ago, and suddenly I had a different book, one that united my obsession with my mother's mountains and my father's island. The thread became me, the insecure self who was the gringo, the foreigner, and the assumed Spanish speaker. Like in most poetry, the pride and shame wrestled for supremacy, and I freed them both into the world.

When I visited Ecuador as an adult, I always got grumpy at the end of the night. My brain hurt from speaking and translating all day. It resisted because Spanish puts up a fight against the English that regularly clatters around within. I tried to sleep it off every night and found myself ready for the next day.

To Dream in Spanish

Practice as an adult with phone calls
to mama y papa. You volunteer to teach
ICE detainees in the jail every Tuesday.
You finally take trips
to the motherland and the fatherland
as a tourist ironically surrounded
by family. Describe your life
back in America with sentences
as simple as charades
laced with wrong syntax and cognates.

Give yourself credit when people ask if
you speak it. Don't worry about
your white boy accent. Say yes
instead of the long answer
about not being raised on Spanish
and how you heard
your parents talking it together like secrets.

> It's okay to fry your brain,
> code switching each day in a country
> that is not yours.
> You won't catch every phrase. Let go.
> Fall into the dreams, en sueño,
> heavy as rivers overflowing
> with accents and tildes,
> when you forget you don't speak Spanish
> only for the night.

Speaking Spanish still intimidates me, and I am afraid to mess up, but I am persistent and definitely not alone. I am the same way with my poems—afraid but willing to fail until I get it right. Language humbles me and instructs me to recognize my limitations as a teacher, poet, and activist, but it is mixed with the victories of what I have saved for us and what a student in my class or a fellow poet might preserve from another part of our community. I still look back and think about all the ghost stories and tales of survival my mother told me about Ecuador and Panama, and her journey to the United States. They are similar to my father's war stories and his same path to Colorado from Puerto Rico, with detours in Germany, England, Panama, Korea, Japan, and Vietnam. They cover such a long distance I don't always know how to capture. Some of these stories I have heard many times, and I still hear them today, with subtle details changing. It wasn't until my first Intro to Creative Writing course that I felt a sudden worry that no one was writing these stories down. The sadness of their voices without anyone there to catch them scared me more than anything. The fear allowed me to ask myself, "Why not me?"

Duende the Poem, or Poetics at the Intersection of Realities and Identities

RAINA J. LEÓN

THERE IS A crossroads: the intersection of space, time, identity, body, spirit, language. It is a pointed star track. Duende is one rail that connects; it can be seen as universal and the interstitial. It ripples even in its stillness. Let us explore the consciousness of this revision of reality (itself for alternating enslaving/dehumanizing or liberating purposes) and the desire for connection through duende, a channeling of the preternatural and the natural. Duende is the magical within the real, the word specifically naming a magical being, about half the size of human beings, who is mischievous and acts as a trickster to good and bad effect. Duende, for all intents and purposes, could just be an elf, but Federico García Lorca (1933) reimagined the duende: "Those dark sounds are the mystery, the roots that cling to the mire that we all know, that we all ignore, but from which comes the very substance of art . . . 'A mysterious force that everyone feels and no philosopher has explained.' . . . So, then, the duende is a force not a labour, a struggle not a thought . . . it's not a question of skill, but of a style that's truly alive: meaning, it's in the veins" (2). Duende retains trickster dimensional power. It exists beyond the limits of space and time, performative in its guerrilla pull. It can be seen as the resistant and resilient response to a pathology that attempts to erase the body; instead, it infuses the art through the telling of lived experience that like a grappling hook, reaches from the creator into the soul of viewer/reader/hearer, draws it closer, and dances with it to bounded and boundless rhythm.

SPACE

When I was around five, we got our first color television. Before then, it was a B/W with an antenna set by duct tape and a dial that had to be secured with a brush handle. There were few women, and the only black faces were on the news: wanted, accused, or dead. The only Latino I saw on television was on reruns of *I Love Lucy*.

Sometime around then, we started watching *Star Trek*. First, we watched the reruns of the original series, where the only person of color regularly seen demonstrated her intelligence through communication and also had the highest skirt. I developed an attraction to logic, started to play chess, learned that recklessness comes at a price (but someone else pays it, if you are Jim Kirk). *Star Trek: Next Generation* (2007) started only a few years after that. "Space, the final frontier. These are the voyages of the starship Enterprise. Its continuing mission: to explore strange new worlds, to seek out new life and new civilizations, to boldly go where no one has gone before!" Jean-Luc Picard (played by Patrick Stewart) says in the opening credits. How revolutionary that "no one," which showed women were not no ones. We were visible, included. Initially, there were three women in leadership: one hypersexualized and intuitive, another intelligent and matronly, and the third a warrior and aggressive with reason. All white women, though one, Deanna Troi, was half-Betazoid. The idea! A woman who was half-alien.

Intuitive, passionate, hypersexualized, initially brainless. Sounds a lot like the historical and contemporary depictions of Latinas, but I doubt that in this future Deanna Troi would identify in this way, though I have to admit that I wanted to claim a connection to her, as she was one of the few women to whom I might look—until Guinan came along, the wise black alien who had lived for centuries and acted as a comforting mother figure to the captain or the mammy of the future.

Worf and LaForge were the only men of color, one an alien, black, always disregarded by leadership and inherently violent, and the other human, intelligent, anxious, and empowered by his blindness to see in ways others could not. Though the depictions of gender, race, and ability did not fully allow for multidimensionality outside of stereotypes (even when alien), at least on the face, there were more women and more people of color on television. In space, if not in televised reality, I could almost see myself.

TIME

Here on earth, for me, space and time are intertwined. Outer space was a place of imagination in a place where, with the arrival of my family, in a mile radius with hundreds of families, there were three Latino families. I was related to them all. Of the black families on my block, until I was in high school, there were only two, ours and our direct neighbor's. This was Philadelphia. White flight began to occur, most notably in the disappearance of Christmas lights. In southwest Philadelphia, an Italian tradition was to decorate the whole house for the entirety of the Christmas season; the lights seemed to burn the sky! By the time I was in high school, of the hundreds of houses, the lights had gone down to less than ten. Going home to Philadelphia now, I generally see less than a handful. White people were afraid of us, too much gesture toward our skin, too much difference in our language. They saw us as the criminals they must have seen, too, on black-and-white screens, even when we were in color.

  Southwest Philadelphia, 1988

  Our eyes focused on swirled vats:
  vanilla ice cream, then cherry water ice,
  more vanilla,
  cherry for a tower of red
  and white stripes that melted
  into pink after heat stroll.

  We had to wait for tall, plastic cups,
  like all the brown
  kids, while Papi grumbled.
  Counter girls sucked their teeth,
  gloved their hands
  but we never noticed that then.

  Children with stain history –
  my brother, fair-skinned and universal
  prize, and me, black and not –

> walked the block with the evidence there,
> cherry crystal-flecked jackets,
> happy. Papi held our hands,
> brooding the cost.

Of course, there is a greater context, a much longer history of dehumanization and oppression rooted as deeply in this earth as it is in a spiritual warfare that seeks to rip the spirit from the body, of the racialized body as a service mechanism rather than a respected vessel of light. Lorca wrote that duende is the "most ancient culture of immediate creation," and here we have an attempt at speaking to a core memory born from conflict within a particular social context. It invokes, too, folk story, the hidden revelations of raven and that dark natural power within the world, a power strong enough to capture the sun and generous enough to bring it back. Time belongs outside of and within the body. It is not linear; rather, it is spiraling and circuitous. All generational traumas and joys exist within the body, passed down through genomes, and in experience we relive our ancestors and predict the futures of our descendants. An aspect of othering today persists in the outsider sense of what beings will, in future, call me grandmother of grandmother. A body is a defiant vessel of time and duende.

BODY

In duende, too, there is a fearlessness in difference, but I recognize that not all will be able to connect to intersectional rhythms. Africans were the first aliens, Kodwo Eshun (1998) reveals. He writes:

> African aliens are snatched by African slavetraders, delivered to be sliced, diced and genetically designed by whiteface fanatics and cannibal Christians into American slaves, 3/5 of their standardized norm . . . the slave was actually manufactured to fulfill a function: as a servomechanism, as a transport system, as furniture, as 3/5 of the human, as a fractional subject. . . . Leroi Jones adjusts the macroscope setting: 'Not only physical and environmental aliens, but products of a completely alien philosophical system.' Inhumans, posthumans owing nothing to the human species." (112–13)

And that stripping of humanity that extends beyond racial and ethnic identity to that of the ever pushed outward, that denial of dignity continued through generations from the Middle Passage, the capture, theft, abduction, mutilation of diverse peoples robbed of history, identity, language, persisted through slavery and into the present day. So many want to brush this history aside and proclaim the ills and strengths of today as independent anomalies. I say, those who cannot see the cords of history cannot hear the chords of history's music. In their attempts to wipe away the soul in connection with the body, they reveal an absence within themselves.

Michelle Alexander (2010) writes in *The New Jim Crow*:

> Conservatives argued that poverty was caused not by structural factors related to race and class but rather by culture– particularly black culture. This view received support from Daniel Patrick Moynihan's now infamous reports on the black family, which attributed black poverty to a black 'subculture' and the 'tangle of pathology' that characterized it. (45)

How this persists in the mouths of teachers who say *those* parents (black, brown, non-English speakers, dispossessed), who don't care about these kids, and who attempt to rise as white saviors. Yes, there is a pathology, an earthbound pathology that reaches through time and space into the essential intersectionality of humanity and the preternatural, sparking a resistance response, the duende. It is the pathology that allows a black man-child's body, killed brutally on a street called Canfield, in a place that ripples through time and experience, Ferguson, to bleed out on the hot asphalt for four hours. Africans were the first captured aliens, and it continues even into our imagining. Uhuru was sexualized, to be of service for the captain's (the virile man) pleasure as any woman; Worf was violent and disregarded (the exotic and strange alien); LaForge was intelligent, gifted with a second sight (otherworldly), and shy. His most intimate relationship was with an android learning to be human. Add two hundred years (original, 2260) or three hundred years (*Next Generation*, 2364) in the imagined space, and the black body is still the racialized other. I find myself even thinking of Troi, half-Betazoid, half-human though she could be received as white, could be said to be a recent depiction of one-dimensional, exoticized and eroticized *Latinidad* within a future imagining. There are so few sci-fi, future forecasts that include people of color.

Here, in this real time and space, we struggle for our autonomy, our right to exist, even for our names. How many times have our stories, my story, reflected those of the past: the fear against riders in the night; the literal or metaphorical fires lit in our front yards; being seen and suspected as criminals—Trayvon—and our killers go free; no whistling of Vivaldi (Steele) can protect us; being mistaken for another black woman or man while someone tries to convince you that you have forgotten that you really are that other person. Even our names are not our names when we are made "sweetie," "boy," "girl," "nigga please," or when we are called by our Anglicized half-selves (Joe and not José, Mary and not María. My own name is an Americanized version of Reina, inscribed so others would say it right.) Fanon (1965) writes, "All that the native has seen in his country is that they can freely arrest him, beat him, starve him: and no professor of ethics, no priest has ever come to be beaten in his place, nor to share their bread with him." (43). Humanity. Add two hundred or three hundred years, and how much will have changed?

It is through a recognition of the boogeyman, the mythological real, the creature upon which the oppressor launches its blame for pathological enactments, otherwise known as systems of oppression, that duende breathes. Lorca (1933) writes:

> The magic power of a poem consists in it always being filled with duende, in its baptising all who gaze at it with dark water, since with duende it is easier to love, to understand, and be certain of being loved, and being understood, and this struggle for expression and the communication of that expression in poetry sometimes acquires a fatal character. (4)

It is through a recognition of the boogeyman and the space/time/body/spirit resilient and resistant response of duende that one avenue of understanding and upsetting of those systems becomes possible. Duende is poem magic, communication unbound, liberating in its story revelation.

Story is not limited; the poem is a starship in which all these elements may coalesce in aspiration of duende.

SPIRIT

Fanon (1965) writes of the violence intrinsic to the process of decolonization, and this also invokes a discussion of the oppressor opposition to decolonization with the violence of ideological warfare. Educational systems are the perfect areas for the flourishing of hegemony—look at the graduation rates for black men and women and English learners—but formal education is not the only site of dehumanization. The pathological separation machine has a master plan of domination over the body (and its coopted and profitable use) through the process of drawing and quartering it, both literally and figuratively. No, there are no physical horses with their ropes, but there are horses of the Apocalypse. How many zombie movies have come out in the last few years? Are we not already on that route, living that reality? Who is the zombie, and who is the human? Where is the spirit in the zombie body? Nowhere, but how is it stripped?

And when the action does not happen through physical pain, it happens through the psychic, through fear. The network (social matrix) teaches us fear through social media: killed like a pig and bled, too, and we see the pictures over and over again. I watch zombie movies to learn how easy it is to be killed when not viewed as human. Our poetics can humanize, revolutionize, and catapult into the intersectional, interstitial realities space.

We should be Travelers, vibrant in the strength of our abilities to interact with space, time, body, spirit, and language. This last evolution would require the cultivation of a boundless tongue that goes beyond grammar and syntax flesh flapping of a fixed multiple of languages or one into star-speak. We are far from that, though I believe in the possibility.

LANGUAGE

When I consider poetics, I do so first from my identity as a black and Puerto Rican, Afropunk, defiant, body-connected, humanizing, and spirited/spiritual womyn. My ancestors were farmers, slaves, slave owners, travelers, soldiers, artists, lovers, dancers, *abuela-santas*, *abuelo- árboles*, teachers, revolutionaries. All of this siphons into the work I do and the work I look to publish. In my capacity as editor of the *Acentos Review*, I feel for the otherworldly, look for the bold (in form, language, internal spark), and connect with those who dare to tilt the world.

Language ultimately can oppress or liberate. In the process of colonization and enslavement, the languages of my peoples were stripped; it is language that situates, connects body to the emotive character of the land and to the community, to a cultural sense of time and knowing, to the historical, cosmological, mythological, and spiritual truths of generations. In the loss of wordsong, peoples can be (mis)oriented by a domineering other-power, which inserts its language, customs, truths through pounding jangle-noise. We know that the use of noise in war can madden; what effect might that violent enforcement of internalizing noise have on a people? Monstrous maddening.

I am interested in the poetics of the *abuela-santa*, the blessed and blessing grandmother who infuses her descendants with a resilience and community-connectedness that shape shifts in form, undermines oppressor languages and the realities that come from speaking/writing the word and world, and reenergizes the world with a blending of languages and realities in a way that explores experience and yet defies placement in the box of time (time-boxing). I am interested in the poetics of *abuelo-árbol* that reveals the intimate land remnants in footprint crevices, spits/sweats/cries nourishment in (dis)jointed prose and grits out/out-grits a cityscape.

Duende in its magic, allure, resistance, ecstasy, sorrow, and the trick of the mundane: that is what I seek to publish and what I seek to write. Particularly, in the way of writing, I live at that intersection right now, writing about transnational black and Latin@ immortals through eco- lyric and character-driven narrative. As an act of resistance against the dehumanization of black and brown bodies, I explore a future in which immortals exist as a reference to generational histories that all humans carry within them. These immortals have an insatiable thirst for water to preserve their bodies, which results in raging desertification. They also thirst for blood to appeases the hundreds of spirits they carry, spirits who can literally take over their bodies to walk again on the earth. These immortals have lived thousands of years, can have children, but these new generations carry the genetic memories of trauma and joy from their parents.

What would you be like as a toddler in the now if you knew what it was to watch Alexandria burn, knew what it was like to see those first ships arrive on your Caribbean island shores? What is it like to be black and alien in and out of time? What are the languages that brings one back into one's right(eous) mind, music, time? These are the questions I explore.

Let us return to earth, where there is a desire for control, for fit, for erasure, using race to kill or incarcerate. In both instances, the result is the same: divorce of the spirit and power from the body to use that body (and the bodies of other black and brown men and women, dominated through fear and othering) for the system's ends. There is a matrix, a netting that is holding us back, and it starts in our very education. Talk this way, walk this way . . . and we might not kill you, that matrix speaks.

Duende is slow and fast, uncontrolled by time; it is trickster at the crossroads, as blues as it is gangastagrass, as funk as it is flamenco. And it responds to blood. There is the sugar-sweet heavy flick-flack of a curtain in the wind. Sekou Sundiata conjures in the 51st (dream) state. The prophetic and the now. LaTasha Diggs, Urayoán Noel, Douglas Kearney, Tracie Morris, Edwin Torres, Thomas Sayers Ellis, among others, who are doing the do, defying, riding the five rails to another dimension.

We have already bled so much to have our mutilators say things like, "This is not about race," when it is so much about race and keeping us buried, drowned, controlled. Duende. Janelle Monáe (2008) sings, "I'm an alien from outer space; I'm a cybergirl without a face, a heart or a mind; I'm a slave girl without a race." Duende. I know what it is to be alien, to be prodded, my hair pulled, my skin rubbed to see if the color would rub off. Duende. I know what it is to be seen and looked at with disgust or not even seen at all and still dance ecstatic my being, still write my right-wholeness, still read and pulse-energized by the work of those standing in a similar poetics stance. Duende. The system would want us all less and less human: a face on a target in a police shooting range, stick figures to bomb. And the system would have us be used only as bodies, servomechanisms: slaves: incarcerated men or superwomen black and brown women who die depressed and alone long before we actually die. Duende. We are still the aliens having to declare that black and brown lives (our lives) matter—black and brown aliens walking down the street, black and brown aliens in academia, black and brown aliens to be dissected on morgue tables (body) or in schools (spirit), black and brown aliens with bodies to be warehoused in incarceration workhouses, black and brown aliens to whom no one listens—and no one cares if we come in peace or not. Duende. Though there are no longer shackles, there are still shackles. I am already so much older than my white female peers. I am living in multiple times and spaces at once. The television is off, but this still ain't real.

NOTE: For those of you who do not identify as Trekkers or Trekkies, the Traveler was a being from Tau Ceti who understood the complexities of reality enough so as to be able to use the power of his mind to alter space, time, and warp fields. He could also alter his appearance and acted as a guide to a young Wesley Crusher.

SOURCES

Alexander, Michelle. 2010. *The New Jim Crow: Mass Incarceration in the Age of Colorblindness*. New York: New Press.

Eshun, Kodwo. 1998. *More Brilliant than the Sun: Adventures in Sonic Fiction*. London: Quartet.

Fanon, Frantz. 1965. *The Wretched of the Earth*. London: MacGibbon & Kee.

García Lorca, Federico. 2007. *Theory and Play of the Duende [Teoría y juego del duende]*. Translated by A. S. Kline. Poetry in Translation. www.poetryintranslation.com/PITBR/Spanish/LorcaDuende.php. Originally published 1933.

León, Raina J. "Southwest Philadelphia, 1988." 2017. In *¡Manteca!: An Anthology of Afro-Latino Poets*, edited by Melissa Castillo-Garsow, 195. Houston, TX: Arte Público.

Monáe, Janelle. 2008. *Violet Stars Happy Hunting*. Track 2 of *Metropolis: The Chase Suite*. Bad Boy Records.

Roddenberry, Gene, dir. 2007. *Star Trek: The Next Generation: The Complete Series*. Los Angeles: Paramount Domestic Television.

Testarudo

An Essay on My Poetic Vocation

ORLANDO RICARDO MENES

SINCE 2000, I have lived in South Bend, Indiana, where I teach in the Creative Writing Program at the University of Notre Dame, having started off as an assistant professor, earning tenure as an associate in 2007, and being promoted to full in 2015. Just the other day, my next-door neighbor Bea, a kind and hardworking woman in her sixties, asked me what I had been doing this summer with all my extra time from not teaching. I answered, "Oh, just reading and writing." To which she replied, "You must have a gift." This is certainly a common idea: that the talent to write is something in-born, God given, and inexplicably innate. My response to Bea was that writing is just something that I do and that I have been doing it for quite a long time through practice, diligence, and perseverance, not unlike my own father's skill in furniture making, and I genuinely remain impressed at having seen my father build a sofa all by himself, from cutting and assembling the wood for the frame to sewing and stapling the upholstery to that frame.

Let us not forget that *poet* in ancient Greek means "maker," so writing a poem requires a command of craft, in this case meaning a facility for shaping words with an eye to form and an ear for rhythm. And just as my father learned to construct a sofa, so anyone with at least an aptitude for poetry can learn the craft of building verbal structures. As a professor who has taught dozens of poetry workshops, I have been amazed at how students, particularly undergraduates, can flourish as poets, even though they had not initially shown a talent for the craft. They just worked at writing poetry as my own father worked at making furniture and as I too have for the past thirty years or so devoted myself to molding words into the sublime confines of the stanza. Talent is acquired through conscious acts of volition, acts of perseverance, acts of faith. In other words, a strong will and an even stronger work ethic will propel even the most diffident writer to achievement. No, I do not possess a gift. All that I genuinely possess is the skill (a combination of knowledge and practice) that I have labored to acquire through trial and error, success and failure, affirmation and rejection, ecstasy and despair. Above all, I am unswervingly stubborn, or pig-headed, indomitable as a bull (I am a Taurus, after all), or as my late mother would have said, *testarudo*.

If necessity is the mother of invention, then too necessity has an important bearing on the poetic vocation, the drive to acquire the craft through an arduous yet also fulfilling process (paradox being a rather constant element in the life of a poet, perhaps to the point of masochism) of learning, forgetting, relearning, pushing out of one's habits, living in state of perpetual uncertainty about one's competence, one's worth, one's relevance, and then into one's old age being obsessed with legacy, the fear of not being remembered as a poet, that one's poetry will be reduced to oblivion. Yes, these preoccupations, whether mild or extreme in form, are not healthy nor are they necessary to write poems. Our sense of accomplishment should be measured more reasonably, more forgivingly, especially if we accept the idea that writing a poem, of whatever quality, is a noble act in itself, but above all, how practicing the craft of poetry integrates us into a long-standing tradition and bonds us as well to other human beings, to lives both different and similar to our own, to the very weft and woof of the social fabric. Nonetheless, poets are particularly prone to narcissism of a rather petty kind, considering that adulation is seldom accompanied by money. I have often witnessed how a poet's experience of success (winning a contest, having a manuscript accepted for publication, having a book well reviewed in a journal, etc.) is accompanied by episodes of self-doubt, self-effacement, and self-abnegation. The pen is married to the whip. Yes, I have chosen this vocation, and I have always said that I need poetry even if poetry does not need me.

So what does necessity mean, anyway? The most persuasive definition that I know of comes from Rainer Maria Rilke's *Letters to a Young Poet*, in which he argues to a military cadet who is spellbound by a strong poet that desiring to imitate this poet is a false reason to become a poet but rather that necessity, which Rilke characterizes as something internal and integrative, should be the sole light that must guide that young poet's decision to embrace the poetic vocation. It is perhaps more a matter of identity, of purpose, of commitment. I do not mean identity as in lifestyle, for instance, being a bohemian, a hipster, a free spirit, an iconoclast. These character traits really have less to do with writing poetry than with adolescent, pseudo-Romantic adulations of the poet as the gifted outsider, the marginalized seer, the antihero who defies bourgeois conventions. To riff on Descartes's *cogito ergo sum*, I would attest to the truth of *I write poetry; therefore, I am*. In other words, the poetic vocation lies in the writing and not in the being. No one is a poet by personality; one is a poet by the act of making a poem.

Wherein lies my own necessity, my own genesis as a poet? I would say that my need to be a poet was intricately connected to my initially fraught relationship with the English language. Though I had attended British schools in Lima, Perú, where I was born to Cuban parents, my knowledge of the English language proved minimal when my family and I moved to Miami when I was ten. Instead of living in Little Havana, we moved way south off West Dixie Highway (US 1), that is 152nd Street or Coral Reef Drive, just a half hour from Homestead. Like other immigrants before and after me, I experienced constant rejection from *los americanos* in our neighborhood and in Coral Reef Elementary. (Read my poem "South Kendall, 1969" from my book *furia*, and you will understand what I am speaking of here.) The children made fun of my English and tormented me for being "Spanish," which is what Latin Americans were called at the time. The alienation and culture shock were severe, and this experience of ruthless rejection has haunted me ever since.

My command of English improved over the years, but I cannot say that I had any mastery of the language. My SAT verbal score was quite low, and I experienced difficulty writing essays for my honors English classes at Coral Gables High School. My essays were heavily corrected by Jenny Krugman, who turned out to be a wonderful teacher, and because of her, I *finally* learned how to use a semicolon, though the D that I got in journalism from another teacher surely deflated my spirits. At the University of Florida, where

I was both an undergraduate and a graduate student, only a single professor praised me for being a good writer or saw any potential in me as a writer (I cannot blame them, really, for my essays did exhibit awkwardness). The exception was Alistair Duckworth, an Englishman with whom I took critical theory in my last year of the MA and who genuinely lauded my essays (maybe it was because of my ideas, or maybe I just felt more comfortable and hopeful as a writer). One of my linguistic handicaps was having an inadequate vocabulary, so I took it upon myself to memorize new words from the dictionary or any other text, keeping a vocabulary journal (or maybe just a list) that I would use to quiz myself just about every day. Therefore, I was fortunate that in this class, I began to experience the necessary self-confidence to transform myself into a writer, a vocation that would empower me to take control of my existence, to bring order to the chaos of my dislocated immigrant life, to affirm my presence (as opposed to feeling absent), to create a voice, both personal and public, through which I could heal.

Therefore, writing poetry is for me a devotional act, a quest for transcendence, a craving for grace. I pray for inspiration before I begin to write, lighting one or more jar candles, while on my desk and on one bookshelf next to my chair I keep framed photographs of my mother, Aída, and her mother, Nena, plus saints' cards, fortune cookie strips, a bottle of holy water, a Fatima rosary, wood shavings from Jerusalem, magical oils and colognes from *botánicas*, a rabbit's foot that my wife, Ivis, gave me, a Native America rooster claw. I realize that my writer's altar might strike many people as superstitiously silly, but I feel safe in that space, free to take risks and be cocooned in my imagination. Something else that helps me get into a creative trance, what some call the "zone" or maybe what Federico García Lorca would say is the abode of *el duende*, is listening to one movement from a classical composition (e.g., Gabriel Fauré's "In Paradisum," from his *Requiem*), using the repeat mode on my computer's iTunes or with my iPod attached to headphones.

For many years, I wrote solely at night, usually from 10 p.m. until 2 a.m., so I would sleep no more than six hours each night. Copious amounts of strong coffee kept me awake during the day. The quiet and stillness of night comforted me, creating the safety of a sanctuary that focused my concentration (in large part, I think, because of the practice of listening to the same music track or even just a recording of beach sounds), thereby allowing my imagination to roam, to leap, and to fly in safety. Somehow, I was better able to quiet, or at least to muffle, the harsh voice of the critic who lives inside me and with whom I have learned over the years to make peace.

His voice has changed from one of sheer negativity ("you're not good enough," "who cares about you're writing," "you'll never get this published") to one of benevolent doubtfulness ("are you sure this works?," "this poem could be much better," "be patient and the solution will come"). If I got stuck on a line, I would just while away the time smoking a cigar and reading poems from Wallace Stevens's *Harmonium*, which would usually unclog my imagination. I cannot think of a better poet to elicit intellectual play and the joy of language. One technique that has given me some degree of objectivity in rethinking or reinventing my poems is to record them and then play them back. I am then better able to select what sounds awkward or unmusical and what needs either elaboration or outright deletion. When the time comes to actually edit and revise, I do engage *el editor* inside me, but as I tell my students that it is important to turn off this critic during the drafting process when it is the creative voice who should be taking control, or else writing becomes an impossibility. Because of the responsibilities of fatherhood, plus being older, I now write earlier in the day, but I still follow the same process and practice the same habits. A predictable method is essential for training the mind to create, what some would call beckoning *el duendecillo*, the little duende.

The first poem that I would say solidified my identity as a poet would be "Cat's Cradle without a String," which I wrote in 1985 and was published two years later in the *Florida Review* (it would reappear in my chapbook *Borderlands with Angels*, published in 1994 and winner of the Bacchae Press Chapbook Contest). My writing process is one that has continued to this day with some necessary modifications. I typed up many drafts using an electric typewriter that had some memory capabilities but really nothing comparable to an actual PC. Later, I would buy a Korean-made Leading Edge computer, along with a daisy wheel printer, the loudest office contraption one can imagine. Revising on a computer proved to be extraordinarily liberating as it took away the drudgery of having to retype the same lines many times over, which I found exasperating, plus it allowed me (because of the decrease in labor, it seems to me) to write the denser, more compressed, more trope-oriented lines of my poems in the 1990's and thereafter. "Cat's Cradle without a String," like many of my other poems of the time, was minimalist, perhaps because of the influence of Raymond Carver and the Ted Hughes of *Crow* or even Laura Jensen's *Bad Boats*. Something else that I did that shaped the ludic quality of this poem was to listen to Laurie Anderson's *Big Science* (on LP) nonstop, besides drinking copious amounts of cheap Publix coffee brewed on a percolator and smoking expensive Gitanes cigarettes (similar to the Spanish Ducados that I used to smoke in Madrid as a teenager) as I created, or maybe improvised, this poem's many drafts. The influence of Spain, where I lived between 1973 and 1975, is also palpable in this poem with its reference to ferrets and rabbits. (Besides having seen dead rabbits in the markets of Madrid, I had also watched Carlos Saura's film *The Hunt*, in the Student Union at the University of Florida, where I studied between 1979 and 1982.) Without a doubt, minimalism was quite in fashion during the 1980s, and I would include the new-wave pop in this category, besides, of course, the classical works of Philip Glass, Terry Riley, and others. In other words, it was this minimalist poetry that I encountered in the many "cool" books and poetry magazines that I bought at Books and Books in Coral Gables, which had monthly open-mic poetry readings just about every month hosted by Steve Kronen and was the *it* place for Miami's literary culture.

Having never taken a poetry workshop at the University of Florida (where I earned a BA and an MA in English), I began to cobble together a poetic education on my own during the early 1980s, reading voraciously in the afternoons and early evenings during the week and just about all day on the weekends, including staying awake well into the wee hours, plus devoting an equal time to drafting poems that, to be honest, were at best juvenile imitations of the dark and nihilistic poems in Hughes's *Crow*. I worked as a high school teacher at the time, and I had to wake up very early to drive to work in my third-hand (or maybe fourth-hand) red VW station wagon with the rebuilt engine, the stiff stick shift, and the bullet hole on the driver's side door that had been patched up with candle wax. I lived in one "cottage" after another (mostly converted stand-alone garages with just a refrigerator and a bathroom) in North Miami, with the exception of the summer months when I backpacked throughout Latin America and kept my belongings in a storage locker and my car parked in front of my mother's apartment on Miami Beach.

I had no girlfriend, did not date, had no social life whatsoever, and just went to the neighborhood bar where, believe it or not, I met another lover of poetry, whose name I cannot remember, a long-haired, disheveled fat man in his late thirties who was one of their regulars. We spent long hours well past midnight drinking booze and talking about the work of Louise Glück, Robert Bly, and Allen Ginsburg. This hobo-looking man and I experienced a strong connection of the mind and the spirit, even though he had no formal education whatsoever and was pretty much unemployed, living off an inheritance from a dead relative, and it saddened me to hear from the bartender that he was living on the street after his money had run out.

One pivotal person in my early poetic education was Eric Leroy, and I consider him my first teacher and mentor. We met in a class on Restoration literature taught by the eminent Aubrey Williams when we were both graduate students in the English MA program at the University of Florida in Gainesville. The year was 1980. I was on the literature track, while Eric was writing a poetry thesis under the tutelage of Dave Smith and the late Donald Justice. Eric was much older than I and so had considerably more life experience, more self-confidence, more bravado, while I was shy and awkward. He had lived in England for many years, had a British accent, and had been married to an English woman with whom he had a daughter, though Erica was actually born and raised in West Virginia. Perhaps his muscular swagger and scruffy beard were part of what he called his hillbilly heritage. His poems, which he read aloud dramatically in his apartment, mesmerized me, especially those in the rhapsodic style of Dylan Thomas, though Eric's poetry would later evolve into a more American plain-spokenness because of Smith's and Justice's influence. Eric and I would hang out at the Pizza and Brew on University Avenue with other young MA writers who were under the spell of Harry Crews, who was then one of the most celebrated contemporary American authors. We would drink pitcher after pitcher of beer talking about writing, the writers we admired, and Harry's womanizing and hard drinking, besides having informal workshops. They spoke with authority and self-assurance, while I felt like an interloper, a hanger-on, a wannabe, which I clearly was. Perhaps because of a combination of shame and pride, I soon began to write poems, or at least what I thought were poems, and they paid attention, which surprised me to no end, in particular to one lost draft with the phrase "the poverty of Spanish textbooks." Eric's affirmation gave me permission to say to myself, *I could become a poet.*

We parted ways after I had graduated with an MA in English from the University of Florida in 1982, and I went back home to Miami, where I lived until 1987, except for that year spent in Orlando working as a high school teacher and feeling miserable because of my students' abusive and rowdy behavior. That year, I got a job as a technical writer at a software company in Jacksonville, Florida, and because Eric lived with his parents in nearby Saint Augustine, we soon renewed our friendship. Just about every Saturday or Sunday we would get together at his home across from the Matanzas River where, chain smoking Winstons and drinking beer, we would talk long into the night about my poems but also about those poets whose work we loved, Dylan Thomas being one of them, of course, but also Rilke, Hart Crane, and Galway Kinnell in particular. I had heard Kinnell read at Florida International University in the early 1980s (so popular was he that the auditorium was packed), and I quickly became drawn to his passionate, sonorous, full-voiced poems. I was on the path to becoming another kind of poet, one drawn to rhapsody rather than one enamored with minimalist nihilism or, to put it more bluntly, the persona of the tongue-in-cheek jerk. (Oh, how embarrassed I was just some weeks ago when I reread these thirty-plus-year-old poems.) Anyway, it was in Jacksonville/Saint Augustine that I composed these new taut and intense poems, which Eric read with an open mind, an ample heart, a keen sense of the beautiful, but which he also critiqued with honesty, even being capable of giving some harsh criticism or tough lessons. I learned from him, or at least tried to learn, how to be more elliptical, to balance the prosaic with the poetic, to be more measured with assonance and alliteration so that these do not inhibit the smooth flow of narrative and of voice. "Don't fuck with language when you don't need to," he would say. "Don't take yourself so seriously."

I wrote few poems that brief year and a half in northern Florida, perhaps because my method of writing was so arduous and my sources of inspiration so constricting. I must have spent twenty or more hours a week at my small office in the living room of my small apartment chiseling and polishing like some mad sculptor one poem for weeks and weeks. Working out one line or one image or even just one word (*la mot juste!*) would be excruciatingly slow, but yet I felt empowered, gratified, exuberant. Sometimes I spent an inordinate amount of time making changes, only to realize many days or even weeks later that the initial draft was fresher, more direct, more genuinely me. (Thank God I was using that Leading Edge Model D computer, or else it would have been impossible to do this in long hand or on a typewriter.) Perhaps this is how one learns to write, and thus one's command of craft has to be hard won, achieved through a long and patient labor, every precious step in this journey to be savored and remembered. I gathered all my drafts into thick folders, some heavily annotated, and I included, too, all those little scraps of paper, index cards, and bookmarks on which I wrote new images and lines that would appear to me as I drove my car, walked along the St. John's River, or read at Denny's drinking coffee. Most of the poems that I wrote were based on places that I visited in northern Florida, such as "Matanzas Bay" in St. Augustine and "A Morning Sally" about Big Talbot Island. (The latter would be published in the magazine *Poem*.) These weekly trips were like pilgrimages of inspiration for me, so Romantically fulfilling, and thus I felt my own humble kinship with Wordsworth in the Lake Country.

Nonetheless, it was difficult to write about these places with which I had no personal connection, no emotional bond, no familial or childhood rootedness. (Many years later, it was so much easier—the words just galloped in my mind—to write poems about Cuba, Perú, and Miami, places that I knew intimately and almost reflexively.) Nonetheless, it was during this period that I learned the value of doing research, learning about the wider world beyond one's self, and I bought many little books of art (printed in Italy) at a small bookstore near the main square of St. Augustine. I gazed at their paintings for hours, taking notes, inventing images, exploring the minds of their artists, enveloping myself in their narratives, which resulted in my first ekphrastic poem, titled "Duty," based on Pieter Brueghel the Elder's "The Fall of the Rebel Angels." I do think that I learned, as best as I could, what Eric had often urged me to do: to write poems about others, to suspend my emotions, and to think more objectively or detachedly.

Even though I had spent considerable time and effort to become a technical writer, I found writing how-to manuals rather dull and working in a cubicle under tight supervision from nine to five each day too constricting, so I quit my job at the banking software company after twelve months. I also did not want to return to teaching high school. Since I had no debts, no family responsibilities, and was still quite young (not yet thirty), I decided to do some traveling in Europe, yet I wanted to save my own money, or at least as much as I could. Eric suggested that I look into the US Navy's PACE (Program for Afloat College Education), which contracted college instructors to teach aboard warships either in the Pacific or the Mediterranean fleet. I contacted someone at the Mayport Naval Base office of Central Texas College, had an interview that day, filled out long applications with intrusive questions, then soon obtained my GS-9 civil service card, and within weeks I was taking an American Airlines flight to Marseille, France, where I boarded the cruiser USS *Leyte Gulf* (CG-59).

For two months I lived on that ship as it traveled from one port of call to another (Alexandria, Izmir, Cannes, Catania) and engaged in several missions (I do not think these are classified), such as chasing a Soviet submarine and crisscrossing Muammar Gaddafy's line of death so as to bait Libya into military conflict. I taught English composition and business writing in the "staging area" between the ammunition locker and the aft five-inch gun, my students mostly young enlisted men who did not foresee a naval career. I slept on a "coffin rack" (with a mustard-yellow curtain) in the overflow compartment that housed six men in two tiers with a red deck light in between that kept me awake at night; in fact, I could hardly sleep, even with ear plugs, because of the jet engines that hummed all day as they powered the ship's screw. Unless anchored at port, the ship was constantly in motion, its top speed thirty-plus knots, so the rocking and rolling gave me awful bouts of seasickness, but the Dramamine pills did alleviate the condition after a few weeks. I never had to wear the infamous "pussy patch" on my neck. I spent most of my time ambling around the ship, learning about the weapons (missiles, cannons, phalanx guns), the Combat Information Center, with all its monitors and screens, where the captain would direct warfare. The food was plentiful and of high quality, but eating with the chiefs at their mess was an experience I will never forget. They were, without a doubt, the most vulgar and obnoxious human beings I will ever encounter (farting contests were frequent), but I must admit that they were much more genuine and convivial than the officers with whom I had little contact. I also read Latin and Greek literature lying on my rack, which was the only place for privacy, so poetry was rarely far from my mind. I kept a journal as a source for future projects, but only one unpublished poem was written as a result. Nonetheless, I should emphasize that sea and water imagery abound in my poetry, so this experience, I suppose, has had some indirect though permanent effect. When walking on the weather decks of the ship, I was impressed by the vastness of the sea, its power to nourish but also to destroy life, a contradiction that is vital to my poems.

On leaving the ship at Catania, Sicily, in April of 1989, I took a flight to Rome and spent over two months traveling by rail across Italy, Switzerland, the south of France, and then on to Barcelona and finally Madrid. Spain's capital had not changed that much since I last visited in 1979, just a few years after the death of Franco. Yes, the euphoria of democracy had disappeared and perhaps there were more foreigners living in the city, but the same cafés and stores that I frequented during the years 1973 to 1975 when my father owned a furniture store near Argüelles were still there, such as Café Punto y Coma and Cervecería Alemana in Plaza Santana. The bar hopping, copious smoking, and loud banter of the Spanish lifestyle were still true. I wanted to live in Madrid again, where I felt so much at ease, so integrated into the city during my teenage years. I thus applied for teaching jobs but got nothing after a few interviews. Believe it or not, these schools wanted a bona fide American, a veritable Anglo-Saxon, a *yanqui*, not someone like me of Spanish descent. Feeling anxious about having no possibility of employment, plus being incapable of living like a bohemian, I returned to my parents' home in Miami the summer of 1989 and soon began teaching English as an adjunct instructor at Miami-Dade Community College, where I had studied after graduating from high school. A few months later, I applied for a permanent position at the Inter-American campus in Little Havana, and I got the job, starting in January of 1990.

The majority of my students were Latin American immigrants, primarily Cubans and Nicaraguans, who had either arrived as teenagers, having then to take ESL classes in high school, or as young adults who had to take these courses at Inter-American whose ESL staff was the largest. The range of courses I taught was remarkably wide, all the way from basic reading and paragraph writing to advanced composition and literary analysis. My schedule each semester consisted of five classes, plus four in the summer, so I had little time to write, yet I still pushed myself to set aside at least three hours each day, mostly between 11 p.m. and 3 a.m., which meant that I often did not have enough sleep, especially when I had to teach early in the morning. (In fact, I had the craziest schedule one can imagine, with classes scattered throughout all times of the day Monday through Friday. One time, if I recall correctly, I had to teach from around 9 p.m. to almost 11 p.m., and then again the next morning at 7 a.m.). Thank God I was full of youthful vigor. Plus, I learned the invaluable lesson that discipline and perseverance are perhaps the two most important traits for a writer in building a career. Even if I felt tired or had nothing to say or maybe was just plain lazy, I would still sit at my computer to draft or to revise or to just while away those hours creatively, which in my case meant doodling with word combinations that could potentially become images, either typing these in my Leading Edge Model D computer or scribbling them in a notebook using a fountain pen to give the process some kind of physical pleasure, all the while listening to classical music (from Vivaldi to Shostakovich).

In other words, I just allowed myself to play and to put on hold the voice of the critic within me, that voice that scolds but also taunts me to improve, to transcend my limitations, to touch the sacred, for I consider the act of writing poetry to be a liturgical experience, a questing for grace in our fallen world. I wrote intense and dark lyric poetry, savoring the heightened, complex language of incantation and its enrapturing (to the point of intoxication) sounds and rhythms. It was then that I read the poetry of Charles Baudelaire, Paul Verlaine, and Arthur Rimbaud, immersing myself in the sublime language, the elevated voice, and the exquisite visions (often tortured) of the rhapsode. I memorized poems by Yeats and Blake, reciting these as I walked the chic streets of Coconut Grove, where I lived at the time, or the disheveled, gritty streets of Miami Beach in the early 1990s, feeling elated to be a disciple of the ecstatic, as if walking on sacred water—a rather naïve and self-indulgent attitude, I would admit, but I must acknowledge its importance in my poetic education. I am fortunate that I would later embrace a more plain-spoken and earthy idiom to write about my childhood and my family, thus learning to balance out the spiritual and the quotidian, the sacred and the profane.

During those two years that I taught at Inter-American (until I resigned and left Miami to pursue a PhD in creative writing at the University of Illinois at Chicago in 1992), I made some vital friendships with colleagues who liked poetry or were themselves poets, such as the Cuban-born Amando Fernández, much older than I, who wrote in Spanish and whose many books had won prestigious prizes in Spain. He was rather dour and cutting with his remarks toward fellow poets, yet I found him to be a fitting role model for his dedication and commitment to a life of poetry, even though he hardly made any money teaching as an adjunct, and I was greatly saddened to learn in 1994 that he had died of AIDS. I still treasure that evening we read our poetry together at Inter-American (with a newspaper announcement, no less). Those poems I read, including several in meter and rhyme, would end up collected in *Borderlands with Angels*. Also, my friendship with Xavier Alfonso-Álvarez and Leah LaPlante were also crucial in my taking a leap of faith into the realm of a more professional poetic life, for I had paralyzing fears that I would fail as an academic poet. Their encouragement and faith in my talent were unswerving, as well as their patience and good humor. I need to mention Lowell Fisher, another colleague and friend from my years teaching at American High School in the middle 1980s. He too graciously found talent in my attempts at writing short stories and pushed me, almost nagged me, to pursue a creative writing degree.

More importantly, it was at Inter-American that I met my future wife, Ivis Teijeiro, then twenty-four years old (I almost thirty-four) and a student in one of my composition classes. I had no idea that this beautiful and vivacious woman liked me, so I mistook her friendliness after class for just the usual chatter of a student engaged with the course. It was not until the end of the semester in May of 1992 that I realized she was attracted to me when the conversation eventually led to my asking for her phone number, and she gave it to me. It was the right time, since I would have felt uncomfortable dating a current student. We developed our relationship during those few months in the summer that I lived in a small and inexpensive efficiency, or studio apartment, in Coral Gables as I prepared to make my move to Chicago. Ivis had been born in Havana, Cuba, but moved with her family as a toddler to La Coruña, Spain, where she lived until the late 1980s when they moved again to Miami seeking new opportunities and a change in lifestyle.

Not only did I fall in love with Ivis, eventually marrying her in 1994, but Ivis's very Spanish character and her love of the Spanish language and culture had a profound influence on me as both as a person and as a writer. For too long I had rejected the Spanish language and just about everything Hispanic. I spoke English all the time, pretending not to know Spanish, a thoroughly unconvincing ruse in Cuban Miami. I was dead set on being perceived as a regular American, even by all those Hispanic students at Inter-American, the most Spanish-speaking campus of Miami-Dade Community College, and no wonder the students would call me *arrepentido* (ashamed) behind my back. Yes, they were right, and I was wrong. I could not run away from the fact that I had been born to Cuban parents in Lima, Perú, where I lived until the age of ten, plus those two years as a teenager in Madrid. We were a family that spoke only Spanish at home. We kept all our Cuban/Spanish traditions. We talked about Cuba incessantly. It was foolish of me to pretend that I was not the dark-haired, dark-eyed ethnic American, the immigrant Other, whose very right to be in this country is still questioned by hard-core nativists. And no matter how American my accent is in English, I would never be accepted as the regular Joe Williams from Dubuque, Iowa.

Of course, Ivis noticed this rejection of my roots, the very essence of my identity, and when she insisted that I speak Spanish, she was humorously surprised to hear a perfectly accented Cuban dialect. And as I became more part of her life, more part of her family, I changed for the better. I began to feel whole, honest, and real. I ate Cuban food. I spoke in Spanish to strangers on the street. I read Cuban American poetry (Ricardo Pau-Llosa, Pablo Medina, and others.). I began to investigate Cuban literature (Alejo Carpentier, José Lezama Lima, Guillermo Cabrera Infante). I developed an intense interest in Cuban history and its tropical flora and fauna. That summer in Coral Gables, I began to experiment with the baroque language of Carpentier's *lo real maravilloso* (the marvelous real), crafting those lush, impacted lines that would later become the hallmarks of my *barroco* poetics. Curiously, my first entryway into this gorgeous language of excess and of the radiating trope was not Carpentier's *Kingdom of this World* (this would happen later as a PhD student) but Shakespeare's *The Tempest*. It was those lines of Caliban's that seduced me into sublime creativity, into an ecstatic journey through Caribbeanness via the tropical and subtropical nature that one finds in Miami's beaches and mangroves, its hammocks, ridges, and sloughs, its copious rains and incendiary sunlight. I will never forget these months of intense drafting and imagining (plus the following two summers when I returned from Chicago to be with Ivis, soon to be my fiancé). I kept various sketchbooks in which I wrote deliriously with a calligrapher's fountain pen. One of these "Caliban" poems, entitled "The Music of Lifeless Creatures," would be published a few years later by the *Antioch Review*, then eventually included in *Rumba atop the Stones* (Peepal Tree Press, 2001), my first collection.

Those seven years that I spent in the doctoral writers' program at UIC would propel me even further into educating myself about Cuba as well as the other Antillean islands. Especially after I had taken my area examinations (believe it or not, Renaissance poetry, modern British poetry, formalist criticism, and poetry of the ecstatic tradition), I began to read every poetic work by Derek Walcott, with whom I found a profound poetic kinship, as I wrote the poems that would make up my dissertation and eventually *Rumba atop the Stones*. I also devoured books by other Caribbean poets, such as Kamau Brathwaite, Eric Roach, and Lorna Goodison, in addition to novels by Wilson Harris (even more baroque than Carpentier!), Rosario Ferré, Cirilo Villaverde, and Reinaldo Arenas. I did intensive research into Cuba's African heritage (of which I knew very little), reading the seminal works of Fernando Ortiz, Lydia Cabrera, and Miguel Barnet. Now on a new Mac with an HP inkjet printer, I wrote about palm trees, cane fields, and strangler figs as I stared at the snow from the window of our apartment on Kenmore Avenue near Loyola University, where Ivis was a graduate student in the Spanish Department. Add to this the influence of John Donne, Richard Crashaw, and John Milton, who were introduced to me by the eminent Michael Lieb at UIC. How was I able to undergo such a transformation from being a purely Eurocentric writer and thinker to one who embraces a multicultural and multiracial Caribbeanness? I would have to say it was the great poet and my dissertation advisor Michael Anania. It was through his encouragement, guidance, and support that gave me, in a sense, permission to become a poet on my own terms.

And I continue to relish in the stupendous irony that it was in frigid Chicago that I grew into the Antillean, tropical baroque poet that I am. And as Mamá would have exclaimed with pride, *¡Qué testarudo eres!*

To Have and Have Not

Uncovering the Cultural Identity in Twenty-First-Century Portuguese American Literature

MILLICENT BORGES ACCARDI

THE LITERARY CRITIC and writer Reinaldo Francisco Silva *(Portuguese in American Literature)* characterized the Portuguese as "the silent minority," and throughout modern times, the literature of Luso writers has been underrepresented and often shifts into varying degrees and categories of marginalization. At best, Luso work has been presented as European or a bastard stepchild of Latinx. At worst, as a Portuguese American writer, I have been labeled "unidentifiable other." As if in a category too small to consider as more than merely part of some unidentified mysterious vastly superior larger whole of humanity.

To have and have not.

A little before I was born, my parents moved cross-country from the former whaling village and mill town of New Bedford, Massachusetts, a bastion of Portuguese culture, to California, and along with that came the late great white-washing of my soul. A soul I longed to reach and take out for a walk long before I knew it was being suppressed. My grandparents were from the Azores.

There were books in my childhood home. Thank God for that. There was reading at bedtime and discussions of Readers Digest. My parents read Dr. Spock and *The Joy of Sex*. One moment of brilliance and perhaps ignorance was the house rule that I could read anything I wanted to read. There was no such thing as children's lit or not getting to check out books in the adult section of the library. It was a free for all, from my grandmother's

Mickey Spillane detective novels with blindfolded women on the covers to abridged versions of *The Thorn Birds*.

Flying the flag of "curiosity," I discovered poetry at a young age, caught between the confines of Catholicism and the freedom of Unitarianism, my childhood stretched wide before me, filled with library books and the knowledge that literature was not only a way to connect with other people; it was the way out. I was bussed to schools where classmates wore Liz Claiborne scarves and went on European ski trips over Christmas. After high school, I worked three waitress jobs to pay my way through City College and California State University Long Beach, with degrees in English and literature. Following graduation, I attended the master's program in professional writing at the University of Southern California, where I found my footing among a cohort of writers. After that came teaching jobs at community colleges and work as a technical writer for every industry from dog food to oil refining.

As a Portuguese American writer, I have published four full-length poetry books, the latest, *Through a Grainy Landscape* (New Meridian Arts, 2021), *Only More So* (Salmon Poetry, 2016), Injuring Eternity (Mischievous Muse/World Nouveau, 2010), and the forthcoming *Quarantine Highway* (FlowerSong Press). *Injuring Eternity* received an honorable mention in the Latino Book Awards for Best Poetry Book (2012) and *Through a Grainy Landscape* has been nominated for a PEN award (2022).

Currently, I curate two literary reading series: Kale Soup for the Soul (Portuguese American writers reading work about family, food, and culture) and Loose Lips (a poets and writers sponsored diversity reading based at the Los Angeles County Library in Topanga), and I founded the Westside Women's Writing Cooperative, which has given readings all over Southern California.

Through a Grainy Landscape confronts the "fullness of vision" of Portuguese identity and serves as a bridge between narratives of the Azores and mainland Portugal with readers in America.

What there wasn't at home (when I was a kid) were books in Portuguese. Books about the Azores and Portugal, books written about people like my family.

Although the Portuguese now carry a presence in the canon of American literature, their placement has often been key, with glimpses of brilliance as in the work of António Lobo Antunes, Nobel Prize-winning José Saramago, and the many heteronyms of Fernando Pessoa. Other than that, the presence has been spotty and unpredictable, with Portuguese writers underrepresented in North America and, quite frankly, mostly unnoticed in the scope of literature itself. In fact, Portuguese writing is often categorized as untested, incomplete, or unproven. One critic went so far as to say that the canon of Portuguese American literature is too small and too immature even to be counted—an opinion formerly held about other marginalized cultures such Cuban, Mexican, and El Salvadorian until a breakthrough book or movie causes the English-speaking world to sit up and pay attention.

In Hemmingway's 1927 collection of stories *To Have and Have Not*, Harry Morgan is the captain of a small fishing boat who transports contraband between Florida and Cuba. Portrayed as essentially a good man, he is forced into the black market. His identity, all but lost by the decisions he makes. To have and have not.

Why is it that Portugal, a country that once birthed the greatest world navigators, has been relegated to obscurity? What about Magellan? With a literature base that often seems to be if not invisible nearly nonexistent? Is the Portuguese identity obscured? How can its place resonate inside the larger umbrella of Latinx, an umbrella that also houses other Lusophone cultures such Goa, Macao, Mozambique, Angola, a number of Caribbean islands, and Brazil.

Writer and Luso advocate Philip Graham said in an interview in *Portuguese American Journal* that Portuguese American literature is "a certain blend of mysticism, lyricism, a sense of community, and saudade. . . . This is literature that doesn't feel American with watered-down Portuguese elements—instead, the work seems to exist equally in an American and Portuguese reality . . . [like] Portuguese culture has somehow colonized American culture, rather than the other way around" (Accardi 2012).

To have and have not.

As a child, my growing literary world was peppered by books: *Little Women*, *The Secret Garden*, The Hardy Boys, *Alfred Hitchcock and the Three Investigators*, and Nancy Drew. It was also informed by the poetry of Emerson and Walt Whitman, which was preached to me every Sunday at the Unitarian Universalist Church in Long Beach, which had ended up being a compromise between the old country's Catholicism and the new world. My dad used to say that everyone in his family had been rotten from Monday to Saturday and then holier than thou on Sundays.

I remember when I had pneumonia in elementary school and was relegated to my parents' bed for weeks, without being able to wash my hair or walk around. These days, I would have been in the hospital, but the times and finances meant that I got to stay home, and staying home meant lemonade spiked with whiskey, Jello, and canned chicken-noodle soup.

It also meant books. I remember reading all of the Wizard of Oz series—and then making a notebook with three-hole paper gathered together with fuzzy pink yarn where I was going to start my own version of the Emerald City. How it was on Cherry Avenue, in the house with a blue roof, smack in the middle of a neighborhood that had once seemed idyllic but had turned into a war zone where people showed up at night on the porch crying and naked and the neighbor on the corner side chased his father around the block, brandishing a butcher knife. It meant gangs and graffiti and my mother being warned not to water her front lawn (because she had once sprayed a drug lord's shoes).

To have and have not.

Now, in my mind, the United States has just started to realize that there is a place called Portugal that is not located in South America, so it is a hard call to make and one that muddies the waters, but what is the proper name for us? Portuguese American (PA for short) or Lusophone? Iberian? Angolan? Dago? Portugee? Latinx, Azorean? Mainlander? Pico? Lisbon-man? Or something else?

Perhaps a reason why Portuguese American Luso-Azorean North Americans and their literature are still unknown and isolated from the canon *is* related to the label. Or lack thereof. The Portuguese are known for their stubbornness and independence. An old joke is when one Portugee starts a marching band, a week later his neighbor has to start one, too. Always, we are separated and torn apart like vegetables in our famous national dish of *calde verde*, kale soup.

So, what to do now?

There are many talks to have. In the meantime, *¡preciso de verdade e da aspirina!* Or, I need the truth *and* an aspirin. Now that we have covered definition and its inherent problems, let's uncover identity in Portuguese American literature. To have and have not. What is had and what is not?

Perhaps Portugal's most famous writer had this to say about the writing process:

> I'm astounded whenever I finish something. Astounded and distressed. My perfectionist instinct should inhibit me from finishing; it should inhibit me from even beginning. But I get distracted and start doing something. What I achieve is not the product of an act of my will but of my will's surrender. I begin because I don't have the strength to think; I finish because I don't have the courage to quit. (Fernando Pessoa, 2002).

In Frank Gaspar's novel *Leaving Pico*, there is failure and strife in a former fishing village between an upscale community of summer tourists counterbalanced by an immigrant population. The narrator, Josie, and his family are controlled by the economy and a great-aunt's own brand of Catholicism:

> [Her] obsession with prayer and the saints and the hereafter infected all of us and kept us in a perpetual spin. But it seemed to pay off for her. It was commonly held among the Picos along our end of Commercial Street that Hettie had gained the favor of certain of the Blessed and that these same saints showed themselves to her frequently in minor visions, something which greatly troubled our parish priest but drew a tight circle of devoted lady friends around her. (Pessoa 2002, 6)

In *Leaving Pico* and other Portuguese American literature, matriarchs play key roles in both plot development and the maturation of identity: Gaspar's poem "Tia Joanna" depicts how domineering an influence a seemingly devout Catholic woman can be to her fisherman husband and family:

> ....The soft kerchiefs
> of the women, the dark cloth
> of their long coats, the kale cooking
> on the oilstoves in the redolent kitchens,
> the checkered shirts of the husbands,

the fish they bring to the doorways....
....
She likes that, thinks of the host she will receive
in the morning, His light shining in her eyes.
But tonight still there is mackerel to pickle
with vinegar and garlic in the stone crock,
her husband's silver hair to trim, the bread
to set rising in the big china bowl
on the stool tucked close to the chimney (Clemente 2013,
   7–8).

The poetry of Sam Pierira explores Portuguese identity as well as the struggles of immigrants. Born in 1949 in Los Banos, a rural town of Portuguese and Italian immigrants in central California called, Pereira explains, early on, "There was a closeness to family and the cultural aspects of life... brought over from Portugal.... The festas, the processions, the religious undertones, were always there" (Pereira 2012e). As a child, the poet was close to his grandmother, often sharing "a nice Coca-Cola, back when it truly was 'the real thing,' some Portuguese cookies that we referred to as 'bulls,' because you could break a tooth eating them, and watching American Bandstand with Dick Clark. My grandmother couldn't understand a word of what was being said ... but she would stand in front of the television, bent over in her dark widow's clothing, and simply laugh, her rosary in hand" (Ibid.).

Pereira's collection *The Marriage of the Portuguese*, reprinted by Tagus Press, one critic claims, emanates "from a place of beauty between two worlds, the old and the new," and critic Frank Sousa declares that Pereira's poems "[make] the Portuguese American experience a little more visible, more an integral part of the American experience" (Pereira 2012e). With poems titled "The Marriage of the Portuguese," "Fado," and "Sugars of Terceira," the "words on a page bring to life, saved from silence and forgetfulness, characters and experiences that are now part of American literary and cultural history" (Pereira 2012d, xi–xii).

From gritty thoughts to lofty imaginings, Pereira brings us to our cultural home as well as to the home in our heart that beats in all of us, as in an excerpt from "A Disease":

> And suddenly our story faltered. It could
> Just be another night in the suburbs. A man
> Grabbing up his cigarettes and wife and calling
> It a day. It's Wednesday. The 14th. Somewhere. (Pereira 2012a)

Thus, Portuguese identity in literature combines struggle, abandonment, culture and assimilation.

From another poem, "Saucers," Pereira explains,

> It started as a recollection in Portuguese:
> A woman's voice, familiar
> Over a collision of dishes. Night
>
> After night, the blending smells of codfish;
> Pinto beans followed by the old world
> Habits of cigarettes
> And pekoe tea sipped from saucers. A gone time.
>
> This isn't nostalgia. It's an actual return.
> Watch my eyes if you need convincing. (Pereira 2007b)

Another first generation Portuguese American poet, Carlo Matos, shares the values of the old and the new, and the struggles of immigration. His family roots can be traced from São Miguel to Fall River, Massachusetts.

He says, "Many of my obsessions over the nature of work come from being an Azorean-American. Even as a young boy, work was something that was on my mind. My parents both worked in the last remaining textile mills. . . . They would warn my brother and I that . . . they'd force us to work with them. Long hours, terrible pay, back-breaking work. I was truly scared. For me, destiny, fate (very important words for an Azorean) was a question of whether or not I could escape the horrors of a soul-killing job" (Matos 2012).

In his poetry collection *A School for Fishermen*, Matos discusses the effects of "work."

> And for every patch of summer dry skin
> there are lovers' fingernails to scratch late into the night,
> scratch your scalp with a grandmother's notice
> when you were a child on her lap demanding nothing. (Matos 2010, 44)

His second collection, *Counting Sheep till Doomsday*, reads like an "insomniac's cookbook," full of discontent and struggle. He admits to having been listening to "a ton of Fado" and says, "It's not a coincidence that the first nine poems are all titled 'Fate'" (Matos 2012).

Another Luso writer, Anthony de Sa, introduces sacrifice to the notion of Portuguese identity in literature. His novel, *Barnacle Love*, is about disagreement between generations, about immigrant parents who travel from Portugal to Canada supposedly to find a better life for their children. It serves up a dish of an unflinching entree of family in conflict, in sadness amid deep regret a father, a son, and two mothers. It is an exploration of identity, self-worth and discovery. Clinging to the old ways.

> The Portuguese call it saudade: a longing for something so indefinite as to be indefinable. Love affairs, miseries of life, the way things were, people already dead, those who left and the ocean that tossed them on the shores of a different land—all things born of the soul that can only be felt. (De Sa 2012, 4)

In a brutal 360-degree interpretation, no faults are glossed over or made "pretty." Instead the successes and faults are intermingled to create believable, intimate identities. Especially the character of Manuel as an aging father who tries to continue amid failure to fulfill a dream to see Niagara Falls.

De Sa elaborates in an interview, "As a child I was bombarded with this precursor, you don't know the sacrifices we made—all these things we did for you. I heard it from my parents, uncles, aunts and family members. I can assure you my friends did as well. We all lived in the Portuguese enclave of Toronto and when we didn't hear it we felt it. It permeated our lives." De Sa says, "One of the thematic questions I pose is what if I choose not to take on [my parents'] dream? What about my dream—what it is that I want for me?"(De Sa 2012, 4)

To have and have not.

The Portuguese identity in literature is awash in regret, sadness, a longing for what was lost, clinging to the old almost irrationally, covered up by a strong work ethic, silence, often a Catholicism built on idolatry and maternal role models.

In his first collection of short fiction, *Almost Gone*, writer Brian Sousa marks progress in the uncovering of Portuguese American identity when he discusses writing as "the ways in which we are tied to our pasts ethnically and culturally and . . . the tension between good and evil" (Sousa 2012b). *Almost Gone* features a close look "at a family of working-class Portuguese Americans from the inside out." And that "In many ways, they could be any set of people facing the challenges that immigration adds to the already complicated world of human interaction—adolescence, love, relationships, loss, regret, betrayal—but in other ways, they are distinctly Portuguese" (Ibid.).

Avoiding saudade, Sousa writes of ordinary day-to-day problems, and he does it in a way that links together multiple generations, thus not only establishing a present but a genuine past also. Sousa claims that he would like his writing to be "meaningful and layered; but . . . entertaining too." Themes of humor, loss, love, sex, violence" because as he puts it, "these are the things that make up the human experience" (Sousa 2012b).

To have and have not.

He explains that while being Portuguese informs his writing in an indirect, evanescent way, amazingly, when he set out to write, "The first character [who] appeared was Nuno, a Portuguese immigrant who would not have been out of place in Cumberland, Rhode Island," where his father and grandfather grew up.

Ultimately, his inspiration emanates from "an interest in the process of assimilation and adaptation that all immigrants share. The idea of memory and tradition, comingled with the loss of these things." His story "One Night in Salvador," which appeared in *Quiddity*, speaks of loss and affectation with one telling passage:

> The streets smell of fried food, of urine, and unfiltered cigarette smoke. Packs cost three real about one US dollar, and are covered in peeling stickers that warn in Portuguese of disease, death, or worse, impotence. There are corresponding drawings, and the one I am the most concerned about shows two cartoon figures embracing but the

man seems to be crying. He couldn't get it done, I guess. I didn't even smoke before I came here the narrator of his story says. (Sousa 2012a)

Portuguese-Canadian novelist Erika de Vasconcelos has written two novels dealing with the elusive Portuguese identity. Born in 1965 in Montreal to recent immigrants, de Vasconcelos was raised with a strong sense of heritage. As a child, she made frequent family trips to Portugal.

In an interview with *Women's Voices for Change*, she speaks of the importance of historical hand-me-downs: "When I became an adult, my mother gave me a typed copy of my great-aunt's journal and I read it avidly. And there has always been in my family a sense of treasuring the past, of holding onto letters, photos, old things. My love of history is definitely inherited from the women in my ancestry" (de Vasconcelos 2012).

Like Brian Sousa, de Vasconcelos claims not to have started out to write about Portuguese identity, but her novel *My Darling Dead Ones* just "happened to be set in Portugal because that is the history that [she knows]." Here, an excerpt from the novel ties in two generations with a single-minded search for identity:

> I have come back. I am walking the streets where my grandmothers walked, seeking out the church where my great-aunt married. A middle-aged man offers to help me find it, grumbling all the way because I haven't got a name. How can you not know what you are looking for? He says irritably. Still, he takes me to a church, and I know this is the one, a white building with wide stone steps as Magdalena describes it that summer, long ago. (de Vasconcelos 1997, 192)

Until the early 1990s, except for Frank X. Gaspar, Sam Pereira, and Katherine Vaz's seminal collection of short stories, *Our Lady of the Artichokes*, Portuguese literary voices in North American had been weak and distant, with Portuguese American literature nearly unknown, nonexistent to a general readership, discouraged by even the best intentioned editors and conventional publishers.

Yet in the early twenty-first century, the climate is evolving. The summer of 2021 brought forth the ultimate, authoritative biography of Fernando Pessoa by Richard Zenith. And, what with the first Luso anthology, *Luso-American*

Literature: Writings by Portuguese-Speaking Authors in North America, a second anthology from Gávea-Brown, and a third from BoaVista Press, the time may be right for a deeper exploration of Luso identity, as well as a breakthrough of Portuguese American literature in the Latinx canon and its inclusion into mainstream America.

So *what is* the Luso identity in literature? Is it the ubiquitous kale soup, fado, saudade? Or is it a new generation of writers developing and adapting and bringing innovation to our growing canon. As Charles Reis Felix said, "The Portuguese are the unknown people. We are lost in this vast country. To be Portuguese in America is to be a stone dropped in the middle of the ocean."

Maybe the Portuguese who were at one time the world's greatest explorers are ultimately successful because we are able to struggle to let go of what is behind us and to move bravely forward into the twenty-first century. Do we struggle to find what we had through our writing, as I have in a series of poems dealing with cultural identity?

The Last Borges

Like God and his Eve,
you never passed on
your secrets; I struggled
to learn. Coitadinho, coitadinho.

Never sure which accent to
migrate towards; which window pane
to breathe on for the best cursive fog.
I shunned the loud
Portuguese fights.

The visiting relatives, named for saints,
Over and over, in the driveway
at night, drunken Uncle John or Paul,
or Robert crashed his truck
into the side of our house:
filha da puta!

While you went to night school
two nights a week—for twenty years,
and ate linguiça sandwiches,
I watched and listened.

I would catch you: sitting at
Rudy the barber's chair
I would sneak up behind to hear
foreign words.

At school, I pronounced our name
as you taught me,
as an Englishman would:
flat and plain, riming it with
a word for "pretty."

After a while it seemed
that someone else
had heard a grandmother's
lullabies at night:
a verse that sounded like
a baby's cries for milk,
wanting the nipple:
Mamã eu quero, Mamã eu quero

As you grow older, papa,
I long for a language that joins us,
beyond our last name,
the space between our front teeth,
and wavy black hair.
Beyond linguiça,
kale soup and sweet bread.

But, the only Portuguese words
you ever gave me do not stand for love.
Que queres, que queres.
What do you want, what do you want. (Accardi 2016)

To have and have not. Meanwhile, the Portuguese identity in literature exists and thrives, with its combination of the old and the new, the Catholic icons, the grandmothers, the codfish cakes, the sweet bread, the immigrants, the fisherman, the whalers, the mill workers, the carpenters, the dairy farms, but it is ultimately more than that, with its heart deeply embedded in the fresh faces of second- and third-generation immigrants looking back to look forward, brimming with memories and sadness, a longing for what we never had: our saudade.

SOURCES

Accardi, Millicent Borges. 2016. "The Last Borges." In *Only More So*, 61–62. Ennistymon: Salmon Poetry.

Clemente, Alice R., and George Monteiro. 2013. *The Gávea-Brown Book of Portuguese-American Poetry*. Providence, RI: Gávea-Brown.

De Sa, Anthony. 2010. *Barnacle Love*. Chapel Hill, NC: Algonquin Books.

———. 2012: "Anthony De Sa's Raw Fiction Tells of Bitter Love and Triumph—Interview." By Millicent Accardi. *Portuguese American Journal* (August 29). https://portuguese-american-journal.com/anthony-de-sa-raw-fiction-tells-of-bitter-love-and-triumph-interview/.

de Vasconcelos, Erika. 1997. *My Darling Dead Ones*. Toronto: Knopf Canada.

———. 2012. "Poets on Writers: Millicent Borges Accardi on 'Wonderful, Powerful Erika de Vasconcelos.'" By Millicent Borges Accardi. *Women's Voices for Change* (September 2). https://womensvoicesforchange.org/poets-on-writers-millicent-borges-accardi-on-wonderful-powerful-erika-de-vasconcelos.htm.

Gaspar, Frank X. 2001. *Leaving Pico*. Lebanon, NH: University Press of New England.

———. 1988. *The Holyoke*. Dartmouth, MA. Center for Portuguese Studies and Culture, University of Massachusetts, Dartmouth.

Gonçalves, Luis, and Carlo Matos, eds. 2015. *Writers of the Portuguese Diaspora in the United States and Canada: An Anthology*. Roosevelt, NJ: Boavista Press.

Graham, Philip. 2012. "Memoir: Philip Graham abroad in Lisbon—Interview." By Millicent Borges Accardi. *Portuguese American Journal* (August 13). https://portuguese-american-journal.com/memoir-philip-graham-abroad-in-lisbon-interview/.

Matos, Carlo. 2010. *A School for Fishermen*. Baltimore, MD: Brickhouse.

———. 2011. *Counting Sheep till Doomsday*. Buffalo, NY. BlazeVOX.

———. 2012. "Professor, Poet, Fighter, Portuguese-American: Carlo Matos." By Millicent Accardi. *Poets' Quarterly* (July 2012). www.poetsquarterly.com/2012/08/professor-poet-fighter-portuguese.html.

Moser, Robert Henry, and Antonio Liciano Andrade Tosta, eds. 2011. *Luso-American*

Literature: Writings by Portuguese-Speaking Authors in North America. New Brunswick, NJ: Rutgers University Press.

Pereira, Sam. 2007a. *A Café in Boca.* Huntington Beach, CA: Tebot Bach.

———. 2007b. "From Saucers." In *A Café in Boca*, 46. Huntington Beach, CA: Tebot Bach.

———. 2012a. "A Disease." In *The Marriage of Portuguese*, 4. Expanded ed. North Dartmouth, MA: Targus.

———. 2012b. "Fado." In *The Marriage of Portuguese*, 7. Expanded ed. North Dartmouth, MA: Targus.

———. 2012c. "Sugars of Terceira." In *The Marriage of Portuguese*, 4. Expanded ed. North Dartmouth, MA: Targus.

———. 2012d. *The Marriage of Portuguese.* Expanded ed. North Dartmouth, MA: Targus. Originally published 1978.

———. 2012e. "Sam Pereira, The Real Thing: Interview with Sam Periera." By Millicent Accardi. *Portuguese American Review* (April 2012). Posting discontinued.

Pessoa, Fernando. 2002. *The Book of Disquiet.* Edited and Translated by Richard Zenith. New York: Penguin Classics.

Sousa, Brian. 2012a. "One Night in Salvador." *Quiddity International Literary Journal* 5, no. 1 (Spring/Summer): 116.

———. 2012b. "Brian Sousa: Sempre p'ra Frente (Always Forward)—Interview." By Millicent Accardi. *Portuguese American Journal* (September 7). http://portuguese-american-journal.com/brian-sousa-sempre-pra-frente-always-forward-interview/.

———. 2013. *Almost Gone.* North Dartmouth, MA: Targus.

Zenith, Richard. 2021. *Pessoa: A Biography.* New York: Liveright.

Invention as Discovery

An Essay on Latino/a Poetics

ANDRES ROJAS

for Michele Boyette and Melinda Rojas

I

I WAS BORN in Cuba, heir apparent to the Spanish of Miguel de Cervantes and Sor Juana Inez de la Cruz, Quevedo and Gabriela Mistral. My schoolmates and I were assigned José Martí's "simple verses" almost as soon as we could read; we had memorized many of them starting in kindergarten. Calderon de la Barca awaited us in sixth grade, Nicolas Guillén and Antonio Machado in seventh. I read Rubén Darío on my own, on a teacher's recommendation.

I would go on to write poetry as an adult but not in my childhood language. When I was thirteen, my mother brought my sister and me to the United States; I was young enough to pick up English quickly and became fluent within two years. The new language came easily to me, and I slipped into it effortlessly. By age sixteen, I no longer dreamed in Spanish. I finished high school in English, went to college in English, lost my virginity in English. Eleven years after arriving in the United States, I found myself in a poetry MFA program. I read poetry, wrote poetry, taught poetry, finished my thesis, and tried to publish poetry all in English. Except for reading and talking about my favorite Spanish-language authors (Federico García Lorca, César Vallejo), Spanish disappeared from my creative life.

Because I was Cuban-born but writing in English, the label Latino/a poet was thrust in my direction. And eventually, I sat down to write this essay about Latino/a poetics.

II

As far as I can tell, *Hispanic* originally meant anyone ethnically Spanish (meaning from Spain) or from a Spanish-speaking country, whereas *Latino/a* indicated a Hispanic from Latin America (Mexico, Central America, the Caribbean, and South America, including Portuguese-speaking Brazil). However, the US Census Bureau now lumps the terms together as one ethnicity ("Hispanic, Latino, or [of] Spanish origin"), not quite a "race" such as the uncomplicated "White" or the aggregate "Black, African Am[erican] or Negro"—some definitions are more exclusive than others—but significant enough to merit its own line in the questionnaire. Per the latest census figures, most Latinos/as are of Mexican descent (63 percent), followed at a very distant second by Puerto Ricans (9 percent) and Cubans and Salvadorians (just over 3 percent each). Of course, *Latino/a* is a US category: there are Nicaraguan or Spanish-language poets in Nicaragua, but there are no Latinos/as poets there. Likewise, there are no Latino/a poets in the Dominican Republic, Panama, or Argentina, only Dominican, Panamanian, and Argentinian poets. For good or ill, Latino/a poets exist only in the United States and write in English, even if they let Spanish visit their poems at times.

Is there such a thing as a distinctly Latino/a poetics? Definitions abound. I like Ilan Stavan's best: Latino/a literature, he wrote, is about "the tension between double attachments to place, language, and identity" (2011, preface). I certainly recognize that tension in my poetry. I would add "loss" to Stavan's list of double attachments: What do I lose in order to gain something? And what do I gain when I lose something? But just as no one exists outside power (apologies to Foucault), no one exists outside double (or triple, or quadruple) attachments to something. It's just a matter of degree. In this respect, how is being a Latino/a poet different from being a poet of any other origin?

Many of my poems do reflect the constant tension of renegotiating an identity that I know is and will remain fragmented. Writing in English in the United States has meant that I have ceaselessly tried to fashion a whole that will more or less hold despite the forces pulling it in several directions. And more than that: I am aware, as an immigrant non-native English speaker, that I can't possibly find protection, at least not for long, in the illusion that a whole, stable identity is possible. Quite the contrary; my identity even as a Latino/a is a constant renegotiation of an illusion, and I know it.

III

Transitioning from Spanish to English is relatively easy; they're both Indo-European languages, share an alphabet and a great deal of Latin and Romance (mostly French) vocabulary, and came conquering to the Americas. To this day, Spanish and a number of "New" World languages appropriated through it remain the largest source of loan words for American English. Consider alligator, barbecue, cafeteria, desperado, embargo, flotilla, guacamole, hurricane, iguana, jade, key (as in a small island), lasso, mosquito, nachos, oregano, patio, quinoa, rodeo, silo, tobacco, vertigo, and of course, Zorro. One may also think of Spanish as a transitional language in the seizure of North American territory from its indigenous populations: present-day Arizona, California, Colorado, Florida, the southeastern corner of Louisiana, Nevada, New Mexico, Oklahoma, and Texas were occupied by Spanish long before American English forced its way there.

Pronouncing English, however, entails a different level of intimacy altogether. I was, as I soon found out, too old even at thirteen to shed my Cuban-Spanish accent fully—I speak English like a foreigner, and people notice. I am often asked where I'm from, often enough that I have a pat response. "I live in Florida now," goes my well-rehearsed answer, "but I am originally from Cuba." Alexis Romay (like me, born in Cuba) has written of using the same phrase: not "I am from Cuba," but "I am originally from Cuba." To paraphrase Romay, our past has become our origin; my first thirteen years are no longer part of me except as the origin of a different me, the current me, the "real" me. Who I am now is no longer from Cuba, though it once was; that "original" me doesn't exist anymore.

And yet it does; my non-native accent, though slight, is there for the world to hear. Some words trip me if I speak too fast ("grahvel" for *gravel*, "dohve" for *dove*). My tongue, on its own initiative, wants to pronounce *crow* like *plow*. Seiko (as in the watch) comes out "psycho." *Focus* is problematic. *Sheets* demands great care. To this day, even after decades of fluency in English, almost every sentence I speak tells me I am not quite at home in my adopted tongue. I joke that I traded a language for an accent.

But it's not a joke; every poem of mine I read aloud, and I recite each one dozens of times as I work on them. It reminds me that I am not the original thing when it comes to English, not really, not one hundred percent. I am something else. I am something other. I may be writing in English now, but originally, I am from another language. And I can't shed that "originally" quite as easily as most of my past.

IV

Identity may be an illusion, but I have to admit it is a useful one, particularly for anyone wanting to bring poems into the world. As a student and would-be writer in the United States, I could not help but notice that my last name didn't quite match those of the authors we studied. We did not cover a single poem by a Latino/a in any of my undergraduate creative writing or literature classes (we did cover one Jorge Luis Borges short story, "The South," though he isn't a Latino/a writer; he was born and lived primarily in Argentina and wrote in Spanish).

I might not have thought consciously about whether I belonged in English, but I remember how important the "Carlos" in William Carlos Williams seemed to undergraduate me; it caught my eye immediately, on first sight, a beautiful thing to behold. When I discovered that his mother was from Puerto Rico, I felt a kinship his last name could not dispel. (William Carlos Williams's mother, Raquel Helene Rose Hoheb—or should that be Raquel Elena Rosa Hoheb Jurrar?—was of Basque, French, Dutch, Spanish, and Jewish descent, a one-person ethnic stew.)

In the absence of Spanish surnames among the writers I was reading and reading into, it became important to me that Jack Kerouac spoke Québécois French at home before learning English at age six; he was not at ease in his new language until his late teens. There is evidence he began *On the Road* in French, a language in which he wrote two unpublished novels. I also noted the twin facts that Joseph Conrad did not become fluent in English until his mid-twenties and Charles Simić until his late teens. Unique among my finds in my search for non-native English writers was Carolyn Forché: though born in Detroit, she became a member of my group of outsiders after Kevin Bezner, a professor at the community college I attended, gave me *The Country between Us*. Forché, I felt, was writing about my experience, and her last name was foreign enough to seem welcoming to me. When I say "writing about my experience," I don't mean her El Salvador poems—they were not about me, though I appreciated someone writing them; the poems that spoke to me directly were the ones about urban blight, poverty, and depression. Her poem "City Walk-Up, Winter 1969" captured my life in the United States, 1980–1988, perfectly, despite our different ethnic backgrounds and her lack of a Spanish surname.

As a graduate student, four or five poems by Pablo Neruda in one class session were as close as we got to a Latino/a poet, though of course, Neruda visited the United States only once and wrote exclusively in Spanish. When Dionisio Martínez came to read at the University of Florida, I made sure to go see him, though I would never read his work; he was the first Latino/a poet to give a reading anywhere near me. This was some six years and a dozen or so poetry readings after I had begun writing poetry myself. But it wasn't until I started to teach creative writing as a graduate student that I went out of my way to find Latino/a poets to include in my syllabus. Actually, I didn't have to search too far: several of the anthologies I had access to included poems by Lorna Dee Cervantes, Alberto Ríos, Sandra Cisneros, and Gary Soto. I made sure their poems made it into my classes.

As for my own work, I often questioned whether I was much too naïve to insist on writing poetry in a language unknown to me during my childhood. The crafting of a poem requires such intimacy with language that having spent my first thirteen years speaking Spanish seemed an insurmountable barrier to writing poetry in English. To this day, it's not only my accent that trips me; sometimes when I scan a line, it's difficult for my non-native ear to get the subtleties of English stresses right. I can manage it with some work, though. Mostly.

And that is what was really at stake during my MFA and for almost a decade thereafter: I knew I did not have (that I would never have) the native ear of, say, W. B. Yeats, Robert Frost, H. D., or Seamus Heaney. I could hear how they made English sing; I just couldn't seem to do it myself. It was one more thing to doubt. Who was I, this accented foreigner with a clunky ear, to dare to try to write poetry in English? Was it not a foolish thing to do, ultimately a waste of time?

But I loved English best as a medium for poetry then, and I love it even more now. It can say so much so efficiently with its abundance of one and two syllable words, not to mention the riches offered up by its fifteen-plus vowel sounds (not counting *y* or diphthongs). Its subtle stresses (as compared to singsong Italian or flat-footed Spanish) roll almost effortlessly along, its rhythms easy to mold into almost anything. To paraphrase Susan Sontag, English is a language that doesn't break when you bend it.

So you're not a native speaker, I told myself. Some native speaker poets have a wonderful ear, some not so much. Go forth and do your best anyway. Who knows what may happen?

Maybe your Spanish roots will add something of value to your poetry. And yet. And yet . . . The question, of course, still remains: Am I the right instrument to perform in such a language? I don't know. All I know is that reading the work of Latino/a poets gave me hope that I might just be able to do something worthwhile in English as so many of them had. I needed a tribe, and thus I invited myself into theirs. Though they had no inkling of the difference they made, I knew they were out there, and that was vital to know as I tried to make my way out there too.

V

Shortly after finishing my MFA, I read Jonathan Weiner's nonfiction book *The Beak of the Finch*. I was struck by the story of a fledgling bird abandoned by his parents and adopted by finches of a different species. This finch grew up among his adoptive kin, learning their particular songs. When it came time to breed, the finch tried out the mating calls he had learned with apparent great success: a female appeared quickly and approached for a closer look.

Unfortunately, the songs the male finch had learned attracted a female of his adoptive kin, not of his own, and she had no intention of mating with a male from a different species. She soon lost interest and flew away. Again and again the finch sang the mating songs of his adoptive species and managed to attracted a female; again and again she flew away after closer inspection: right songs, wrong singer. A pity; here was a beautiful male in the prime of his breeding life who would never pass on his DNA. I underlined and pondered this passage often.

Soon thereafter, I happened to read Reinaldo Arenas's autobiography, *Before Night Falls*—in Spanish, of course. In it, Arenas spoke of Cuban American writers who lived in New York, wrote in English, and thought of themselves as part of the Anglo-American literary tradition. Mules, Arenas called them, hybrids who produce nothing worthwhile, have no authentic voice, and will leave no legacy. This passage, too, I underlined and pondered.

I am happy to report that since then, I have gone on to "discover" Latino/a poets enriching Anglo-American letters with their work: Ricardo Pau-Llosa, Rigoberto González, Eduardo C. Corral, Ada Limón, Ruben Quesada, Rosebud Ben-Oni, and Natalie Diaz, to name a few. (I include Diaz because while she seems to identify primarily as Navajo American, her father is of Spanish descent, she has a number of Mexican relatives, and she grew up listening to her paternal grandparents speak Spanish.) Twenty years after I finished my MFA, Richard Blanco became the first Latino/a poet to read at a US presidential inauguration. Two years after that, Juan Felipe Herrera became the first Latino/a US poet laureate. The question of whether at least some of us belong in English seems to have been answered.

I have tried not to ask too much of my Latino/a poet discoveries. They represent a cornucopia of voices and identities, and I don't expect any special gestures from them: they may or may not use Spanish in their poetry; they may or may not write about migrants, or *balseros*, or political prisoners. I don't expect them to say "I am Latino/a" in every poem. It's enough that their last names are like mine, that like me, they came to American culture via a Spanish one, even if at various removes, and that like me, they are trying to make poetry in English. They were my friends when I needed them, though I have met less than a handful of them in person. I can only hope to return the favor to others who may feel they have no business writing in English, whatever other language they speak and whatever ethnicity they hail from.

VI

After having identified myself as a Latino/a poet (I came from Cuba, I wrote poetry in English), I of course began to question how much of one I actually was: I was granted legal residency upon arrival at the United States, and my subsequent path to citizenship was relatively painless; I can pass for white if I don't speak; I have never felt the institutionalized racism faced by African Americans and Hispanics more obviously brown than me; I have very seldom experienced personal racism. Moreover, I don't use Spanish in my poetry, and most of my work is concerned not so much with exile or immigration or discrimination but with privileged, commonplace interests—the origins of consciousness and the inevitable cycle of birth, love, loss, and death. I am more interested in Old and Middle English than in Spanish, and my allusions run to the Bible and classical antiquity rather than to the Afro-Cuban culture into which I was born. So be it, I told myself. I am originally from Cuba, the United States is my home now, and I write in English. That will have to do. That will have to be Latino/a enough.

By then I had already shed my initial illusion that I could be one thing: the kid from Cuba who became a culturally assimilated Latino/a. Instead, I had come to think of my identity as inevitably hybrid; I had an intimate relationship with both Benny Moré and Charlie Parker, Celia Cruz and Billie Holiday, La Lupe and Nirvana, but I sensed that I didn't fully belong to any of them. I felt the tragedies of the American Civil War and of the Cuban wars of independence equally, and I understood both the Bay of Pigs and Playa Girón, yet I felt like a less-than-fully-vested citizen of either history.

I felt, in short, like I was no one thing fully, and that was close to feeling that I was nothing. I was partly a person originally from Cuba and partly a person reborn in the United States, and thus neither one completely. I was fluent in Spanish and English, but my non-native English accent and my clumsy written Spanish were testaments not so much to my belonging to both but to my not belonging wholly to either. I both was and was not a Latino/a poet, and so my poetry was neither hot nor cold and thus likely to be spit out. I wanted to belong somewhere, even if that somewhere was two places at once, but I suspected that I did not belong anywhere.

While muddling through (and muddling through, and muddling through) various Derrida readers, I was seized by his concept of identity as a "possible-impossible" aporia: identity as an irresolvable conflict rather than a negotiated compromise. Reading Derrida, I was struck by the idea that I was not even only partly both Cuban and Latino/a; rather, I might very well be neither, only an iteration of the interplay between the two. And that interplay, which could turn out to be permanent, was as close as I could get to an identity or a place of rest (I am indebted to Jack Reynolds for the insight that, per Derrida, whether genuine identity is either a possible or an impossible ideal is ultimately undecidable). I was not partly both the kid from Cuba and the Latino/a adult, to the extent I was a Latino/a adult at all. I was not even the conflict between them. What I was was the undecidability of that conflict: not the process itself but its refusal or even inability to resolve itself.

After Derrida, I was grateful that I didn't have to resolve that conflict. In fact, the possibility that such a conflict could be ultimately unresolvable was liberating. I was the (irresolvable?) playing out of the contradiction, among many others, of being both a Latino/a poet and not being one. And thus I belonged somewhere, even if that somewhere was an undecidable contradiction.

I have come to think of Latino/a poetics as an open prairie in which we may gather the tribes rather than as a walled citadel to be scaled or defended. As Martín Espada has written, Latino/a poetries frustrate the expectation that "literature born amid social and economic crisis by nature must be didactic and polemical, obsessed with simplistic affirmations of identity and written in a raw idiom unconcerned with nuance." (1997, ix) That such nuance exists in Latino/a poetry is partly the result of a poetics of irresolvable conflict and thus enormous, maybe even infinite, possibility: here we are as we were, as we are, and as the conflict between the two tenses will continue to make us; here is what we will do with what we have and what we will not do, for now at least, and the possibilities inherent in both. Welcome to the tribe of the future.

Welcome, in other words, to invention as discovery and to the struggle between them, to exodus as settlement and the playing out of both further into the future. Welcome to uprooting as a new rooting and to the variations that will arise thereof, unintended, unforeseen, and out of our control. Welcome to poetics that refuses to decide between this and that and which are not just both this and that but also the multiplication of the two, and all the conflicts and further possibilities such a multiplication creates. Welcome to Latino/a poetics, the poetics of identity set free from its own self-policing and unable to resist challenging any such policing from within or without.

SOURCES

Espada, Martín. 1997. Introduction to *El Coro: A Chorus of Latino and Latina Poetry*. Amherst: University of Massachusetts Press.
Stavans, Ilan. 2011. Preface to *The Norton Anthology of Latino Literature*. New York: W. W. Norton.

Notes on Writing Poetry and the Function of Language

EVA MARIA SAAVEDRA

I

IT'S SUNDAY NIGHT. For whatever reason, most of my panic attacks occur at the beginning of the week. I doubt everything. I start to think that my life is lacking something, that I must have made a wrong turn somewhere. I call my partner to tell him that while I'm happy with our relationship it's not for me. He'll usually spend an hour or two on the phone talking me through my worry and reassures me that I'm fine, most importantly that we're fine. The problem on this Sunday night in January is that he does something unexpected: he agrees with me. He tells me that he's started to feel as if he should be dating an activist like himself. I'm speechless and so I end the conversation with a curt goodbye. We reconcile within a month, but what he said sticks with me.

II

Writing poetry for me is like picking at a barely healed scab. I know I'll bleed a bit afterward but it's compulsive. That scab on my knee or elbow is just so unattractive. Who wants evidence of their clumsiness hanging out on their skin?

III

White men have the luxury of writing about whatever they want. I'm envious of them because of this. Most times, I feel that I have to prove myself or that my right to be a poet has to be earned. White men don't worry if what they have to say is valid. I worry about this every time I sit down to write. It's as if most of them never had to learn to think before they speak, and the place where this is most evident is in writing workshops. In undergrad, one white male poet decides to question my use of Spanish in my poems. It's not enough to simply make the comment, but he feels the need to say it's unnecessary and irrelevant. I'm not sure he knew that by saying that he really meant to say my voice was unnecessary and irrelevant. In grad school, another white male poet tells me my poetry could be so much better if I used the Spanish in my poems to engage canon or the only way another language is worth anything is if it's interacting with old white dudes. I'll take it a step further: white men have the luxury of disconnecting themselves from the real world completely. They don't have to worry if the night before was the last time they'll be able to sleep in their beds. I live in fear of everything. Opposition on my lips will always be read as anger, as a threat. So I check myself constantly. What I want to say is I write in English and Spanish because why not? Why shouldn't white people be made to feel like intruders for once? When a white male professor tells me I should invent my own language, I tell him I've invented the language of fuck you.

IV

Once, I wrote a poem about my fear of intimacy and my inability to connect with someone in a meaningful way. Afterward, I felt so flooded that I drank an entire bottle of white wine, cooked some plantains for dinner, and sat cross-legged in front of the television while I ate and sobbed for close to an hour. When I'm writing, I'm confronting myself entirely, the good, the bad, all of it. It makes me feel like such shit sometimes.

I think of the page as my only opportunity to be honest. I've been called deceitful several times, and I wish I could say it weren't true. If I could take a moment, I lie when the truth is too much to handle. For example, I've lied about the specifics of pregnancies and infidelity to my partners, and often. There is something difficult in saying, *No I could never want your child because you're white, so I got rid of it the second I realized your spawn hijacked my uterus* or *I fuck other men because there is something you could never give me*. I like to think of my lover as home, and to me, home will always be brown skinned, revolution written into palms, a mouth that speaks more Spanish than English. I've lied to you because I'm a coward. I'm sorry.

v

On Saturday I wake up my sister. I wake her up even though I know she went to bed at 3 a.m. and the last thing she wants is to be up at 8 a.m. She rolls over and grunts. I decide to leave her alone for another few hours. I convince her to go see the new Jesse Eisenberg movie with me because in the trailer, I'm most struck by the scene in which Jason Segel tells Jesse Eisenberg he doesn't want to be him. Shamefully, I'll admit I know nothing of David Foster Wallace's work, but I know what it's like to have that conversation. Knowing someone else once felt the same way comforts me. When we arrive at the movie theater, I wonder how many of the people surrounding me are Wallace fans and how many of them are aspiring writers. I want to understand the parts of me that are poet because I blame them for the things I haven't been able to completely get right in my life. I want to learn how to turn those parts on and off. I'm convinced that I could lead a more fulfilling life this way.

No seas grosera, Viejita tells me. I think the body of a poem is an opportunity to drop as many f-bombs on paper as possible. I just like the word *fuck*. It's perfect. It's short, but it cuts deep. *It's the equivalent of your anticuchos*, I tell her. They both embody the perfect balance between vinegar and meat, bite and substance. Besides, if I don't say it, then who will? She smiles at me. I see that glimmer of defiance in her. I think of her crossing a desert and how she slept with a married man once just because she could. We won't let our people be taken. We won't go silently. Think of this as me kicking and screaming. I'm putting up my best fight.

VI

Last year on Valentine's Day I ordered myself some Indian food and asked for extra samosas. I wanted to eat my feelings, read some Tracy K. Smith, and cuddle with my cats. I had just finished stuffing myself when I receive a text message from B., *Happy Valentine's Day. If you don't have plans would you want to grab some food?* I didn't respond until an hour later. I say sure, and he suggests we eat at my favorite restaurant, Peaches. When I arrive I find myself upset. I remember a few weeks earlier. I'm angry with myself for letting my white ex- boyfriend's comment get to me. When we sit down for dinner I notice I'm disinterested in anything he has to say. Except for an occasional nod or a polite smile, I keep quiet for most of the meal. He is in the middle of telling me about how he's taken to playing poker when I say, *Good art should make people question. As writers and artists it's our duty to make society question race, gender, sexuality—everything. There are writers that talk about beauty, but I've never considered myself to be among them. I've always wanted my words to change something. What you said the last time we spoke hurt me, it showed me that you don't respect me as a poet.*

VII

When I was younger I barely spoke. Looking back on it, I'm not sure if it was due to shyness or to the fact that I always felt uncomfortable. In first grade my teacher thought I didn't know English, and because of this she suggested I take remedial ESL classes. My mother and father fought for me then. They insisted she was wrong and refused the classes. As I grew older I came to enjoy my silence. At the age of twenty-two I'm on a plane on my way home from Texas after spending two weeks away from my family to attend a writing workshop. Earlier I had wandered around the airport bookstore and ended up buying *The House on Mango Street* by Sandra Cisneros. When I read the introduction I start crying. I've always loved books, but it was the first time I ever felt myself reflected back at me. This is the first time I consider my voice to be worth anything, and I return to my life feeling more at ease with my writing. Later I participate in a Tupelo Press's 30/30 Project for the month of December 2014. I write a poem every day for that month. When the month is over, B. asks me to take a break from writing. Apparently I haven't been very agreeable lately, and he thinks my writing is the cause of it. I call him ignorant. He says nothing. We all have our own language; it's not my fault you haven't found yours yet.

VIII

I'm not sure people realize what language can do. On most days I have to remind myself that I exist and therefore I matter. I'm not an immigrant. I don't know anything other than this country. I don't know what it's like to give up the known for the unknown, but I watch my family struggle with it every day. They raised me speaking Spanish; they tell me they raised me Peruvian. They remind me often that I learned English from watching the television as if it's this strange synthetic thing. For as long as I can remember I've viewed my life in terms of twos: inside and outside, illegal and citizen, English and Spanish. This hasn't affected me too much, the rules are simple: Spanish at home and English in the outside world. It hasn't affected me too much up until recently. I watch the news and hear about Trump's immigration reform plan. The narratives are always the same: illegal immigrants take jobs away from American citizens, or the people crossing the border are criminals. When I hear illegal, I think of my Viejita and my Tía because they crossed the border except that contrary to what most people believe they crossed the border for love. If I had the opportunity to face all the people who buy into Trump's hateful rhetoric I would say I'm just as much a citizen as any one of you are. I have just as much a right to be here. Do you realize that you're ostracizing citizens like me just because our history is different from yours? Isn't there strength in numbers? If you agree with this, why cut us out?

Aren't we important too? Language should be used for something productive; it should seek to include.

Stealing the Crown

LAURIE ANN GUERRERO

There must be those among whom we can sit down and weep and still be counted as warriors.

—ADRIENNE RICH

MY GRANDFATHER, GUMECINDO Martinez Guerrero, was born in South Texas in 1931. He had a third-grade education; he quit school at age eight so that the ten cents a week he earned would supplement his family's earnings in the Texas cotton fields. He learned carpentry in the 1950s in California's San Joaquin Valley and lived there with my grandmother for a short time.

He became a master of his craft. He was forty-seven years old when I was born in 1978, and I watched him build many things: the house he lived in, the house I grew up in, buildings all over Texas, even toys for his four grandsons and me, his only granddaughter—always with the materials and tools he had, what was accessible. He was mindful. He was deliberate. There was a kind of light that he walked with, that he worked with—nothing was above him and nothing was beneath him. And there was a special kind of magic when he spoke. He shined. He was brilliant.

I cared for my grandpa during the last five years of his life. We spent most of our time exchanging stories. I learned the mythology of the Guerrero family; he learned what was important to me: equality, education, rewriting prescribed narratives. I learned how to make pies like his mama made; he learned self-compassion. He made me rethink my ideas of men; I made him rethink his ideas of women. We were an odd pair. Sometimes we fought. Mostly, we loved. It was perfect.

When he died in 2013, I felt a sense of drifting—it was as if parts of my body, my brain, my voice wanted to follow him into the clouds. Then began the slow deconstruction of everything I had, until then, known to be true and right: my sense of self, my sense of future, of past, my sense of identity as a Guerrero, a warrior.

I knew I needed to contain everything I had, all my pieces, however I could—if not for my own sake, then for the sake of my children, my students. I only knew to turn to writing. It has been two years since he has passed. In that first year, I wrote a heroic crown of sonnets for him that has since been published, but it has taken these two years to really understand my need for a form I had been so adamantly against using.

What I knew for sure was that the sonnet was an unyielding form, and I needed something as steadfast as he was to get me through the greatest loss of my life thus far. I keep thinking, what did he think would help get me through the loss of him? I keep thinking, he never even knew the word *sonnet*—little song. And what little songs did he know that I will never hear?

But it was the sonnet, that vessel, that was the only thing I knew that was experienced enough to guide me through grief, what I have never known. What could I possibly try to understand of lost love that the sonnet didn't already know? The sonnet became for me a teacher, a rigid mentor who expected my complete seriousness. It demanded that I work hard, that while trying to capture, capture, I not get so lost that I forget I am working. In this way, the sonnet was very much like my grandpa: it expected me to work hard, to never give up, to be able to put my name, our name, proudly on something that was well crafted, maybe even beautiful. But functional, always. In this case, these sonnets functioned to keep me from losing my pieces.

These sonnets functioned to help me understand the blessing of work. Something that my grandpa, Gumecindo, knew well.

SONNET AS VESSEL: PLAN FOR BUILDING

There is much to be said about the first year of grief—small victory that the earth, in fact, did not swallow me or that the reverberating and growing black mass that has entered my body did not devour my bones. I had begun to think, heading into December for sure, five months after he died, that the sonnets were a pathway I was excavating or stepping stones that would lead me out of the morose and inexhaustible air I suddenly found myself in. And for one whole year, I worked very hard at the compartmentalizing of my grief—the organizing, the dissecting, the rearranging, the counting of lines and days, inventing new ways of spinning straw into gold.

You gotta work hard, I could hear my grandpa say under his breath, under the earth. This was good. And for months, as I wrote from my bed, enveloped in my black mass, or as I lingered in thought, silently, in hallways at parties, at events I had committed to, in groups or alone, I worked the poems. Constantly, I worked the poems.

I found myself apologizing to so many people for being "absent," for not fully participating in my life, which was part of their lives. I thought to be gentle with myself—to allow myself to indulge in whatever it was that would make me smile a little or laugh. If it didn't, I didn't need to be in its presence. It was that simple. And so, I worked the poems.

It was like this: my grandpa, who had given me most of his stories, was suddenly gone from this world. *The bad ones are going to the grave with me*, he said once. And I, who had done all I could to keep him healthy, keep his medications in line, his bills paid, didn't know what to do with all my free time. I remember lying on the bed days after he passed, feeling overwhelmed with an overabundance of love for him. He was no longer there to consume it, and it threatened to suffocate me or squeeze the life out of me so that all the parts that made up who I was were suddenly disengaging, seeking a new shelter away from me—maybe they wanted to follow him, maybe they, my hands, my heart, my brain, never belonged to me. Maybe the makeup of who I am existed only if and when I could touch my own history. He was my whole history.

I needed to contain myself. I thought immediately of sonnets—sonnets, which I had, until then, despised for their arrogance and institutionalization. So damn full of rules and inflicting of centuries of conformity. And challenging—both mentally and spiritually—as a brown woman who has watched so many of her own, grandfather included, suffocate under the weight of induced borders, labels, lines we ought not cross, assimilation in language and culture. Why would I, or anyone like me, choose to corral our voices, our spirits into a small box of someone else's making—especially when we're still having to exist in such a contrived manner in so many other aspects of our lives?

But it was this challenge that lured me. It was exactly the thing I needed to get up and get to work—employ the brain and not the heart. If I could force myself to write a sonnet, if I could switch gears for a minute, gather my brain close enough to work, then maybe I would be able to gather up the other parts of my body that I felt I was losing, too. This was important, as I had children to tend to, students. And some days, I knew, if I had to work, then maybe I'd even take a bath, comb my hair.

SONNET AS SUSTENANCE

> *If a woman wants to be a poet,*
> *she must dwell in the house of the tomato.*

—ERICA JONG

In the field between the house I grew up in and grandpa's house, vegetables bloomed—mostly tomatoes. It was my job, before dinner, to help with the watering. We dug trenches around the base of each tomato and serrano plant, and at the end of each row, grandpa extended the trench to reach the top of the next row. The water followed in a rhythmic trickle, circling each plant until it pooled over into the next. It was beautiful to watch.

I was a little girl crawling on my hands and knees ahead of the water as guide. Grandpa always stood at the head of the first row adjusting the hose or inspecting the perimeter to see what needed picking. We did this as he told me stories.

He held stories in his body—stories of picking cotton, baking pies, stringing up cabrito over a fire. He told stories about his brothers and sisters, about love and death. He told stories, because he never really learned to write. I see now that because we spent small amounts of time together—the hour between homework and dinner, Saturday morning before chores—and because he had told his stories for years, they were tight, well thought out, precise. The pacing was always perfect, and his tone always turned just right. When I discovered poetry, I recognized my grandpa's style: whole worlds in bite-sized bits. Grandpa, who learned how to record and revise in his head because he didn't know how to write, was the first and greatest poet I knew.

I've been thinking about that tomato garden for two years. How efficient it was, how calculated. And, too, how this kind of system is one that is passed down from previous generations, inherited by those who would have to find a way to feed themselves, adjusting and readjusting to the elements, to modernisms. The tomato garden was grandpa's sonnet.

And while I had a hard time finding an access point into the sonnet, I was well aware of the workings of a tomato garden. I knew, then, that what I had chosen, this working of sonnets, was like a return to that field between our two houses. The challenge that I had taken on excited me, brought the only kind of engagement that could bring me comfort. I thought, too, about the heroic crown and how the last line of one sonnet would pull you into the next, just like the water trickling over to the next row of tomatoes. I wrestled with the idea of using the form for a man who would never know it. I thought about how he created, how he sustained himself: he used what he had. It was then that I really understood the magnitude of my own education. I knew how to write. In English. I knew poetry. I knew sonnets. I, too, used what I had.

I began to think of building sonnets as my grandpa built houses and gardens. I knew I didn't want to write sonnets that looked or sounded like what anyone was used to—I wanted them to feel indigenous, easy, from the earth. I remembered my grandfather in his workshop, how he often left edges of a table, a birdhouse, a slab of sheetrock a little roughed up, never perfect. On the kitchen hutch he made for me of reclaimed wood, he left an emptied wasp's nest intact and attached: *character*, he said. I wanted sonnets like that. Roughed up and with wasps nests attached. Dampened with rainwater, smelling of dirt. My sonnets are not perfect—in the English or Italian sense—but charactered, like us . . . working class, rough, Tejano . . . maybe even beautiful.

SONNET AS RESTING PLACE

We need a dead (wo)man to begin.

—HÉLÈNE CIXOUS

There were realities I could not fathom, even as I stood there watching my grandpa's casket sink into the same dry Texas land he walked weeks before, where he was born, where I was born, where we shared meals and grew things; his body will stay there forever, he will decompose.

The fact of decomposition consumed me, and soon I walked the earth very aware that there was decomposition happening all around me. That there were probably bones and strands of DNA under the soles of my feet at any given moment—from this century or that.

Sometimes I didn't know why I was writing anymore. I wanted to lay flat on the earth and be with the decomposing things of the world, including my grandpa. It seemed the decomposition of him composed the earth. I wanted to do that. I wanted to help build the earth.

But I had to keep working. I arrived in El Paso to do a couple of readings at El Paso Community College and UTEP sixty-one days after grandpa was buried. I had never been, and I had never been so close to Ciudad Juárez, so close to the brutal femicides that had taken place there, just a few short miles from where I was. I could look over the wall and see Mexico, and probably everywhere I looked, someone was decomposing. This felt familiar. But while the land where my grandpa lay was quiet, this land was pulsating.

I remember the violet peaks and red sand of El Paso. And I fell in love with the ocotillo, a cactus I was unfamiliar with. I remember thinking that the folks in El Paso were such a sad bunch—the waiter at the restaurant, the store clerk, the mothers with their little babies trailing them in the streets, and the men who looked like they might collapse if they had to lay one more brick, swing one more hammer. El Paso was quiet, but I was so split open by my own grief that I was privy to sounds I don't think I would have heard otherwise; I could hear, faintly and in the distance, the screams of women. And maybe then, I knew what the people of the border knew.

Maybe you have to know grief to know the border. Or maybe you have to know the border to truly know grief.

The students I met from Ciudad Juárez were the ones I most wanted to talk with. How many of them had lost a sister? A daughter? A niece? Mother? Did they feel the pulsating ground? For the first time since I lost my grandfather, I felt that there were people around me who knew what I knew. More so, knew a kind of loss that I could not comprehend. I found myself wanting to pull their stories out of them, but I hadn't the strength nor the right.

I couldn't stop myself from imagining the brutal deaths of all the women of Ciudad Juárez: mothers and daughters and sisters. I lost myself, recalling details, specifically, from Valerie Martínez's book about the murders, *Each and Her*: a nipple, a shoe. All the Marias. Maybe there was a Laurie Ann? I was so close to the border—on the border, in fact—and I could hear my dad's voice, who had just lost his, insisting as he did just days prior: *Don't be alone, Laur. Don't you dare cross over. Stay on this side.* This made me angry—who was I that I might be spared? And who are you, man, to utilize your right to protect your child? And who are you, man, trying to protect me, a woman?

But I stayed. I stayed in El Paso imagining my life if I had been born on the other side; the loss I had experienced, on this side, was nothing. It was part of life. There was nothing unnatural about our loss. On I went; I imagined my own brutal, horrific death. I imagined the details they'd have to tell my children, my mama and daddy, which left me weeping alone in El Paso in September. I cried for every loss on both sides of the border that night.

I carried El Paso and Cuidad Juárez with me throughout the writing of my crown of sonnets, named in honor of my grandpa, Gumecindo. But who am I to honor one man and not all these women?

And with whom do I feel the most solidarity, really?

And note the decomposing bodies that build the earth . . . how dare I wish to build any damn thing.

But it was these women on the other side of the border who offered different lenses through which I might see the death of my grandfather and the man himself. I felt many things. I was embarrassed that I was so distraught after the loss of him. I felt shamed—by my own tears, by the recognition of his full and glorious life, that he had eighty-two years to make magic and did, often. That I had never heard him scream.

Then I thought, in their death, perhaps they would find each other. And where I had been grandpa's one and only, now maybe he would have so many granddaughters to love and be loved by. And I was jealous.

And with whom did I feel the most solidarity, really?

Then I thought, maybe now they'll have someone to protect them in death the way they didn't have in life. And then I was disgusted by my own internalized sexism. And how dare I wish to build any damn thing?

And I didn't want to write the sonnets anymore. Grief is a ruthless and complicated monster.

But I knew that—as a woman, a living woman—I had been brought to that border place to contemplate both sides, to feel the grief, to get angry, to be ashamed, and to understand that like the ocotillo, there were many things I would not be familiar with and that they would exist regardless, with or without me. The border both ravaged me and centered me: so many bodies building the earth.

I could only have understood this in El Paso.

I went back to the business of my grief, knowing that the geography of my life rendered me lucky. Social, personal, political, and cultural histories were converging here. And, too, the intersections of time and space, race and class, gender and occupation meant my job as a Tejana poet meant I had to write sonnets. I had to write sonnets in defiance—with my sadness and fear and jealousy and loyalty and anger and fear and prejudice and speechlessness and ignorance and Texas pride and shame and fear and fear that I also inherited. I had to steal the crown.

SONNET AS RECONCILIATION

> *. . . when we mourn our losses we also mourn, for better or for worse, ourselves. As we were. As we are no longer. As we will one day not be at all.*

—JOAN DIDION

In 2012, I learned that my first full collection was going to be published, and I rushed to grandpa to tell him my news. When he opened the door, he knew immediately that the dream I had been waiting for since I was a very little girl had come into fruition and he hugged me tight, tight: *You got it?* he asked. *Yes, you got it. You got it.*

I didn't have to say a thing.

We celebrated with coffee and pan dulce, and he recounted all the times he got after me for writing my name on the studs of buildings he was building, for scribbling Beatles' lyrics, lines from Sylvia Plath, Gloria Steinem quotes on my bedroom wall when I was a kid: *puro graffiti*, he used to say. But on this day, he beamed: *I shoulda known you were gonna be a writer!* he said over and over that one day in 2012 . . . *you wanted to write on every damn thing, yo se.*

That was true: I wanted to be a writer, but I also wanted him to love me—to see who I was and love me for it.

When I was working on the crown of sonnets, I often curled up in grandpa's armchair, trying to conjure his old-man smell, his gruff voice—half in English, half in Spanish. I'd bury my own cold hands under the heat of my own sad legs, dangle them off the left arm of his chair like it was his arm. I pressed my face against the wide and chesty cushion—it was almost his chest.

> When he was alive, he never held me like this.
> When he was alive, I was his right-hand man.
> When he was alive, I was all Guerrero, all warrior. I learned how to fight young.
> There was no kind of fight I didn't have in me.
> Never thought my right-hand man'd be a girl, he'd say.
> We shocked each other all the time.

When he died, things were different. And when I read the above quote for the first time in Joan Didion's *The Year of Magical Thinking*, the possibility of becoming someone other than who I was baffled me. I was taught to live up to my name. But all I really knew is I felt very tiny. Very soft. Very weak.
    I hated it.

Grandpa never saw me like this. I wondered, could he love me weak?

But I have been split open. It has taken me two years to understand that the fight in me—which helped me claim my education, helped me seek equal access, helped me demand respect, even helped me redefine the role of women in my family—has transformed into something I do not recognize.

Which is to say, I have been transforming into something I do not recognize. If my name means warrior, and I grew up fighting, then the word fight is no longer charged with the anger or the spite or the defiance it once was.

Watching my grandpa die, and then existing in a world without him, has only led me to understand the kind of transcending love that can exist between two people—beyond time, beyond space, beyond the named boxes we have created for ourselves in which to exist. Like sunlight that comes in through a window—if the building is destroyed, the light will still exist in that space. Such is our love. I didn't understand this before now.

Now, the word *fight* conjures in me love. If I am to fight now, let me fight for love like

that.

In my grief, in my being gentle with myself, I have allowed my split-open self to experience both beauty and heartache as if I am brand new. I want to be tender and deliberate. And, too, I want, with grace, to release what is no longer mine. Sometimes these ideas contradict each other.

I, too, am large.

Sometimes I think there is not enough room in the world for all my love—was this why I tried to capture it in fifteen little fourteen-lined poems? And anyway, who gives a shit about fourteen-lined poems when there is loving to be done? It is just a little song we might listen to, a little room we can enter and then leave. Does my grandpa exist in the poems? No. Does anyone?

But I think through writing. And I love this, too. It is where I go to reconcile ideas and sorrow, to relive harmony or to raise my dead. It is where I can distill the histories that move my hands to do the work, where I write new definitions for words like warrior or fight or grace, where I learned to understand my own ego and need to claim things as my own—people, places, even poetic forms.

I write. It's how I learn who I am.

Knocking on Heaven's Couplets
The Nature and Function of Poesía

NATALIA TREVIÑO

URGE

I WENT ON a retreat this past summer to Italy to go and write poetry. What an indulgence. What a cliché! The opportunity was there to live in a wonderful house in a town called Giove, just forty minutes from Rome. I wanted time and space to play with the poems I felt coming, poems about the Virgin Mary, my grandmother, dealing finally with her death and her life, and some miracles that have been associated with the journey through these new poems. I wanted to fully engage with the poetry and do nothing else.

FEAR

For me, planning this trip took great courage, even if it seems like it was a no brainer. I am married, a mom, a teacher, and not big on traveling alone, not big on that at all. But my teenage son was old enough to handle time away from me. Because he had been to Italy, he understood my motivation to go. My husband was not an obstacle at all. He was supportive, not thrilled, but kind and encouraging. My parents were both alive and healthy as could be. No one was on a respirator, and no one was leaving in the middle of the night causing a Silver Alert.

All of this meant I could easily go if I could get the huevos to do it, and so logic and reason caused me to book my ticket. If emotion had been in charge, though, I would not have done it. I was full of fear. In fact, I booked my ticket knowing it did not mean I was going. Just like being pregnant never really meant I was going to have a baby for sure. I was pregnant four times. I had one child and lost three babies. With the first loss, I learned that pregnant does not equal baby. And for me, a ticket to Europe does not equal trip. My e-ticket was not my actual ticket. My real ticket was my father's blessing. He was my only resistance, the one true obstacle to my going. He was that powerful.

PRETEXT

I had the money saved to do this, the time I had to open up to go; the elements in my life for this to happen were all open and ready for this trip to become a reality. I daresay the Virgin Mary was coaxing me to go, but that series of miracles really belongs in another essay. My father had anxiety about most of my career and writing-related activities. If I drove downtown for a poetry reading, I was asking to be murdered. If I went to AWP again, I was going to get fired from my job. If I got my MFA in a low-residency program, my son would become an orphan from the many plane rides I would need to take because at least one of them would inevitably crash. If I went on a short vacation with a friend, my husband would surely leave me. I had twice seen his anxiety take him to the hospital. Trouble breathing, high blood pressure. No real explanation. He got worried, he went to the ER, so telling Dad about Italy was my only huge mountain to climb for this trip, but thankfully, I did climb it about three weeks before I left. After much whining and procrastinating about telling him and fearing his reaction, he held back on the frightening predictions about my trip, told me how wonderful it would be, asked me where I would be traveling to while there, and then reminisced about his time in Italy back in the early sixties, before he married my mother.

Usually, his predictions about hurricanes, terrorists, and other disasters would come about forty-eight hours after I told him I would be taking a trip. So I knew his initial positive response to my trip would shift into fear, and then it would shift into a call for me to cancel. And then there would be guilt, and then worry I was causing him possibly too much anxiety, enough to take him back to the ER, and then a very likely canceled plane ticket. Forty-eight hours turned to seventy-two, and then to several hundred hours, and silence. He refrained. There was no resistance. Not one word. No headlines or links to articles about Isis emailed to me. No texts asking if I was sure I needed to go, asking why I needed to be gone if I am just going to write, no nearly tearful voicemails about how I need to think of my son, my marriage, my safety. He had given it a full blessing from the moment he heard about it.

COMPOSITION

That would be the last time I would worry about telling him about a trip. His heart stopped suddenly the day after I arrived home from my trip. The anxiety I mentioned? I beg to think that it was not the cause. Thankfully, I had spent that day with my parents, wanting to see them immediately after I got home! I was proof, proof my trip was a good idea. Was his death a perfect mercy, an answered prayer for instant death after his amazingly health-conscious life? I beg to think that was the cause. I will never know. The first thought, though, shatters me. I hate to even mention it, but as I consider the nature of poetry, I think about this story, how it is like a poem, a natural poem, a poem made out of life itself and death too. And for me poetry and his end of life are eternally linked, as they should be. After all, isn't poetry there to assist us with wonder about the impossible? To give language about the unknowable? To give clarity above all? If not, then many of us would be out.

 This story makes me think, what is it about poetry that made me want to undertake a journey that could literally risk my father's life? Before I traveled, there was urge, fear, pretext, and then decision and action. Is this also the process of poetry? Is composition always happening in our lives? Of course it is. Is poetry? Yes, I believe it is too.

FEAR AND RESULT

I had to remind myself over and over again that he was not ill, that I was not risking his life. And yet I told many friends that I was going on a trip that might kill my father. I could feel it, and I felt that if I said it, my fear would back off. Dad had just mowed the yard before I left, for Christ's sake, and he told me it made him feel exhilarated, and then, well

He took his last breath just three weeks later, just over two hours after he sent me a YouTube video about how to download this type of file to that type of drive, so he could see my photos of this trip. He wanted to see the photos at his own pace on his own computer and fully expected them on a flash drive by the next time I saw him.

ISN'T POETRY JUST ANOTHER TYPE OF FLASH DRIVE?

Why was poetry so powerful for me that I wanted to be thousands of miles away from my own study and bed to write from another desk, or while leaning on another headboard, all morning or all night long? Why would I go to such lengths and expense? Why did this poem turn out to be so sad? Is it God's poem? Is God writing us just as I write this essay, to learn? To store us so that we can be observed at his pace? I want to answer that question by looking at what is poetry, anyway?

ANSWER

When thinking about the nature of poetry, I am reminded of my rhetoric class in which we study Aristotle for about five seconds. He was concerned with the nature of things and their function, and in his work *Physics*, he developed the idea of the four causes in order to know the nature of something in the physical world. The first question he asked was, What is the material cause? This is the thing it is made of. Poetry is basically made of what Heather Sellers calls word packages. Crudely put, it is made of literary devices. The second question he asked is, What is its formal cause, the thing that formed or designed it initially, that made it possible to exist? I would say inspiration. Inspiration leads to poetry, and form and structure ultimately shape it.

Next he asked, *What is its efficient cause*, the thing that brought it into matter, the producers of it? This would have to be the poet or the higher power that the poet is channeling, yes? The poet is the cobbler at work here and hammers at it. The *efficient* cause may also be what Stephen King calls the seat of the pants in the seat of the chair, the act of composing, revising, workshopping, revising, until wham, it is done. The shoe fits over a most grateful foot.

Aristotle's last question was, What is its final cause, the thing's purpose? Why was it built? To teach and delight, right? As Horace put it in his *Ars Poetica*, "The aim of the poet is to inform or delight, or to combine together, in what he says, both pleasure and applicability to life." This is why I I have to include my father in this essay. If the nature of poetry cannot combine applicability to life, then I am done.

BETTER ANSWER

Anzaldúa, Mora, Corpi, Cisneros, they might have another say about the final cause of poetry. I think even Aristotle would tell me to get back to work, stop comparing poetry to physics, On this question of the nature of poetry, what can I possibly add to what Anzaldúa said about poetry, divinity, and creativity in her work *Borderlands*? Is it really useful to you for me to be in conversation with her on this matter here on these pages?

What could be more important than to listen to her and then apply her theory to justice, to creativity, to the mastery of our long awaited and transcendent time as Latinos with a voice and a unique experience that can actually heal the wounds of world? She said this in many languages and through multiple disciplines. She can easily be the final word on the nature and purpose of poetry. For her, poetry is beyond binary, is functional, and is sacred: "In the ethno-poetics and performance of the shaman, my people, the Indians, did not split the artistic from the functional, the sacred from the secular, art from everyday life . . . The ability of story (prose and poetry) to transform the storyteller and the listener into something or someone else is shamanistic" (1999, 66).

Shamanistic. A shaman is a person who does divination, healing, and who might even influence spirits. There are many forms of the shaman, and by calling it shamanistic, Anzaldúa is pointing to the spiritual place from which poetry comes, the God-space, the sacred, the realm that is impossible for humans to understand, and with this poem, offer clarity and healing, as all good shamans do.

WE ARE UNDER CONSTRUCTION

I spent one day in Rome while I was on my retreat. I did not want more, and I could not afford more, because the days were for writing, and they kept shrinking like cling-wrap with each passing moment. I had to do Rome in a day, and I knew that there was too much to see, do, want, cherish, and of course bask in while there. When I am going to a place like that where I know I will be overwhelmed, I just let go of control. I let go. I could research like mad, arrive at all the places on a set schedule, know everything about the place before I get there, decide to taste all the right things, and organize the itinerary like a travel agent would, but that is not traveling for me. The unknown unfolding is much more interesting to me than the known desire or outcome.

I even approach my writing this way, which makes it terribly fun to do even if my drafts look like a construction site, and please, I have to say to myself as I tinker with the draft, "Excuse our mess, we are under construction." Since it was Rome, though, I knew I wanted to at least see the Vatican, at least go the site and see what the building looked like. If it was possible, take a moment with *la Pietà*, a sculpture I marveled at in college, in grad school, and now that I am into Mary, even more. I knew I wanted to visit the Sistine Chapel too because of course, it is the Sistine Chapel. My son had seen it on his high school trip. I had to keep up with him at least. My sister-in-law who took me to Rome is practically a Roman native, though Californian by birth. Neither of us knew what I would get to see, how we could handle any kind of crowd, and of course how we would handle the inevitable attack on the Vatican that my dad predicted months before when my son was visiting this exact same spot. Tensions in Rome were actually building in March and during the late spring, and I told my Dad, "I am only going to Rome for a few hours." He was paranoid, yes, but never without a good dozen news stories to back up his claims. As we walked up to the white columns, we saw thousands. The line to get into the Vatican, someone told us, was eight hours long. Vatican out. St. Peter's, *Pietà*, see you next time. The Sistine Chapel, then, still a possibility since it is another building entirely and all the way on the other side of the Vatican where no one goes. Right. But it had to be explored at least. Is this like writing a poem? I hope it is clear that we are writing a poem here with this story, that we are going for something, not sure why, but pulled in by the idea of a mental orgasm with beauty. Is that it? We walked around the block to the side entrance to the

Vatican Museum, which *houses* the Sistine Chapel and tons of other art my sis in law assured me would knock my socks off. The train ride there knocked them off already. My socks were long gone. I just wanted to see the Sistine and get the heck out of this big and scary city, get back to our safe house in Giove, and go and write some more about Mary.

My formal cause, then, if we are to examine the nature of this journey, and yes, all poems I also believe are journeys, was to explore art I had studied deeply long ago, and I have given up being picky long ago, so this chapel, this object that yes is the ultimate tourist spot and no isn't totally about Mary had a hold of me as I walked up the long uphill sidewalk, feet already starting to ache from the walking from the train, to the Trevi Fountain, to the Pantheon, to the best gelato in the world, Crispini, right next door to, yes, another Basilica dedicated to Mary, Basilica di Santa Maria Sopre Minerva, all about her, an astonishing tribute to her, yes, candles lit for my great-aunt and my grandmother and then for all of us down here in any kind of murk or suffering, done. Through hawkers selling pricey tours and using fear mongering to get me to buy with them, through doors and floors, and lines, I finally got headphones and was about to see this thing quickly so I could go home and write about it.

You can clearly see that this is not how we should go about writing a poem. That I had no plan, no patience, and was far too aware of my physical limitations to immerse myself with the sacred, so that I could transfer it all as a good shaman could.

CALIBRATING THE BODY

If you have ever been to the Vatican Museum, you already know what happened. If you have never been there, take note. There is no such thing as a quick walk in to see the Sistine Chapel any time soon after you endure the line and the ticketing processes.

The museum is more like a million-foot-long corridor that is actually a human channel, able to process thousands of people second by second, walking to the same exact destination as you, which is at the end of thousands and thousands of works of art that are priceless, and thousands and thousands of steps behind thousands of people who are in the same state of heaven as you, ankles hurting, necks up, mouths agape, and, yes, stopping to take in yet another several-hundred-foot-long set of tapestries before the next small room filled with more priceless pieces takes yet another breath away. Breathing slowly, enjoying the shit out of this space, even though my body was crying out for a rest, I waded through the shocking collection of sculptures and paintings that of course, each in its own right, was the result of a fabulous creative effort that occurred not very long after our old friend Aristotle was talking about art, poetry, and drama, and of course, physics and science. If art is a shaman, then this museum is a shaman's convention, much like the AWP book fair, but where you are reading every book that is on display at light speed because your eye can actually take it in all at once.

It did seem, after hours of walking, wading, stopping to gasp, taking a photo, weeping to myself, listening to the tapes about the rooms and who painted this set of frescoes and why, that the palatial corridors got smaller, and then the stairs came. The signs "Capella Sistina" became more frequent. I was getting close, just as you do when you get close to a poem being done. You feel it. The rooms are not as vast. The cuts and stanzas are more manageable, and you are about to behold this wonderful room in one reading, and then, I don't know if this happens to you, but it sometimes happens to me, and it did here this day, a massive collection of modern art donated to the Vatican appears in a nondescript gallery. Afterthoughts? Matisse. Picasso. Chagall. Rare drawings of the Virgin. Modern sculptures. It was practically an assault of what my senses could take, on my time. It was terribly unfair. I had to make cuts, choices. I am here for one thing only, I said to myself. No distractions. Oh, but look how he painted her, so voluptuously, so sad. I had to keep moving. I had a train to catch. And then more rooms of modern art I had to walk by because my throbbing feet could literally not handle this walk any more. And yes, I wore smart shoes, but maybe they were not smart enough for this walk. I know I wasn't, and sometimes it is like that, when the poem is smarter than you, and you have to let go enough to trust it to say what it wants to say.

Then, after steps up and down, the walk opened up into a chapel covered in story. My son's description of it floated in my head. "Mom, look. There is his *hand. There* is the crack. There is a brain that looks like a heart. There is so much, and it's not a big room at all, Mom, is it? It's not what you would expect." I heard guards repeating loudly and in English the phrase, "No photos. Silence." Oh, English, thank you for echoing your rules through these sacred artifacts.

It was understandable. These men were corralling at least two thousand people who were in various states of awe, wonder, craning their necks, and I had to wonder, were they all possibly in as much pain as me? Their feet? They had to take this walk too, and probably more slowly because, yes, I was whipping by people as much as I could, but no. I stopped and stopped, and stopped. It was just. Too. Much.

Why am I talking again about my pain and not this glory? What does that have to do with the topic? Isn't it clear that the pain is a metaphor by this stage? That the pain all along has been in the background of this creation of this trip. And that without this pain, I would simply notice less. And I am not saying the pain is essential or good because, no. It was not good. I felt old and alone. I was old. I was alone. We have to be alone when we write, and well, if we are old too, we are allowed to stride, right? And wear comfortable shoes?

The headphone narrator man said something that will help me as a poet for the rest of my life. This is not a great paraphrase, but he said something like, *What Michelangelo believed was that the human body was the only way to understand God*, and that is why the people are all nude or 99 percent nude. Of course this is true. Of course poets have known this for years, for generations. Use the body. Bring the poem to life by evoking the body into the images or the narrative. That was it! That was my bright spot in Rome, that was worth all the trouble, and that is something I could have read in any art history book because headphone man is only giving generic and flattering information about these Renaissance artists.

So I walked out never to return again, satisfied with my trip to St. Peter's, Rome, and even held three rosaries in my hand, which I bought on mile one of the corridor and was hoping someone close to the Pope would bless. Unfortunately, no prete was available in the Sistine, or at the exit, and headphones soon were dropped in a thank you bin, and I was out. Lesson complete.

THAT WAS NOT THE LESSON

As I was making my way out, I saw a small counter selling something, which I spotted because I was hoping somewhere around me there would be a man in cloth who could bless my little rosaries, someone in a shop maybe ready to bless it for maybe two more euro. What they were selling was not blessings, but tickets, tickets to climb to the cupola. The cupola. The interior of St. Peters. High up. I had less than thirty minutes and about 14 percent battery in my phone. I decided it was a must. I was being led. I opened my phone to tell my sis-in-law I might be a little longer, and she had already texted saying we should meet a little later. Permission.

Payment. Up.

The guy who took my ticket said, "Are you ready? Good luck." And I thought he was kidding around because I mean, if they sold tickets, then it was obviously not that bad. Now, this moment of cockiness and certainty is exactly what a poet sometimes feels when dealing with what they think is a poem they are controlling. They went with their inspiration. They bought the ticket. They have a plan, and they even have time to go and finish the thing off, even though they have just been granted unlimited time with the Sistine Chapel. They are greedy, want more, want it all. That was me. That is a lot of creative people.

I walked up several round staircases and landed inside the most incredible space I have ever or will ever know. I was surrounded by a few hundred meters of a blue and gold mosaic, meant to be seen from the ground of, yes, the inside of St. Peters. I was at the top of it. Inside. It was kind of easy, and I got to be *this* close to heaven.

Interestingly, this space is suicide proof with a cage surrounding the walkway around the entire inside of the dome. I touched the walls. I looked down. I looked up, and I was amazed, and I think this is what we feel when we are near finished with reading or writing a wonderful poem. We are looking at its form close up, looking at the makings of this masterpiece, and we are literally touching the images and colors of the message on its walls. There are no good pictures of this space. It is too round, too impossible to capture with my dinky iPhone 5. So I walked all I could around it, looked down and had my first glimpse inside the Vatican from its duomo, from its highest interior point. What in the world allowed me to do this? Courage? Fear?

Composition? The four causes? was done. I had seen it all, and if I was fast, I could maybe go down and see the *Pietà*. I mean, it was right there, so close to this heavenly dome. I went back out and looked for a way, and I saw yet another ramp that went up the side of the duomo. It was an empty ramp, but there was no sign that said "Keep Out." Something was telling me that as long as there was an opening to go up, I should take it. Battery dying and all. And by battery dying, you know what I mean, right? I mean, this story is real, it's nonfiction, but it is also a story about the nature of poetry, about finding it through the writing of it. That is the only way. When there is a chance to go up, the poet has to say yes because the poet is one end of a very powerful magnetic pole, and the poem is the opposite end of that magnetic pole, and the two poles want to touch. The pull between them comes as lines, and those magnetic lines are a force in nature. It cannot be stopped even when the poet is a weenie full of fear, pain, and pretext. Pre-text. You see what I mean right? There is pre-text before there is text.

INTENTION IS THE ROOT OF ALL BAD POETRY

This is where I now understand the real nature of poetry. It is not in what you intended to behold. It is much greater than you could have hoped for, and you still do not know what it is, what is up that ramp, what you can behold. Poetry is like that, too, because it is such a shape-shifter, because in it, anything can be manifest in order to make sense out of the chaos in which we live. Even a small humorous poem sheds light and can be, as my great grandmother's friend Soledad said to her, "a revolution of ideas" that can change the world.

I did not know what was ahead, but it was up, and I was already as up as I could have imagined. What more up could there be? As I walked forward, the incline was kind, long, and I could feel I was walking along the perimeter of the cupola that I was just bursting over, and, truly, how much more could I burst? I was on the outside of this duomo. Can you use that when thinking about the nature of poetry, going up to the center, and then outside of it, and climb, climb. I think I am getting to what I mean here.

I wanted to see. Was there another one, a smaller duomo? Italy is all about layers. The buildings look like cakes, after all. I had no idea where I was headed, and I did not really know if I had permission to go up since I was the only one on this white corridor.

And this is how we must take to writing, too, open to the possibility of going up, possibly without permission, and yes, even when you have already seen the Sistine Chapel, when you have already touched the walls of St. Peter's enormous and glistening duomo. There is so much adventure in trusting that there is more, much more that is beyond our expectation or comprehension. This little ramp up the side of the duomo was teaching me that, and humbling me with each painful throbbing step.

ONLY THIS MANY STEPS TO GO

The ramp eventually turned to stairs that were wide and comfortable, and going up at an incline that most ambulatory people can easily do. Sure, it was uphill, but there was inspiration, hope, and wonder fueling my bodily battery to keep going, and of course these fossil fuels can keep us up until 2 a.m writing poetry, giving us that boost to proceed because ahead there has to be something. Otherwise there would be no ramp, right?

Then the stairs started to get steep, and then they started to tighten into spirals, and then the incline was not an incline but became what felt like a vertical plane. There was room for one climber at a time. By this point I did see a handful of people coming down. I knew I had permission. In fact, I saw a couple when I was in one of the vertical and tight spirals, a much older couple than me, and they were coming down, and the wife was holding her cane. I felt both a stabbing shame for fearing my own ability to keep climbing and a boost of courage. If they could, then, I . . . And then the husband said to me, "Don't give up. Only a hundred and fifty steps to go." I wished I had not heard that. I wanted to be there, there where the climbing was done. My legs had become lead by this point, and I had already stopped to rest them a few times. We squeezed by each other, and I thought to myself I could take a few hundred steps if I count to ten fifteen times. No need to pull back now, and even so, what was I going to see?

Then the ceiling above the spiral staircase became quite short, shorter than me, and I am short, and it was so low that I had to turn my head in order to climb. This is where my being five feet tall really helped, though I wondered how many people who are much taller than me and who have neck and back issues would turn away right there. I wanted to. I thought about it. I was getting out of breath. I stopped again. I told myself that stopping and looking out the tiny windows would renew the energy in my legs. My thighs no longer could lift me, and my feet were throbbing again, but again, there was that pull that is beyond reason, beyond pain. Poetry is the thing that called me, though at the time, I thought it was just a good view of something really cool. But it was poetry that was waiting above and nothing else.

OUR *ANTEPASADOS* ARE RIGHT WHERE WE NEED THEM

I saw names carved into sections of stone as I became dizzy with the smallness of the spirals and the tightness of the staircase, and the turning of my head downward to fit. There, I saw the name of a woman. Was she a great mother? Then the name of a man, a patron, an important priest? a pope? Were there bodies buried up here, crypts? There were small windows, and a climber could see outside, and just out the window, on a sort of wing extending from the building, another man's name on the decorative wing of the cupola, the upper cupola, And his name is written on top of the stone, so that it can be seen by God himself because from where I was looking, I could not even make the name out. Someone was out there with the wet concrete after climbing these spirals long before I did. I kept on.

The old poets, our *antepasados*, who came before us, who made poetry with corridos, with gardens, with huevos rancheros, who made the music of our people. We may not know or remember them as their art was not firmly cast into a concrete structure, but they are known to the universe, to the pull, and they are on that climb with us. They are gently encouraging us to keep climbing and get closer to that thing that other pole that wants to unite with us.

And there, when the calves I do not even think about were screaming at me to stop, there was a space not quite as wide as a door, and I walked up a few more steps to now be outside. Open air. On top of this world. I was looking at Rome from its cultural center, from one of its highest point. I was looking at the architectural design of the city from the inside *out*. The day could not be more clear. The gardens could not be more symmetrical, Vatican City spread from the rounded arms that hold St. Peter's Square. I was looking at the Earth from what was believed the highest point, to be God's own perspective.

I was surrounded by people, though we could all move freely. I photographed them. I photographed myself. I photographed Muslim women so my dad could see that the Muslim people at the Vatican were just like me, peaceful and relishing at being at the top of St. Peter's Basilica. There were Oriental Asian students, Spanish men, German families, all of them taking selfies the moment they came through that door, elated, proud.

All of us surrounded by an anti-suicide fence because when you are that close to God, you do. You want to leap. I could have leapt. I was already in God's poem. I was already in heaven.

KNOCKING ON HEAVEN'S CUPOLA COUPLETS

Being as close to heaven as I would ever get on this holy site, I was in awe of the brave architect poet who pulled himself through urge, pretext, and fear. Then he went to composition to build a temple all the way to heaven. And he did what poets do, graced us a new perspective by accessing what the gods and God can see. He gave us what poets hope to achieve and hope to give: clarity.

And with our poems, we have the same charge. To go from unclear to clear. Those are the two magnetic poles, and the poet is that magnetic charge that brings the poles together from urge to text, line by precious line.

SOURCES

Anzaldúa, Gloria. 1999. *Borderlands/La Frontera: The New Mestiza*. 2nd ed. San Francisco: Aunt Lute Books.

Contributors

Francisco Aragón is the son of Nicaraguan immigrants. His books include *After Rubén* (Red Hen Press, 2020), *Glow of Our Sweat* (Scapegoat Press, 2010), and *Puerta de Sol* (Bilingual Press, 2005). He is also the editor of *The Wind Shifts: New Latino Poetry* (University of Arizona Press, 2007). His work has appeared in over twenty anthologies. A native of San Francisco, CA, he is on the faculty of the University of Notre Dame's Institute for Latino Studies, where he teaches courses in Latinx poetry and creative writing. He also directs the literary initiative Letras Latinas. A finalist for Split This Rock's Freedom Plow Award for poetry and activism, he has read his work widely, including at universities, bookstores, art galleries, the Dodge Poetry Festival, and the Split This Rock Poetry Festival. For more information, visit www.franciscoaragon.net.

Millicent Borges Accardi, a Portuguese American writer, is the author of four poetry collections, *Only More So* (Salmon Press, 2016), *Injuring Eternity* (Mischievous Muse, 2010), *Through a Grainy Landscape* (New Meridian Arts, 2021), and *Quarantine Highway* (FlowerSong Press, 2022). Among her awards are fellowships from the National Endowment for the Arts, Fulbright, CantoMundo, California Arts Council, Foundation for Contemporary Arts, Yaddo, Fundação Luso-Americana (Portugal), and Barbara Deming Foundation. She founded the popular Kale Soup for the Soul reading series, cocurates the Los Angeles poetry series Loose Lips, and has interviewed over fifty writers, artists, and musicians. She lives in Southern California, in the hippie enclave of Topanga Canyon.

Contributors

Daniel Borzutzky is a poet and translator who lives in Chicago. His most recent book is *Written after a Massacre in the Year 2018* (Coffee House Press, 2021). His 2016 collection, *The Performance of Becoming Human* won the National Book Award in Poetry. *Lake Michigan* (2018) was a finalist for the Griffin International Poetry Prize. His other books include *In the Murmurs of the Rotten Carcass Economy* (2015); *Memories of My Overdevelopment* (2015); and *The Book of Interfering Bodies* (2011). His translation of Galo Ghigliotto's *Valdivia* won the 2017 National Translation Award, and he has also translated collections by Raúl Zurita and Jaime Luis Huenún. He teaches in the English and Latin American and Latino Studies Departments at the University of Illinois at Chicago.

Rafael Campo teaches and practices internal medicine at Harvard Medical School in Boston. His eight books of poetry and prose have won many awards, including the National Poetry Series prize, two Lambda Literary Awards, and a Guggenheim fellowship. His work has appeared in the Best American Poetry anthology series and in many periodicals, including *American Poetry Review*, the *Nation*, the *New Republic*, the *New York Times*, *Poetry*, *Salon*, *Slate*, and elsewhere. In 2018, Duke University Press and Hippocrates Press (UK) copublished *Comfort Measures* Only, a volume of his new and selected poems. For more information, please visit www.rafaelcampo.com.

Brenda Cárdenas is the author of *Boomerang* (Bilingual Press) and the chapbooks *Bread of the Earth / The Last Colors*, with Roberto Harrison; *Achiote Seeds/Semillas de Achiote*, with Cristina García, Emmy Pérez, and Gabriela Erandi Rico; and *From the Tongues of Brick and Stone*. She also coedited *Resist Much/Obey Little: Inaugural Poems to the Resistance* and *Between the Heart and the Land: Latina Poets in the Midwest*. She recently completed a new manuscript titled *Trace*. Cárdenas's poems have appeared in many anthologies and journals, including *Kinship: Belonging in a World of Relations*; *Hope Is the Thing: Wisconsinites on Perseverance in a Pandemic*; *Grabbed: Poets and Writers on Sexual Assault, Empowerment, and Healing*; *Ghost Fishing: An Eco-Justice Anthology*; and *POETRY*. Cárdenas served as faculty for the 2021 CantoMundo writers' retreat and as the 2010–12 Milwaukee Poet Laureate. She currently teaches creative writing and US Latinx literature at the University of Wisconsin-Milwaukee.

Contributors

Steven Cordova's collection of poetry, *Long Distance*, was published by Bilingual Review Press in 2010. His poems are forthcoming in *Hunger Mountain Review* and *Pleiades Magazine* and have appeared in *Bellevue Literary Review*, *Callaloo*, *The Journal*, *Notre Dame Review*, and *Los Angeles Review*. From San Antonio, TX, he lives in Brooklyn, New York.

Blas Falconer is the author of three poetry collections, including *Forgive the Body This Failure*, and a coeditor of two essay collections, *The Other Latin@: Writing Against a Singular Identity* and *Mentor and Muse: Essays from Poets to Poets*. His poems have been featured by *Poetry*, *Kenyon Review*, and the *New York Times*, and his awards include fellowships from the National Endowment for the Arts, the Tennessee Arts Commission, and *Poets and Writers*. He is a poetry editor for the *Los Angeles Review* and teaches in the MFA program at San Diego State University. Visit him at www.blasfalconer.com.

Sean Frederick Forbes is an assistant professor-in-residence of English and the director of the creative writing program at the University of Connecticut. *Providencia*, his first book of poetry, was published in 2013. He serves as the poetry editor for *New Square*, the official publication of the Sancho Panza Literary Society, of which he is a founding member. In 2017, he received first place in the Nutmeg Poetry Contest from the Connecticut Poetry Society.

Laurie Ann Guerrero was born and raised in the Southside of San Antonio. She is the author of four collections, including *A Tongue in the Mouth of the Dying* (Notre Dame Press, 2013), *A Crown for Gumecindo* (Aztlan Libre Press, 2015), and *I Have Eaten the Rattlesnake: New & Selected Poems* (TCU, 2021). She served as poet laureate of San Antonio from 2014 to 2016 and the poet laureate of Texas from 2016 to 2017. She is an associate professor and the writer-in-residence at Texas A&M University, San Antonio.

Juan Felipe Herrera is the author of many collections of poetry, including *Every Day We Get More Illegal* (City Lights, 2020), *Notes on the Assemblage* (City Lights, 2015), *Senegal Taxi* (University of Arizona Press, 2013), and *Half of the World in Light: New and Selected Poems* (University of Arizona Press, 2008). He is a recipient of the PEN / Beyond Margins Award and a

National Book Critics Circle Award. Herrera served as a chancellor of the Academy of American Poets from 2011 to 2016. In 2015 he received the *LA Times* Book Prize's Robert Kirsch Award for lifetime achievement. Herrera served as Poet Laureate of the United States from 2015 to 2017.

Raina J. León, PhD, is Black, Afro-Boricua, and from Philadelphia. She believes in collective action and community work, the profound power of holding space for the telling of our stories, and the liberatory practice of humanizing education. A poet and writer, she is the author of *Canticle of Idols, Boogeyman Dawn, sombra : (dis)locate,* and the chapbooks *profeta without refuge* and *Areyto to Atabey: Essays on the Mother(ing) Self.* She has received fellowships and residencies with Cave Canem, Obsidian Foundation, and Vermont Studio Center, among others. She is a member of San Francisco Writers Grotto and the Carolina African American Writers Collective. She also is a founding editor of the *Acentos Review,* an international online quarterly journal devoted to the promotion and publication of Latinx arts. She educates current and future agitators/educators as a professor of education and is a frequent guest speaker nationwide. She is an emerging visual artist and digital archivist, particularly with StoryJoy, which she cofounded with her mother, Norma Thomas. She is the lead coordinator for Nomadic Press in Philadelphia and a senior researcher and editor on various grants in education and literature. Find her online @rainaleon.

Sheryl Luna's *Magnificent Errors* (Notre Dame Press, 2022) received the Ernest Sandeen Poetry Prize from University of Notre Dame. *Pity the Drowned Horses* (University of Notre Dame Press, 2005) received the Andres Montoya Poetry Prize and was a finalist for the Colorado Book Award. *Seven* (3: A Taos Press, 2013) was a finalist for the Colorado Book Award. Recent work has appeared in *Poetry, Huizache,* and *Saranac Review.* She has received fellowships from Yaddo, Anderson Center, and CantoMundo. She received the Alfredo Cisneros del Moral Foundation Award and was inducted into the Texas Institute of Letters.

Valerie Martínez is a poet, educator, collaborative artist, and community activist. Her award-winning books of poetry include *Count, Absence, Luminescent, World to World, A Flock of Scarlet Doves, Each and Her, And They*

Called It Horizon, and *This Is How It Began*. Her book-length poem, *Each and Her* (University of Arizona Press, 2010), winner of the 2012 Arizona Book Award, was nominated for the Pulitzer Prize, the National Book Critics Circle Award, the PEN Open Book Award, the William Carlos William Award, and the Ron Ridenhour Prize. Her work has been widely published in journals, magazines, anthologies, and media outlets, including *The Best American Poetry*, the *Washington Post*, and the Poetry Foundation's Poetry Everywhere series. Valerie has more than twenty years of experience as a college/university professor. For the past thirteen years (with the nonprofits Littleglobe and Artful Life), she has worked with children, youth, adults, elders, and families in a wide range of arts and community engagement programs. From 2021 to 2022 she was the lead consultant for the City of Santa Fe's CHART (Culture, History, Art, Reconciliation, and Truth) project. Learn more: www.valeriemartinez.net.

Carlo Matos is a bi+ author who has published twelve books, including *As Malcriadas or Names We Inherit* (New Meridian, 2022) and *We Prefer the Damned* (Unbound Edition Press, 2021). His poems, stories, essays, and reviews have appeared in such journals as *RHINO, PANK, DMQ Review*, and *Diagram*, among many others. His books have been reviewed in such places as *Kirkus Reviews, Boston Review, Iowa Review, Portuguese American Journal*, and *Word Riot*. Carlo has received grants and fellowships from Disquiet ILP (Portugal), CantoMundo, Illinois Arts Council, Sundress Academy for the Arts, and La Romita School of Art (Italy). He is a founding member of the Portuguese American writers collective Kale Soup for the Soul and a winner of the Heartland Poetry Prize. He currently lives in Chicago, is a professor at the City Colleges of Chicago, and is a former MMA fighter and kickboxer. Find out more at www.carlomatos.blogspot.com. Follow him on Twitter @CarloMatos46.

Orlando Ricardo Menes is professor of English at the University of Notre Dame, where he teaches in the MFA program and edits the *Notre Dame Review*. He is the author of seven poetry collections, including *The Gospel of Wildflowers & Weeds* (University of New Mexico Press, 2022), *Memoria* (Louisiana State University Press, 2019), and *Fetish* (University of Nebraska Press, 2013), and is the winner of the 2012 Prairie Schooner Book Prize in

Poetry. His poems have appeared in several prominent anthologies and in such literary magazines as *Poetry*, *Southern Review*, *Prairie Schooner*, *Yale Review*, *Harvard Review*, and *Hudson Review*, among many others.

Juan J. Morales is the son of an Ecuadorian mother and Puerto Rican father. He is the author of three poetry collections, including *The Handyman's Guide to End Times*, winner of the 2019 International Latino Book Award. His poetry has appeared in *Crazyhorse*, the *Laurel Review*, *Breakbeats Vol. 4 LatiNEXT*, the *Acentos Review*, *Copper Nickel*, *Pleiades*, *terrain.org*, *PANK*, *POETRY*, and elsewhere. He is a CantoMundo Fellow, a Macondo Fellow, the editor/publisher of Pilgrimage Press, a professor of English, and the associate dean of the College of Humanities Arts & Social Sciences at Colorado State University Pueblo.

Tomás Q. Morín is the author most recently of the poetry collection Machete (Knopf, 2021) and memoir Let Me Count the Ways (Nebraska, 2022). He translated Pablo Neruda's The Heights of Macchu Picchu (Copper Canyon, 2014), as well as the libretto Pancho Villa from a Safe Distance. With Mari L'Esperance, he coedited Coming Close: Forty Essays on Philip Levine (Prairie Lights, 2013). His work has appeared in the New York Times, the Nation, Poetry, Slate, and Boston Review. He is a Civitella Fellow and a National Endowment for the Arts Fellow. He teaches at Rice University and Vermont College of Fine Arts.

Adela Najarro is the author of three poetry collections—*Volcanic Interruptions* (Jamii Press, 2022), *Split Geography* (Mouthfeel Press, 2015), and *Twice Told Over* (Unsolicited Press, 2015)—and a chapbook, *My Childrens* (Unsolicited Press, 2017), which includes teaching resources for high school and college classrooms. Her poetry appears in *The Wind Shifts: New Latino Poetry* (University of Arizona Press, 2007), and she has published poems in numerous journals, including the *Rumpus*, the *Acentos Review*, *Puerto del Sol*, *Nimrod International Journal of Poetry & Prose*, *Notre Dame Review*, *Crab Orchard Review*, and elsewhere. More information can be found on her website www.adelanajarro.com.

Contributors

Ruben Quesada is a poet, translator, and editor. He is the author of *Revelations* and *Next Extinct Mammal* and the translator of a collection of selected poems by Luis Cernuda titled *Exiled from the Throne of Night*. He has served as an editor and coordinator for *The Rumpus*, *Kenyon Review*, *AGNI*, *Pleiades*, and the National Book Critics Circle board. He lives in Chicago, Illinois.

Andres Rojas was born in Cuba and came to the United States at age thirteen. He holds an MFA from the University of Florida and is the author of two chapbooks and a full-length book of poetry, *Third Winter in Our Second Country* (Trio House Press, 2021). His poetry has been featured in the *Best New Poets*, *AGNI*, *Barrow Street*, *Colorado Review*, *Diode Poetry Journal*, *Massachusetts Review*, *New England Review*, and *Poetry Northwest*.

Eva Maria Saavedra is a Peruvian American poet, educator, and mother. She was born and raised in New Jersey where she currently resides with her son. She received a BA from SUNY Purchase and an MFA in writing and translation from Columbia's School of the Arts. Her chapbook, *Thirst*, was selected by Marilyn Hacker for the Poetry Society of America's 2014 New York Chapbook Fellowship. She is working on her first full-length manuscript of poems.

ire'ne lara silva is the author of four poetry collections (*furia*, *Blood Sugar Canto*, *CUICACALLI / House of Song*, and *FirstPoems*), two chapbooks (*Enduring Azucares and Hibiscus Tacos*), and a short story collection, *flesh to bone*, which won the Premio Aztlán. She and poet Dan Vera are also the coeditors of *Imaniman: Poets Writing in the Anzaldúa Borderlands*, a collection of poetry and essays. ire'ne is the recipient of a 2021 Tasajillo Writers Grant, a 2017 NALAC Fund for the Arts Grant, the final Alfredo Cisneros del Moral Award, and the Fiction Finalist for AROHO's 2013 Gift of Freedom Award. Most recently, ire'ne was awarded the 2021 Texas Institute of Letters Shrake Award for Best Short Nonfiction. ire'ne is currently a writer-at-large for *Texas Highways Magazine* and is working on a second collection of short stories titled, *the light of your body*. Visit her at irenelarasilva.wordpress.com.

Contributors

Michael Torres was born and brought up in Pomona, CA, where he spent his adolescence as a graffiti artist. His debut collection of poems, *An Incomplete List of Names* (Beacon Press, 2020), was selected by Raquel Salas Rivera for the National Poetry Series and named one of NPR's Best Books of 2020. His honors include awards and support from the National Endowment for the Arts, McKnight Foundation, Bread Loaf Writers' Conference, CantoMundo, VONA Voices, Minnesota State Arts Board, Jerome Foundation, Camargo Foundation, and Loft Literary Center. He iss an assistant professor in the MFA program at Minnesota State University, Mankato, and a teaching artist with the Minnesota Prison Writing Workshop. Visit him at www.michaeltorreswriter.com.

Born in Mexico, **Natalia Treviño** grew up in South Texas, where Bert and Ernie taught her English. She is the author of the poetry collections *VirginX* and *Lavando la Dirty Laundry*, which has been published in a dual-language edition in Albanian and Macdonian. Her work captures the voices of women who emerge despite everything that works tirelessly against them. Natalia has won several awards for her poetry and fiction, including the Alfredo Cisneros del Moral Award, Dorothy Sargent Rosenberg Poetry Prize, Literary Award from the Artist Foundation of San Antonio, Menada Literary Award from the Ditët e Naimit Festival in Macedonia, and several others. Natalia is a graduate of the University of Texas at San Antonio and the University of Nebraska at Omaha. She is a professor of English and an affiliate Mexican American studies faculty member at Northwest Vista College.

Index

About to Happen (Vicuña), 25
abuela-santa, 145
abuelo-árbol, 145
Accardi, Millicent Borges: childhood and exposure to literature, 163–64, 165–66; cultural difference established by, 86; old country traditions desired by, 82–83, 173–74; as Portuguese American writer, 163, 164–65; work, attitude concerning, 84–85
accent, speaking with, 179
accessing deep memory (term), 40
Acentos, 90
Achilles (Greek mythical character), 12
action, calling world to, xiv
activism, 58, 60, 61, 71
ACT UP veterans, 59
adaptation, 171
addict (term), 62
"Adrift" (poem), 44
adult literature, 163–64
advocacy organizations, 60
aesthetic, changing, 62
affiliation, strategies of, 54
Africa/Afrika, invoking of, 63–64
African American and Latino cultures combined, 93
African American and Mexican American communities, relations between, 27
African American communities, policing of, 34
African American writers, 64
African diaspora, 70

Africanness, 64
Africans as aliens, 141–42
Afro-Caribbean writers, 64
"Afro-Latino" (term), ix–x
Afro-Latino poets, 63–70
Afro-Latino voices, 94
Against Forgetting (Forché), 75
agency, taking back sense of, 74
Aguililla, Michoacán, 18–19
Alcalá, Rosa, 98–99
Alexander, Jeffrey C., 72
Alexander, Michelle, 142
"All Dharmas Are Marked with Emptiness" (poem), 87
Almost Gone (Sousa), 171–72
Alurista, x–xi
Alvarez, Julia, 63, 93, 98
ambiguity, 68
"American" (concept), ix
American acculturation, xvii
American commercialism, 120–21
American culture, assimilation into. *See* assimilation
American dream, 99
American English, Spanish influence on, 179
American experience, xiv
American idiom, xv
American literary tradition, Latinx impact on, xvii
American literature, xiv, xv, xvii
American poetics, 95–96
American poetry, trends in, xvi

223

American rule, resistance to, 121
"Amerindia" (Latin American macro-self), x
Anania, Michael, 162
ancestors, calling on, xi
ancestral language, loss of, 53
Andean culture and civilization, 25
"And Seeing It" (poem), 49–50
Angels of the Americlypse (Giménez Smith and Martínez), xvii, 91
"Angie Appropriates a Bar or Two" (poem), 85–86
Anglo-American literary tradition, 182–83
Anglo-Saxon worldview, jobs reflecting, 88
Anteparaiso (Zurita), 30–31
antepasados, 213–14
anthologies, publication of, 90–91
Anzaldúa, Gloria E.: border theme addressed by, 94, 108–9; on poetry, divinity, and creativity, 205; Rio Grande described by, 78; as second-wave feminist, 22–23; stories told by, xvi; "wounds" reference by, x
Aragón, Francisco, ix, xi, xvii, 40–47, 90–91
Araguz, José Angel, xi
Arbol de Blues (painting), 27
archetypal tensions, 91–92
Arenas, Reinaldo, 162, 182–83
Aristotle, 204–5
Ars Poetica (Horace), 205
"Ars Poetica" (poem), 129
art: activism *versus*, 61; folklore *versus*, 68; life changed through, 61; making, 1–2, 6–7, 87–88; poems inspired by multiple kinds of, 27–28; and politics, relationship between, 120, 121–23; role in making people question, 189
Arteaga, Alfred, 16–17
artist's work, understanding, 27
assimilation: in language and culture, 193; Latinx poet experience of, xvii; Portuguese American experience of, 87, 88, 169, 171; Puerto Rican resistance to, 121
associated language (term), 53
Associated Writing Programs conference, 90–91
associative meaning, xvi
"At the Base of the Blues Tree" (poem), 27
Auden, W. H., xvii, 4
author tools, limitations of, 2
autobiographical writing, 103–4
autonomy, struggle for, 143
Aztlán (Southwest homeland), x

Baca, Jimmy Santiago, xvi
Barcelona, 40, 42
Barnacle Love (de Sa), 170
The Beak of the Finch (Weiner), 182
beautiful *versus* ugly, art distinction between, 16
beaver and poet compared, 4
Before Night Falls (Arenas), 182–83
being, liberation of, xii
belonging, 54
Ben-Oni, Rosebud, ix–x, 183
Bezner, Kevin, 180
bilingual linguistic repertoire, 109–10
bilingual readers, 21
binary structures, 68
BIPOC poets, 128–29
black and brown aliens, 146–47
black and brown bodies, dehumanization of, 145
black diaspora in Caribbean, 63
black family, reports on, 142
black female presence, ignoring of, 66
black-Latino intersection, 69
blackness, 64
black Puerto Rican poets, 144–47
The Black Unicorn (Lorde), 66–67
Blake, William, 106, 159
Blanco, Richard, 91, 95, 96, 98, 183
Blocker, Jane, 22, 23–24
Bloom, Harold, 105

body: calibrating, 207–9; domination over, 144; fusion with earth, 23–24; interaction with, 144; overview of, 141–43; spirit and power divorced from, 146
boogeyman, 143
border: in blood, 81; crossing, 13; girls killed on, xi; grief and, 196; killing on, 75; loss on both sides of, 197; as metaphor, 94, 108; ravaging and centering by, 198; straddling, 99; transcending, 94
border crossers, 73
Borderlands/La Frontera (Anzaldúa), 108–9, 205
A Borderlands View on Latinos (Hernández-Wolfe), 74
Borderlands with Angels (Menes), 152, 160
border patrol officers, artistic depiction of, 17–18
borders, negation of, 23–24
Borges, Jose Luis, 93, 110, 180
Borzutzky, Daniel, xi
Boucher, Madam, 42–43, 47
boundary crosser, trickster (mythical creature) as, 64–65
"Bridge over Strawberry Creek" (poem), 41, 44–45, 46–47
British rule, 68–69
British West Indian culture, 68
Broken Souths (Dowdy), 32–33
Brooks, Gwendolyn, 63–64, 65
brother (term), 61
"brown" (term), ix–x
brown identity, ix–x
Brueghel, Pieter, the Elder, 15, 156

"Caliban" poems, 162
Campo, Rafael, xi, 90–91, 92–99
Cárdenas, Brenda, xii, 9–28
Caribbean, 63, 165
Caribbeanness, 162

Carpentier, Alejo, 161, 162
Catholicism, 49, 164, 167–68, 171
Catholic poets, 45–46
"Cat's Cradle without a String" (poem), 152, 153
Cavafy, C. P., 45
centaur, poetry as, 6, 7
Centennial Museum (University of El Paso), 20
Cervantes, Lorna Dee, 14, 50–51, 181
change, art relationship to, 61
Chávez, John, 91
Cheeke, Stephen, 11, 13
Cheyenne Mountain, 135
Chicago, 33–34
Chicago police, 34
Chicana, xii, 109
Chicanismo, xi
Chicano, x–xi
Chicano/a project, 14
"Chicano poetry," x
Chicano studies, 114, 128
childhood sexual abuse and molestation, 49, 72, 75–76
children born out of wedlock, 101, 102–3
Chile, 33–34
Chilean dictatorship, 32, 33, 34
Chilean nation as imaginary "republic" site, 33
Chilean poems, US reception of, 30–31, 32
"Chilo's Daughters Sing for Me in Cuba" (poem), 95
Chin, Timothy, 68
Christ, crucifixion of, 5
Cisneros, Sandra: as canonical author, 63; on final cause of poetry, 205; marketing of, 93; poetry of, teaching, 181; stories told by, xvi; works by, 189
City of a Hundred Fires (Blanco), 95
"City Walk-Up, Winter 1969" (poem), 181
Ciudad Juarez, 196–97

"Claiming an Identity They Taught Me to Despise" (poem), 68–69
clarity, 214
class consciousness, 82–89
class in America, 88
Cliff, Michelle, 65, 67–70
Cloud-Net (Vicuña), 25
"code switching," xvii
"cold country," 66, 67
Coleridge, Samuel Taylor, 105, 106
collaboration, artist/poet, 15–22, 28
colonialism, 67–68
colonization, 75
comfort zone, leaving, 74
community, trauma within context of, 73
complex identities, xiii
composition, 203
confidence, restoring, 74
Conrad, Joseph, 180
contemporary Latinx poets, xvii
contradictions, negotiating, 68
Cordova, Steven, 58–62
Corral, Eduardo, 14, 183
Correa, Eustaquio, 121
Corretjer, Juan Antonio, 120, 123, 125, 126
Cortez, Carlos, 25
Cortez, Jayne, xvi
Counting Sheep till Doomsday (Matos), 170
The Country between Us (Forché), 180–81
Couto, Nancy Vieira, 85–86
creation, xii, 80
creation process, 7–8
creative desire, image for, 65
creativity and destructiveness, balance between, 69
Crews, Harry, 154
cross, stations of the (metaphor), 4–5
"Crossing Boston Harbor" (poem), 95
crossroad, trickster at, 67–70
crossroads, poet at, 64

Cuba: cultural imperative of, 95–96; exile from, 22, 23, 24; songs, 92–93, 96
Cuban American poetry, 161
Cuban American poets, 177, 178, 179–80
Cuban American writers, 182–83
Cuban children, 22
Cuban immigrants, 150, 179–80
Cuban literature, 161, 165
Cubans, Latinas/os as, 178
cultural consciousness, 107
cultural forces, xi
cultural groups, trauma of, 75
cultural histories, 76
cultural identity, 173–74
cultural landscape, xv
cultural norms, familial, renunciation of, 125
cultural reclamation, 14
cultural self, damaged, ix
culture(s): binary structure operation within and between, 68; estrangement across borders, 97–98; hatred of own, 73; juggling, 109; learning from writers from other, 70; trauma relationship to, 74; trickster's developmental growth within, 65
curiosity, 1

dance, garments incorporated into, 20
Darío, Rubén, 105, 177
dark water, 79–80
The Daughters of Freedom, 123
Davis, Jimmy, 27
dead, naming, 35–37
dead white men, 108
Deanna Troi (television character), 139, 142–43
death, euphemisms for, 62
Death, poetic depiction of, 17
death of a loved one, 192–94, 195–98, 199–200, 203–4
de Burgos, Julia, 63, 122–23, 125, 126

Index   227

deceit, creating and unmasking, 66
decolonization, oppressor opposition to, 144
decomposition, 196, 197
dehumanization, 141, 144
De Kansas a Califas & Back Again (Cortez), 25
Delgado, Brenda Berenice, 36, 37
Delgado, Lalo, 14
depicted experience, xiv, xvi
depression, 6
Derrida, Jacques, 184–85
de Sa, Anthony, 170
destructiveness and creativity, balance between, 69
detachment, 95–96
de Vasconcelos, Erika, 172
"A Devil Inside Me" (poem), 22–23
diaspora of diverse peoples, 65
Diaz, Natalie, 183
Dickenson, Emily, 93
Didion, Joan, 198, 199
"dig into the dark" (metaphor), ix, 2
Directions to the Beach of the Dead (Blanco), 95
"A Disease" (poem), 168–69
dissidence, 31
dissociation, 73–74
domestic violence, 122
Don Clemente characters, 16
Doty, William, 69
Douglass, Frederick, xii
Dowdy, Michael, 32–33, 34
dream, ocean in, 79
dreamcatcher, 6
dreams about poems, 62
dreams *versus* creativity, 6
Drucker, Johanna, 26
Ducksworth, Alistair, 151
duende: abode of, 151; alien identity and, 147; body as vessel of, 141; creating, 152; creative bursts and exposures through, x; enabling existence of, 143; as resistance response, 142; as trickster, 138, 146; wound, attraction to, 81; writing and publishing, 145; writing with, 80
duendecillo (term), 152
Dunbar, Paul Laurence, xv, xvi
"Duty" (poem), 156

Each and Her (Martínez), 35–36, 197
earth, body fusion with, 23–24
economic violence, 33, 34
education as tool of oppression, 144, 145
Edwards, John, 53
efficient cause of poetry, 204–5
Eisenberg, Jesse, 188
ekphrasis, 12–14
ekphrastic poetry: examination of, xii, 10–12, 13–16, 17–28; paintings as inspiration for, 156; places as theme in, 40
El Barco de La Ilusión (XEJ radio comedy segment), x
El Caballero (game character) as conquistador, 17
"11th Birthday" (poem), 86
Eliot, T. S., 105, 108
El Mojado (the wetback) (print-poem pair), 17–18
El Paso, 196, 197, 198
El Salvadoran culture, 165
El Salvador poems, 180–81
emotion and story, creating mosaic of, xvii
emotions, separation between ourselves and, 80
end of life, poetry and, 203
English language: awkwardness of, 99; hegemony of, 68; as Latino/a poet dominant language, 178; merits of, 181–82; relationship with, 150; as second language, 177, 178–80; and Spanish language, pull between, 109
English-only demands, 109
English-only legislation, 102

environmental wreckage, 24, 34
equality, fight for, 54
erasure, experience of, 101, 106–7
Eshun, Kodwo, 141
Espada, Martín, 33, 63, 93, 128–29, 185
establishment, poet relationship with, xvi
ethnic (defined), 54–55
ethnic foods, 82, 86
ethnic groups, trauma of, 75
ethnicity, 52–54, 55, 56, 73
Ethnicity (Hutchinson and Smith), 53
ethnic language, 52–53
ethnic "requirements," xi
Eurocentric ideals, 124–25
events of world, poetry as response to, xv
exile, experience of, 23, 24
expressive language, Latino reverence for, 92–93

"Fado" (poem), 168
Falconer, Blas: cultural forces, war cited by, xi; ekphrastic poems written by, 14–15; as gay person, 123–24, 125–26; Puerto Rican heritage, 119–21, 122, 126; on reclaiming and honoring injured self, ix
"The Fall of the Rebel Angels" (poem), 156
families, separation from, 130
family rejection, 123–24
Fanon, Frantz, 143, 144
fear, 201–2, 203–4
"Federico's Ghost" (poem), 129
Felix, Charles Reis, 173
female-voiced speaker, hunger for, 65, 67
femicides, 196
feminists, 22–23, 94
Fernández, Amando, 160
fighter, identity as, 199–200
final cause of poetry, 205
Finnegan, Ruth, xvi

first-gen themes, 84
first person, writing from, 74, 75–76
Fischer, Barbara, 13, 23
Fishman, Joshua, 52–53, 54–55
flor y canto (flower and song): festivals, 14; genre, 19–20
folklore, 68
Forbes, Sean Frederick, ix–x, 63–65, 70
Forché, Carolyn, 75, 180–81
formal cause of poetry, 204
fragment of *memoria,* 41–42
freedom, 61, 67
free verse, xv
"Freeway 280" (poem), 50–51
French, study of, 42–43
Frost, Robert, 4, 93, 181
fuck (term), 188

Gaelic, 53
Gárate García, Catalina, 20–22
García, Rupert, 16, 19
García (Aguirre), Cuca, x
García Manzaedo, Hector, 20
García Márquez, Gabriel, 129
Gaspar, Frank X., 87, 88, 167–68, 172
Gávea-Brown, 173
gay (term), 61
gay Afro-Latino poets, 63–70
gay bilingual Cuban American poets, 98
gay Catholic Latino poets, 45–47
gay Chicano writers, 69–70
gay Latino poets, 123–24
gay poets, pioneering, 45–46
Geha, Katie, 13–14
generational histories, 145–46
generations, disagreement between, 170
gift, loss of, 6
Giménez Smith, Carmen, xvii, 14–15, 22–23, 24–25, 91
Ginsberg, Allen, 45, 153
Gioia, Dana, 45–46
girls, lists of killed, xi, 35, 37
globalization, 32–33, 94

Glow of Our Sweat (Aragón), 45
Gomez, Gabe, 52
Gone with the Wind (movie), 103
González, Kevin, 98–99
González, Rigoberto, 63, 69–70, 99, 183
Goya, Francisco, 7
graffiti artists, xi, 111, 112–13, 114, 115–16, 117–18
Graham, Philip, 165
grandparents, Spanish-speaking, 92
grief, 192–93, 196, 198
Guadalupe Hidalgo, Treaty of, 102
"Guantanamera" (song), 96
Guerrero, Gumecindo Martinez, 191–92, 193, 194, 195–96, 197, 198–99, 200
Guerrero, Laurie Ann, 14–15, 191–200
Guerrero, Rose, 20
Guinan (television character), 139
gun violence-related deaths, 31

"halfway" figure, operating as, 68
Harmonium (Stevens), 152
Harry Morgan (fictional character), 165
Hayden, Robert, 65
healing, 72, 80, 205
heat, 8
Hefferman, James A. W., 11–12
hegemony, 144
Hemingway, Ernest, 165
herida abierta (term), 78, 81
Hernández-Wolfe, Pilar, 74
heroes, bad behavior from, 60
Herrera, Juan Felipe: on being student, 113; ekphrastic poems written by, 14, 15–20; as Latino/a US poet laureate, 183; prosopopoeia used by, 17; stories told by, xvi; violence against women addressed by, 35, 36–37
hip-hop culture, 93
Hirsch, Edward, 123
Hispanic (defined), 178
historians, artists as, 114
historical hand-me-downs, 172

historical knowledge, xvi
historical scene, 108
history, writers and poets as curators of, xiv
HIV-positive (term), 62
Hofer, Jen, 35, 37–39
Holocaust, 75
home, displacement of, xv
homoerotic, exploring, 45
honesty, obstacles to achieving, 187–88
Horace, 205
horse (metaphor), 5, 7
horse, artist as, 7
The House on Mango Street (Cisneros), 189
human emotions in literature, xiv
human experience, xiii, xiv, xvi, 171
humanity, xi, 141–42
hunger, 7–8, 65, 66, 67
The Hunt (movie), 153
Hurston, Zora Neale, 68–69
Hutchinson, John, 53
Hyde, Lewis, 64–65
Hynes, William, 69
hyper-vigilance, 73

ICE detainees, 130
IDEA Project, 130–31
identity: ambivalence of, xv; claiming, x, xi; class role in construction of, 86, 88; learning through writing, 200; poetics of, 185; search for, ix–x, 184–85
ideological warfare, 144
idiomatic expression, xv
The Iliad, 12
illusion, language used to create, 102
I Love Lucy (television series), 139
image, 5, 12, 14
immigrant families in conflict, literary treatment of, 170
immigrant non-native English speakers, 178
immigrants: longing and loss experienced by, 175; rejection experienced by, 150; struggles of, 168, 169, 171

immigration reform, 190
immortals, 145–46
Incan poems, 135–36
information, knotted cords used to store, 25
injured self, ix
Injuring Eternity (Accardi), 164
injustices, 107, 129
In Play and Theory of the Duende (Lorca), 80
inspiration, 10, 27–28, 108, 156, 204
Instan (Vicuña), 25
Inter-American campus, Little Havana, 158, 159–60
internalized racism, 73, 125–26
internalized sexism, 197
intimacy, fear of, 187
Inverness Almanac, 40
in xochitl in cuicatl feasts, 14
Isla de Providencia, Colombia, 64, 70
Italy: immigrants from, 124; trip to, 201–4, 206–14

Jamaican poets, 67–70
Jones-Shafroth Act, 121
"Jorge the Church Janitor Finally Quits" (poem), 129
Juárez, Mexico, 98
Jung, Carl, 65
justice, fight for, 54

Kahlo, Frida, 15
Kale Soup for the Soul (literary reading series), 164
Keats, John, 106, 110
Kerenyi, Karl, 65
Kerouac, Jack, 180
Kim, Hyesoon, 31–32
Kingdom of this World (Carpentier), 161
King's English, hegemony of, 68
Kinnell, Galway, 155
Kirby, David, 30–31

knowledge, challenges of acquiring, 1
Korean history and politics, 31–32
Krugman, Jenny, 150

La Campana (the bell), 19
La Dame à la licorne (The Lady and the Unicorn) (collection of tapestries), 66
La desembocada, 78, 81
LaForge (television character), 139, 142
La Migra (the immigration officer) (print-poem pair), 17–18
"La Muerte" (poem), 17
The Land of Look Behind (Cliff), 67–70
language: border walls of, xii; commonality of, xvi; constructing collage of, 104; education through, 107; emotional charge of, xvi; human culture characterized by, 26; illusion created through, 102; interaction with, 144; inventing own, 187; limitations of, 104; loss of, 53; negotiating, 110; overview of, 144–45; spoken at home, 49; use of, 190
Language and Ethnicity in Minority Sociolinguistic Perspective (Fishman), 52–53
language fragments, xi, 43
"The Last Borges" (poem), 173–74
Late Rapturous (Gaspar), 87
Latin@, condition of, 99
Latin@, enthusiasm for all things, 93
Latin America, erased history of, 106
Latin American dictators, 75
Latin American writers, 106, 108, 110
Latinas, 107–8, 139
Latinidad, 51, 55, 56, 107–8, 142–43
Latino/a: black, intersection with, 69; defined, 94, 178; identity as, 178; term, 61
Latino aesthetics, xi, 92–99
Latino/a literature, 106

Latino and African American cultures combined, 93
Latino/a poetics, definition and overview of, 178
Latino/a poetics, inclusive nature of, 185
Latino/a poets, reading, 182, 183
Latino/as: Anglo perception of, 140–41; influences on, 93; past traumas experienced by, 73; Spanish knowledge of, 127–28
Latino/a story, forgotten or ignored parts of, 102
Latino/a subjects, 107
Latino/a writers, 106, 108, 110
Latino communities, policing of, 34
Latino identity, meaning of, 55
Latino people and culture, Africa relevance to, 64
Latino poem "markers," 50–51
"Latino poetics" (term), ix
Latino poetry, reviews of, 91
Latino writers: assumptions concerning, 93–94; connection to Spanish-speaking writers in Latin America, 32–33
Latino writing, reviews of, 93–94
"Latinx Aesthetics" (term), ix
Latinx, xii, xv; community, xvi, 56; culture, xiii; cultures and arts, 11; diaspora, 55; ekphrasis, 14; ekphrastic poetry, 12, 15–28; identity(ies), xiii, xvii; literature, 49–52; poetics, xi; poetry, x; poets, xiii; predecessors, xvii; writers, 129
leaders, bad behavior from, 60
Leaves of Grass (Whitman), xv
Leaving Pico (Gaspar), 167
León, Raina J., ix, 139–41, 143
León-Portilla, Miguel, 14
Leroy, Eric, 154, 155, 156
lesbians of color, 67
Letters to a Young Poet (Rilke), 149–50
LGBTQ experience, 123
liberation, 67

life, poetry applicability to, 205
life and death, cycle of, 110
life of individual, evolving, xvi
liminality, works evoking, 22, 23
Limón, Ada, 99, 183
line, poems generated from single, 3–4
linguistic and cultural duality, 109
Lipman, Pauline, 33–34
literary antepasados, 70
literary critics, classifications made by, 2
literary devices, 204
literary forms, recognized, xvi
literary landscape, xvii
literary world, Latino/as place in, 75
literature: marginalization in, 75; as news, xiv; possibility of, 105
lived experience, 138
local violence, 35
Loizeaux, Elizabeth, 18, 28
Loose Lips (literary reading series), 164
Lorca, Federico García, x, 80, 138, 141, 143, 151, 177
Lorde, Audre, 65, 66–67, 70
lo real maravilloso (the marvelous real), 161
Los Banos, California, 168
"Los Muertos" (poem), 35, 37–39
losses, mourning, 198
lotería (game of chance), 16–20
Lotería Cards and Fortune Poems (Herrera and Rodríguez), 15–20, 22
Luna, Sheryl, 96–98
Luso-American Liturature, 172–73
lyric poetry addressing trauma, 72–76

machismo, 94
Manifest Destiny, 102, 106
maquiladora industry, 35
marginalization, 75, 99
marginalized cultures, 165
marginalized groups, 75
mark making, 26

"The Marriage of Figaro" (poem), 87
"The Marriage of the Portuguese" (poem), 168
The Marriage of the Portuguese (Pereira), 168
Martin, Trayvon, 143
Martínez, Dionisio, 181
Martínez, J. Michael, xvii, 91
Martínez, Valerie: ekphrastic poems written by, 14–15; ethnicity explored by, 48–57; on Latinx poet proliferation, xiii; "Other Tribe" (term) used by, ix; violence against women addressed by, 35–36, 197
Mary, chapels dedicated to, 207
"Matanzas Bay" (poem), 156
material cause of poetry, 204
maternal role models, 171
Matos, Carlo, 82–89, 169–70
matriarchs in Portuguese American literature, 167–68
Melendez Kelson, María, 10–11
Melville, Herman, 7
memoria, landscapes of, 40–47
memory, loss of, 170
Mendieta, Ana, 22–25, 27
Menes, Orlando: as English language learner, 150; on Navy ship, 157–58; as poet, 148–49, 150, 151–56, 157–58, 159–60; in Spain, 153, 158; Spanish language, attitude concerning, 160–61; as teacher, 148, 153, 155, 156–57, 158–59; words used by, xiv; as writer, 150–51
men of color, television depiction of, 139
Mesa Refuge, 40
mestizaje, 57
metaphors, 26
Mexican American and African American communities, relations between, 27
Mexican American culture, shaming within, 73

Mexican-Anglo relations, 111–12
Mexican: border (*See* border); culture, 165; dance, 20; land ownership, loss of, 102; territories, annexation of, 102; war, 102; women, artistic depiction of, 20–22
Mexicans: Anglo perceptions of, 116–17, 134; as border crossers, 73; friendship among, 112–13; Latinas/os as, 178; life after high school, 118; status of, 103, 113, 114
"Mexicans Begin Jogging" (poem), 51
Miami, literary culture of, 153
Michelangelo, 209
migrants, border crossing deaths of, 18
migrant workers, 77
Milk and Faith (Giménez Smith), 22–23
mill workers, 85–86
minds, merging of, 28
Mind the Gap project, 27–28
minimalism, 153
minorities, finding own, 75
Mitchell, W. J. T., 12
"mixed race" (term), ix–x
Monáe, Janelle, 146
Montoya, Tomás, xvi
Moraga, Cherríe, xvi, 22–23
Morales, Juan J.: Latinx writers, exposure to, 128–29; parents, relationship with, 132, 137; racism experienced by, 129; Spanish knowledge, 127–28, 129–31, 136–37; as teacher, 128, 130–31, 132, 137; as writer, 132–34, 135–37
moral imperatives, 55
morals, writing without, 61
Morín, Tomás Q., ix, 1–8
"A Morning Sally" (poem), 156
mouth of the river, 78, 80
Moynihan, Daniel Patrick, 142
multilingual poems, 26
multiple identities, ix
murdered women, names of, 35–37
Museum Meditations (Fischer), 13

music, listening to, 151, 159
"The Music of Lifeless Creatures" (poem), 162
My Darling Dead Ones (de Vasconcelos), 172
Mystic Pizza (movie), 83–84

Nahuatl language, 26
Nahuatl poetry, 14, 26
Nahuatl *x*, 17
Najarro, Adela, xi, 100–101, 102–8
names, struggle for, 143
naming, examination of, xii
narrative form, 68
narrative style, 50–51
nation, poetry tied to, 30–31
Native American ancestry, 49
Native Americans, genocide of, 103
necessity (defined), 149–50
Negrón, Rosalyn, 54, 55
neoliberalism, 32–33
neoliberal policy labs, 33–34
Neruda, Pablo, 63, 92, 93, 128–29, 130, 181
Neves, Paula, 86
The New Jim Crow (Alexander), 142
news, xiv, 59
Nicaragua, 106
Nichols, Travis, 13
nonprofit advocacy, 60
non-white poets, xv
Northern California landscapes, 40
"Not Here" (poem), 33

Oak and Ivy (Dunbar), xv
Obama, Barack, 91, 95
ocean in dreams, 79
ocean without boundaries, 80
Olvera Street, Los Angeles, 112
"One Night in Salvador" (poem), 171–72
Only More So (Accardi), 164
On the Road (Kerouac), 180
oppression, 23, 74, 99, 141, 143

oppressor languages, undermining, 145
oral tradition, xvi
Other, x, 142, 161
otherness, experience of, 48–49, 77
"Other Tribe" (term), ix, 49
Our America (traveling exhibit), 15
Our Lady of the Artichokes (Gaspar, Pereira, and Vaz), 172

Pachuco, x
pain, response to, 80
painting, poetry compared to, xv
panic attacks, 186
parental separation or divorce, stories about, 102, 103
partisipasión (invented word), 26
"Passing" (sequence), 68–69
pass/passing (term), 62
patolli (game of chance), 16, 17
Paz, Octavio, 63, 98
"peopleness" (term), 54, 57
people of color, 139, 143
Pereira, Sam, 168–69, 172
periodico canto (sung newspaper), 121–22
personal change, first-person perspective as means to, 75
personal histories, 76
personal recollections, xvi
personal stories, 51
Pessoa, Fernando, 165, 167, 172
Philadelphia, 140–41
physiological changes during creation process, 7–8
Picard, Jean-Luc, 139
Pictures from Brueghel (series of poems) (Williams), 15
Pietà, 206, 210
Pikes Peak, 135
Pinochet regime, 34
Pity the Drowned Horses (Luna), 96–98
place, writing about, 40–44, 46–47
Plath, Sylvia, 96–98, 105

Plato, 12
plena (musical genre), 121–22, 126
plural society, 99
poem, searching for, ix
Poems on Various Subjects (Wheatley), xv
poem writing as journey, 206, 207–4
poetic composition, xvi
poetic subject, democratization of, xv
poetic vocation, 148–50, 151–56, 157–58, 159–60, 161–62
poetry: limitations of, 103–4; nature of, 204–5, 211; origin of, xvi, 3–4; writing, 186
Poetry like Bread (Espada), 128–29
Poets on Painters (Geha and Nichols), 13–14
politics: art and, 120, 121–23; life changed through, 61; poet relationship with, 58, 59–60, 62
polysemic signs, 17
Portugal, 165, 166
Portuguese American literature, 166–75
Portuguese American poetry, 82–89
Portuguese Americans: cultural loss experienced by, 82–83, 87; film depiction of, 83–84, 88–89; literary depiction of, 88–89; names for, 166; working-class experience of, 84–88
Portuguese American writers, 163, 164–65
Portuguese as silent minority, 163
Portuguese identity, 166–72, 173
Portuguese language, 82–83
Pound, Ezra, xiv, 6
poverty, cause of, 142
power: dark natural, 141; divorce from body, 146; of poetry, 4; reclaiming sense of, 72, 74
power systems, 125
Precarious/QUIPOem (Vicuña), 25–27
pregnant woman, poetry depicting, 21
pretext/pre-text, 211
Prieto, Miguel, x

primary world, xvii
Princeton Encyclopedia of Poetry and Poetics, xvii
prison inmates, poetry written by, 130–31
privilege, blindness stemming from, 74
prosopopoeia, xii, 17, 18
Providencia (Forbes), 70
Providencia, Colombia, 64, 70
pseudo-bohemian, true bohemian *versus,* 88
psychic, 144
psychogenic fugue, 73
psychological growth, 65
public characteristics of ethnicity, 53–54
Puerta del Sol (Aragón), 41
Puerto Rican poets as activists, 120
Puerto Ricans, 178
Puerto Rico: English spoken in, 129–30; independence movement, 120, 121, 125; socioeconomic conditions, 119–21; U.S. annexing of, 121

Quarantine Highway (Accardi), 164
Quechua language, 26
queer voices, 94
Quintana, Roberto, x
quipu (information storage system), 25, 27

race: killing or incarcerating based on, 146; myth about beauty and, 125; shame over, 73
racialized body, 141
racism: "cold country" referring to, 66; experience of, 129; immigrant experience of, 22; internalized, 73, 125–26; reality of, 54; stories of, 123
racist machismo, 94
Radin, Paul, 65
rage, expression of, 93
rape, 74
rasquachismo, 9–10

reading and writing: activism *versus*, 61; aesthetic, changing during, 62; life of, 58; moment striking, 59
rebozo (Mexican shawl), exhibit on, 20–22
Rebozo Rojo (dance), 20
Rebozos (painting and poem exhibit), 20–22
recovery, process of, 74
relationships, 186, 187–88
research, 156
Residencia en la tierra (Neruda), 128–29
resiliency, 74
resistance, 60
rider, artist as, 6–7
right to exist, 143
Rilke, Rainer Maria, 149–50, 155
Rio Grande, mouth of, 78
Rio Grande valley, 78
Rivera, María, 35, 37–39
Rivera, Tomás, xvi
Roberts, Julia, 83, 84
Rodríguez, Artemio, 15–20
Rojas, Andres: identity, conclusions about, 184–85; language challenges of, 178, 179–80, 181, 182; as Latino/a poet, 183–84; literature studied by, 177, 180–81
Romantic poetry, 106
Romay, Alexis, 179
Rome, 206, 209, 213
room of one's own, 62
The Roots of a Thousand Embraces (Herrera), 15
Rumba atop the Stones (Menes), 162
Russian River, 43, 44, 47

Saavedra, Eva Maria, xii, 186–90
Salvadorans, 178
Sanchez, Sonia, xvi
San Felipe (hurricane), 122
San Francisco, 40, 41
San Quentin (California state prison), 18–19

San Quintín, Baja California, 18–19
satire, 61
"Saucers" (poem), 169
saudade (term), 170, 171, 173, 175
Saura, Carlos, 153
A School for Fishermen (Matos), 85, 169–70
secondary worlds, xvii
second-wave feminists, 22–23
self, destruction of, 69
self, poems finding new, xii
self-blame for abuse, 72
self-doubts, 186
self-imaging, xii
self-respect, 74
Selznick, David O., 103
"Sendero Chibcha" (artwork and poem), 25–26
"Señorita X" (poem), 35, 36–37
sentiment, Latin@ penchant for, 99
sexism, 123, 197
sexual abuse survivors, 49, 72, 73–74, 76
sexual awakening, 44–45, 47
sexual orientation, shame over, 125–26
Shakespeare, William, 161
shaman (defined), 205
shame: internalizing sense of, 72; letting go of, 76; in trauma and culture relationship, 74
Silko, Leslie Marmon, xvi
silva, ire'ne lara, ix, 77–81
Silva, Reinaldo Francisco, 163
Simic, Charles, 180
sincerity, commentary on, 60
The Siren World (Morales), 135–36
sister (term), 61
Sistine Chapel, 206, 207, 208–9, 211–12
Sitges, Spain, 42
slavery, 66, 103
slaves, 141–42
Smith, Anthony D., 53
Smithsonian American Art Museum, 15
social and political movements, xvii

social change, 75
social class, 87–88
social function, xv, xvi
social mobility and access, 53–54
social service organizations, 60
sociopolitical and ethical concerns, 11
sociopolitical commentary, 17
sonnets: as reconciliation, 198–200; as resting place, 195–98; as sustenance, 194–95; as vessel, 192–94
"sopping gut" (term), 24
Sorrowtoothpaste Mirrorcream (Kim), 31
Soto, Gary, xvi, 51, 181
Sousa, Frank, 168, 171–72
South, 103, 129
South Korea, 31
space: battling for, xi; interaction with, 144; television depiction of, 139; and time, 140
Spain, 124, 153, 158
Spanglish, 94, 101, 104, 109
Spanish-American War, 121
Spanish language: ambivalent feelings concerning, 92–93; connection to, xiii; English language, transition to, 177, 179–80; and English language, pull between, 109; as Latino poem characteristic, 50–51, 99; love of, 160–61; in North America, 179; punishment for speaking, 128; spoken (or not) at home, 49, 63, 77, 127, 161, 190; teaching and learning, 127–29, 130–31, 134–35, 136–37; use in poems, 187
Spanish-only demands, 109
Spanish settlers, monument of, 112
Spanish-speaking writers in Latin America, 32–33
speech, self-reproduction in, xvi
spirit, 144, 146
"spoken word" poetry, 93
sports as poetry theme, 132–33
stable hand, job as, 5
standard English (defined), 109

stanza *versus* new poem, 3
starship, poem as, 143
Star Trek (television series), 139
Stavans, Ilan, 94, 178
stereotypes, 22
Stevens, Wallace, 152
story(ies): forgotten or ignored, 101–3; images telling, 12; poetry as, xi, xv, 5, 100–101; telling own, 75; term, 100
storytelling, xvi, 68, 194
St. Peter's Basilica, 206, 209, 210, 211–12, 214
string, photographs of, 25, 26–27
subject matter, Latino poem identification through, 50–51
suffering, 4–5, 75
"Sugars of Terceira" (poem), 168
survivor (term), 62
survivor's guilt, 72
Swaziland, 48
swimming, 79–80

Tafolla, Carmen, 14–15, 20–22
Taylor, Lili, 83
Teijeiro, Ivis, 160–61, 162
Tejana poet, 198
Tejano music, 94
The Tempest (Shakespeare), 161
"Temporal" (song), 122
testarudo (term), 149, 162
text, pre-text before, 211
The Lady and the Unicorn (collection of tapestries), 66
"The South" (short story), 180
"This Particular Season" (poem), 52
Thomas, Dylan, 154, 155
Thompson, Dunstan, 45–46
thread, photographs of, 26–27
Through a Grainy Landscape (Accardi), 164
"Tia Joanna" (poem), 167–68
time: interaction with, 144; overview of, 140–41; poems as record of, xiv
"To Autumn" (poem), 110

"To Dream in Spanish" (poem), 136–37
To Have and Have Not (Hemingway), 165
tomato garden, 194–95
tongue, liberating, 67–68
Torres, Lidia, 44, 45
Torres, Michael: as graffiti artist, xi, 111, 112–13, 114, 115–16, 117–18; as writer, 114, 117, 118
"To the Diaspora" (poem), 63–64
tradition, xvi, 170
transcultural experience, 10
translation, poetry in, 30–33
transnationalism, 32–33
transnational republic, Imaginary, 33
trauma, 72–76
trauma survivors, 75
Traveler (science fiction character), 144, 147
Tree of Life (Mendieta: series of works), 24
Treviño, Natalia, 201–4, 206–14
trickster (mythical creature): as boundary crosser, 64–65; at crossroad, 67–70; duende as, 138, 146; role of, 69
The Trickster (Radin), 65
Trump, President, 190
"Two Girls from Juarez" (poem), 96–98
"Two Poets Named Dunstan Thompson" (poem), 45

ugly, artistic depiction of, 16
Uhuru (television character), 142
unacknowledged man or woman, xv
understanding, 103–4
undocumented immigrants, artistic depiction of, 17–18
Unitarianism, 164, 165
United States: history, stories about, 100, 101, 102, 107; Latino/as as category in, 178; poetry and translation in, 32–33; Puerto Rico annexed by, 121
"until laughter did us part" (line), 3
Untitled (performance film), 22, 25
urge to travel, 201

US Navy's PACE (Program for Afloat College Education), 157
US presidential inauguration, 183

Valadez, Roberto, 27
Valdez, Germán (Tin-Tan), x
Valdez, Patsi, 10–11
Vallejo, César, 105, 110, 177
Vatican, 206, 210–14
Vatican Museum, 206–8
verbo-visual texts, 26
Viajes a los Estados Unidos (Prieto), x
Vicuña, Cecilia, 25–27
violence: awareness of ramifications of, 74; Chilean government as cause of, 33; facing and processing, 75–76; international and transhistorical, 32; as poetry theme, 24, 31; survival, resistance, and resilience in aftermath of, 75
visual arts: ekphrastic, 27–28; games, use in, 16–20; Latino/a poet interpretation of, 12; museums focusing on, 14; poetry inspired by, 10; sociopolitical and ethical concerns addressed through, 11; tongue spoken by, 21
vocabulary journal, xiv
voice: finding, 68; hunger to create, 65; worth of, 189

Walcott, Derek, 162
"Walking Around" (poem), 129
Wallace, David Foster, 188
war, 24, 74, 75
water, pushing through fear of, 80
A Weakness for Boleros (Torres), 44
Weiner, Jonathan, 182
We Prefer the Damned (Matos), 88
Westside Women's Writing Cooperative, 164
Wheatley, Phillis, xv, xvi
Where Is Ana Mendieta (Blocker), 22
white flight, 140
white male oppression, 66

white men as poets, 187
whiteness, legal, 68–69
Whitman, Walt, xv, xvi, 105
Wild West, Hollywood version of, 103
Williams, William Carlos, 5, 15, 110, 180
The Wind Shifts (Aragón), xvii, 91
witnessing, poem as, xiv–xv
women: breaking with silence imposed upon, 107–8; deaths in Ciudad Juarez, 196–97; oppression of, 98; rape, protest against, 25; violence against, 24, 35–39
women in leadership, television depiction of, 139
women of color, 125
women prison inmates, 131
women writers, 51, 65, 105–6
word and image, relationship between, 14
words: and belonging, 77; invented, 26; multiple connotations within, 103; power of, 102, 105; as tools, xiv
Wordsworth, William, 105, 106, 156
Worf (television character), 139, 142
work: attitudes toward, 84–85, 88; blessing of, 192; nature and effects of, 169–70
work ethic, 111, 116, 171
working out, 58–59
world, creating own, 65
world, poetry enlarging view of, xiv

"The World in 2001" (poem), 84–85
world literature, 70
wound, Rio Grande as open, 78
wounds, healing, 72, 205
Wright, Charles, 4
writer, split consciousness as, 68
writers, community of, 115
writers of color, 51
writing: fear of, pushing through, 80; feeling at ease with, 189; process of, 167; purpose of, 60; success, requirements for, 148, 159; thinking through, 200; timely, importance of, 6; without morals, 61
Writing for Art (Cheeke), 11

X (letter), symbolism of, 17

yarn, photographs of, 26–27
The Year of Magical Thinking (Didion), 198, 199
Yeats, H. B., 159, 181
Yerba bruja (as plant and symbol), 120
Yerba bruja (Corretjer), 120
You, Mia, 31–32

Zenith, Richard, 172
zombie movies, 144
Zurita, Raúl, 30–31, 32, 33

www.ingramcontent.com/pod-product-compliance
Lightning Source LLC
Chambersburg PA
CBHW020236170426
43202CB00008B/102